RAIN

John Knight

ONLEY PUBLISHING

"I will be to the people of Israel like rain in a dry land."
(Hosea 14:5 Good News Bible)

First published in Great Britain 1987. Reprinted 1999
Revised new edition 2011

ISBN 9780955310874

Cover design by Trevor Boys and Mark Dixon

Printed and bound in the UK by the
MPG Books Group
Bodmin and King's Lynn

Designed and published by:
Onley Publishing
60 Onley Park
Willoughby
Rugby
CV23 8AW

AUTHOR'S NOTE

All Scripture references in the text (except where otherwise indicated) have been taken from the Good News Bible.

The present Zimbabwe has changed its name several times during the last century. It was known as Southern Rhodesia when we entered it in 1936. From 1953-63 it amalgamated with Northern Rhodesia and Nyasaland to form the Federation of Rhodesia and Nyasaland. On the dissolution of the Federation in 1963 – on the granting of Independence to Northern Rhodesia (renamed Zambia) and Nyasaland (renamed Malawi) – Southern Rhodesia became simply Rhodesia.

Just before the end of the guerrilla war, which covered a little more than the 1970's – Prime Minister Ian Smith tried to accommodate black aspirations by stepping down as Prime Minister and appointing Bishop Abel Muzorewa in his place. He also sought to pacify both black and white groups by renaming the country Zimbabwe-Rhodesia. Neither action satisfied the freedom fighters. After the Lancaster House Agreement in 1979, Britain granted Independence to the new Zimbabwe in April, 1980, with Robert Mugabe of ZANU PF as its first Prime Minister.

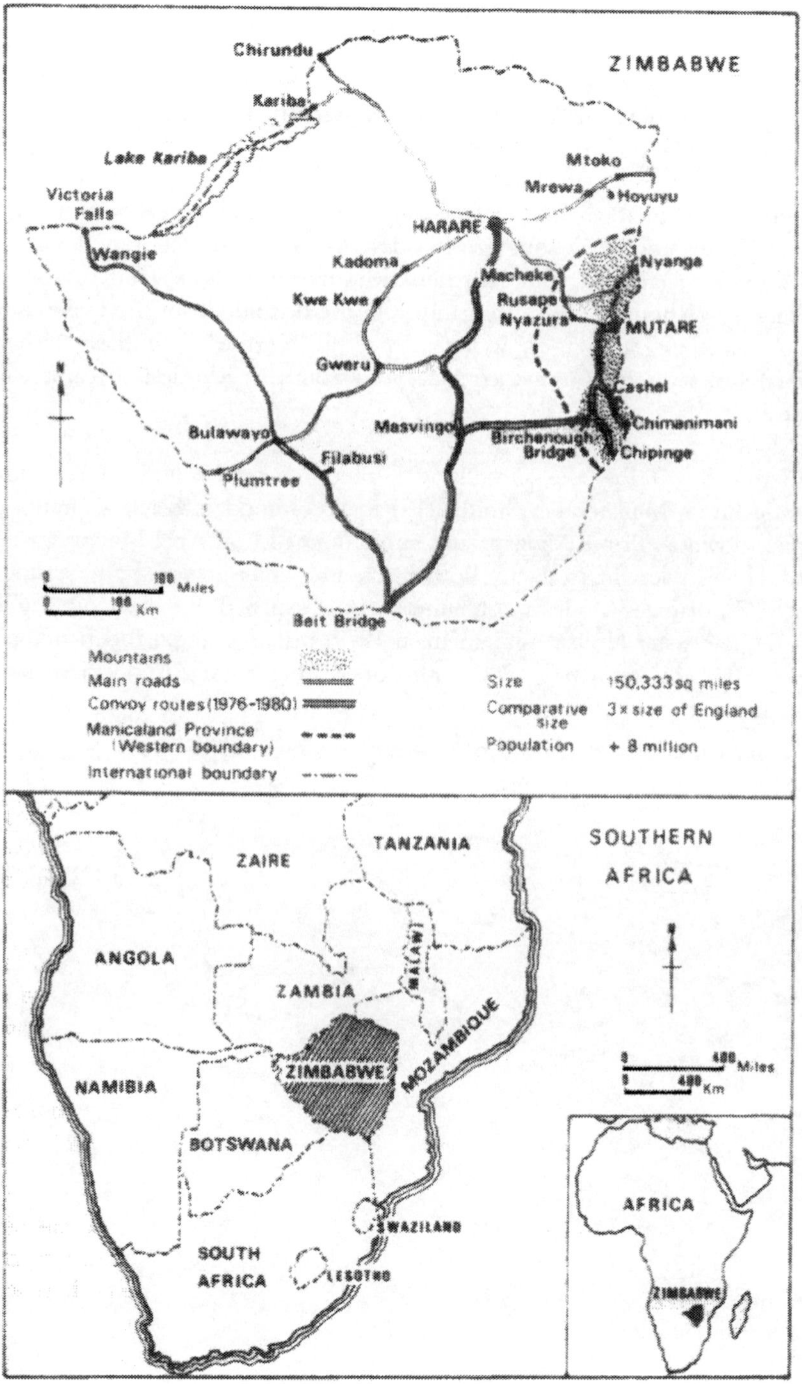
ZIMBABWE
Chirundu
Kariba
Lake Kariba
Victoria Falls
Wangie
Mtoko
Mrewa
Hoyuyu
HARARE
Kadoma
Macheke
Nyanga
Kwe Kwe
Rusape
Nyazura
MUTARE
Gweru
Cashel
Masvingo
Chimanimani
Bulawayo
Birchenough Bridge
Chipinge
Filabusi
Plumtree
Beit Bridge
N
0 100 Miles
0 100 Km
Mountains
Main roads
Convoy routes (1976-1980)
Manicaland Province (Western boundary)
International boundary
Size 150,333 sq miles
Comparative size 3 x size of England
Population + 8 million
SOUTHERN AFRICA
TANZANIA
ZAIRE
ANGOLA
MALAWI
ZAMBIA
MOZAMBIQUE
ZIMBABWE
NAMIBIA
BOTSWANA
SWAZILAND
SOUTH AFRICA
LESOTHO
0 400 Miles
0 400 Km
AFRICA

FOREWORD
by Michael Cassidy

If you are a candidate for spiritual adventure, then John Knight's *Rain in a Dry Land* is for you. It is a veritable twentieth century Acts of the Spirit and parts of the book partake of the dimensions of a Christian thriller. In fact, I can't remember when I have been as enthralled by such a wide range of Christian experience and insight, all within the compass of one story. Moreover, by virtue of the wide canvas on which John paints, the book has something for everyone, whether new minister or old hand; whether missionary, aspiring ordinand, Christian worker, ordinary layman; whether housewife, seeking teenager or young disciple.

John's thoroughly readable story nevertheless goes deep into what the Christian life is all about. Beyond that, it succeeds remarkably in bringing together personal biography, spiritual quest, doctrinal reflection, ecclesiology, evangelism, healing, personal and congregational renewal, giving, stewardship, social concern, prophetic witness, family life, discipleship, missionary adventure plus glorious evidence of God's involvement in the affairs of man. It is all here – and more – in breathtaking range. And all written with compassion, humanity, lightness of touch, and humour.

However, what struck me most here was the extraordinary testimony to the faithfulness and living active power of God, our contemporary. If you doubt the miraculous this book will put an end to your doubts. Not only in his personal experience of God's miraculous power, but in the mind-boggling evidences of God's supernatural workings and protection of His people in the 'Rhodesian' guerrilla war, John brings us incontrovertible evidence of a God who is alive and well and on the job in our tattered twentieth century world.

What's more, the humble and honest quest described here for personal and congregational renewal, for preaching power, for counselling effectiveness and for pastoral relevance will particularly encourage every minister and pastor who knows dryness, or discouragement, or simply the desire to do better.

Personally, what challenged me most was John Knight's resolute determination to obey God whatever the cost, or risk, or consequence. And often for him and his family this was considerable.

This makes the book dangerous to pick up, because not only may it be the gentle tonic you need, it may also be spiritual dynamite to blast you into a new place in your discipleship. The book is hugely enjoyable. But be warned. It may be more…

ABOUT THE AUTHOR

John Knight was born in 1936 near Penzance in Cornwall and emigrated to Southern Rhodesia (Zimbabwe) as a baby and educated there until 1948. He completed his schooling at St John's College in Johannesburg before attending Leeds University and Mirfield Theological College from 1958 to 1961. He then returned to Rhodesia where he was ordained into the Ministry. For the next 25 years he held a number of appointments, and became Dean of Mutare Cathedral for a number of years before being forced to leave the country. He spent 10 years as Team Rector of Emmanuel, Northampton during which time he also served 5 years as Rural Dean. The next eight years were spent ministering to three village Churches – Greens Norton, Bradden and Litchborough before he retired to Brackley at the end of 2005.

John has also written *To Reign or Not To Reign.* This book is his positive response to the doubt and unbelief so prevalent in the Western Church today where basic doctrines of faith and Biblical credibility are often questioned, even denied. Is it surprising then that many in our 'pick-and-mix' society believe anything or nothing?

In addressing the issue of doubt and unbelief, John challenges and encourages the reader to develop a faith consistent with Biblical experience. Having said that, *To Reign or Not to Reign* is not a dry theological treatise one might expect as there are many wonderful testimonies to God's healing love and grace, as well as personal anecdotes to encourage the reader.

An extract will be found at the back of this book.

CONTENTS

CHAPTER ONE

THE DESECRATION OF GOD'S HOUSE

It was 7.30 a.m. on Sunday, 16 February 1986. Many of us were in St. John's Cathedral, Mutare (Zimbabwe), at the first of our Sunday morning Communion services. None of us had any knowledge of the stunning events that would follow two hours later. I had just read the Gospel for the day and was ready to preach. Yes, stranger than fiction perhaps, but at that moment I was led to change the theme I had earlier decided on, and spoke instead on the subject of 'violence only begets more violence'. With hindsight, I believe God used that time to speak to me more than anyone else... In addition, many listeners later drew comfort from this sermon when they received news of the desecration of the Cathedral.

In elaborating on the theme, I pointed out that Scripture would have us carefully note: '"Vengeance is mine", saith the Lord.' It was Jesus who gave us, His followers, a command that when anyone 'attacked' us, we were to turn the other cheek! I suggested that there was always such a temptation for us to want to defend 'our good name' and to want to hit back – verbally at least – against any who would lay false accusations against us, or any who hurt us by word or deed.

I reminded them that Jesus was our most perfect example. Deserted by all His friends, He found himself hanging on the Cross. Without any verbal expression of anger, or of the injustice of it all, He looked down on all those standing there mocking and jeering Him and said, 'Father, forgive them, for they know not what they do.' I pointed to the fact that the first Christian martyr, Stephen, followed his master's example when he himself was being stoned to death. He commended his murderers to God with the words, 'Lord, lay not this sin to their charge.'

Those thoughts were still fresh in my mind when, two hours later, a vast mob stormed in and desecrated God's House during the next service. And because God had been so gracious in this way, we were ready with the right attitude of non-retaliation, and with a constant flow of prayer for forgiveness on the lips of all God's people kneeling there in the Cathedral at the time. Perhaps the best way of describing the events that surrounded that desecration, is to simply reproduce the report drawn up by myself as Dean of the Cathedral with the help of the Cathedral Council. We did this ten days after the event, after meticulously checking all the facts. The report read as follows:

Tekere seizes Z$1.25 million of Church property: Police forbidden to intervene: Law and Order non-existent in Mutare: constitutional right to freedom of worship abrogated.

1. 8.50 a.m. 500-strong mob move on to St. John's Cathedral property.
2. 8.55 a.m. Senior Officer of Central Intelligence warned leaders:
    - they had illegally invaded Church property,
    - they were causing a disturbance of the peace while Church services were taking place, and
    - he ordered them to leave the property.
3. 9.00 a.m. The mob ignored the CIO. He gave them 15 minutes to leave, or else! (An empty threat as police previously ordered by officials not to intervene.)
4. 9.15 a.m. Church Service commenced despite noise outside.
5. 9.20 a.m. Edgar Tekere (Chairman of Zanu PF Manicaland) entered the cathedral.
6. He talked to the Churchwardens while the service was in progress. He was asked to stop the noise outside and invited to attend the service. Tekere said he had no wish to listen, and that he was ordering his mob to take possession of the property and drive us out.
7. 9.25 a.m. Tekere gave a brief speech to the demonstrators and, with the service still in progress, the mob poured into the Cathedral, singing political songs, with many of them armed with sticks. The 500-strong mob:
    - rocked and turned pews over to get the congregation out;
    - danced on the altar, beating out the candles with newspapers;
    - knocked one priest over at the altar and dragged him down the full length of the Cathedral flat on his back; another priest also manhandled out of the Cathedral;
    - children being led to safety thrown in all directions by the mob;
    - one elderly lady, severely buffeted, carried out by parishioners in a state of shock.
8. 9.40-11.40 a.m. The Dean, assistant priest and about twenty parishioners stayed to try and discover what the crowd wanted. No clear picture emerged except false stories told to squatters at St. Augustine's Mission that the Bishop wanted the land for his own (mythical) cattle.

9. 11.40 a.m. Mob started process of selecting two parishioners 'to be beaten until the Bishop's whereabouts were revealed'. We walked through the mob and left as they fought over their choices.
10. Police refused to act. Several times the police were asked to remove the illegal mob from the Cathedral, to protect parishioners, and to restore church property to the lawful owners. The police explained that strict orders 'from above' ruled out any action to protect lives and property, for this was 'Tekere business. Tekere obviously above the law. Permission was also refused for us to enter the Cathedral and lock up valuables, and permission refused us to switch off power to Z$60,000 pipe organ.
11. 12.30 p.m. Assistant Commissioner (Police) advised the Dean and his family to leave their home immediately as Tekere had given orders to invade their home. Although asked to do so, he regretted police were forbidden to intervene…
12. 2.00 p.m. Two church members – the Bishop's caretaker and another young man – caught by the mob in Main Street outside Church Offices. While being held by his thugs, Edgar Tekere personally brutally assaulted them in public. When they failed to give the information required, they were bundled into Tekere's car and driven off. Police in full view of the incident took no action to intervene. The young men were later hospitalised in Mutare General Hospital. Police not only did nothing to intervene but further, have apparently done nothing to lay charges of assault, battery and forcible abduction against Tekere.
13. 2.00 p.m. Mob rampages through assistant priest's garden throwing stones, banging on doors and windows demanding entry. Riot police removed the mob. (Not a designated house?)
14. 2.00 p.m. Mob took possession of Bishop's House. (Ten days later we were still barred from entry. On Thursday, 20 February, the S.P.C.A. Inspector went to feed the dog, puppies and chicken – unattended since Sunday. The mob forcibly evicted her and said the animals were to be left to starve to death or die of thirst.)

Monday 17 February to Wednesday 26 February:

Daily many have failed to gain entry to Church property. Many requests made to the police to intervene. They consistently refused because of 'orders from above'. Only three have gained access to the Cathedral during the period – a lawyer who described the Cathedral as being in 'a filthy and disgusting state', and a person who revealed himself to be a member of the British House of Lords (together with his wife) who insisted on entering the Church to pray. One parishioner was assaulted on entering the Cathedral to pray – believing the mob had left – and laid charges at the Police Station. A message was relayed from Police Headquarters in Harare saying he had no right to enter (his own!) Cathedral without prior police permission!

On Tuesday, 25 February, the Church re-possessed the Parish Office for four hours. The police refused to drive off the mob that tried to attack the offices. The mob leader said he had instructions from Tekere to break the door down if the staff did not get out, and threatened the women with rape. The staff left peaceably.

A PLEA. Every responsible citizen in Mutare is appalled at this outrage. The people are crying out to our Government to come to our aid as a city and ensure that justice is seen to be done. Many policemen have told us of their horror at what is going on, and of the evil system of 'orders from above' that make them powerless to act. Some policemen who have wanted to help have been threatened with arrest if they do so. If those who perpetrate such lawless acts believe we are guilty of any crime, let them bring us to court, and let mob rule (when you can't get what you want legally) cease for ever in our beautiful new Zimbabwe.

As at midday, Friday 28 February, the church had still not regained any of its properties.

Report prepared by Dean and Church Council of St John's Cathedral, Mutare, Zimbabwe. END OF STATEMENT.

A 'Stop Press' was added a few days later:

Police finally ordered to drive out those illegally holding our property late Saturday, early Sunday, 1 – 2 March, 1986. The Dean and his family returned to their home on Sunday 2 March – fifteen days after leaving with little more than they stood up in. The Bishop and his family hope to return soon. Thanks to thousands who supported St. John's and the Diocese with their love, prayer and messages. 'They' can take our property – but they cannot stop the *living* Church. People will be heartened to know that all church services continued 'as usual' underground.

Tuesday 4 March: Mutare Ministers' Fraternal came out in total support of our cry for an end to the obvious breakdown of law and order, and the threat to freedom of worship in this country, and called on Government to urgently remedy the situation.

The desecration of the Cathedral, with the eviction of clergy and people from all Church property for fifteen days, was staged to threaten the life of the Bishop – or, at the very least, to intimidate him to such an extent that he would resign as Bishop. Although the reason given for the invasion was the support of the leadership of a school in rebellion against the Diocese, the main reason appeared to be a local political one. The principal character behind this was Edgar Tekere. He had been a Cabinet Minister in Robert Mugabe's first government after Independence was declared in April, 1980. Tekere was later charged with first-degree murder after he personally led a gang of his thugs, heavily armed with automatic weapons, against a farmer in the Goromonzi area near the Capital. It was a commando-style affair with a farmer being chased across his farm, into his house, and gunned down in cold blood at point blank range. The judge and his two assessors were unable to reach an unanimous decision (the assessors being in fear of their lives if they voted for a guilty verdict) on the murder charge, but such was the revulsion in the country against such a cold-blooded and calculated murder, and at the blatant way Tekere took the law into his own hands to obtain what he could not get legally (the possession of the farm), Robert Mugabe removed him from the cabinet.

It was not very long before the party in power appointed Tekere to a powerful position as chairman of the party for the whole of the Manicaland Province, covering the eastern border area of the country. Soon afterwards he used a large threatening mob – in weeklong demonstrations that closed down the Civic Centre of Mutare – to bring about the enforced resignations of all the duly elected city councillors. As a consequence, our city was left in limbo without an executive arm until Tekere put forward his list of 'approved' candidates to be voted for several months later. This was the man who led the demonstrating thugs into the Cathedral, ostensibly backing the cause of the rebellious school leadership he had befriended, but really for his own ends – to try and remove the Bishop from his duly elected position.

In order to understand how we saw God's hand in preparing us for these days and in discerning his protection over us, I need to go back in time.

CHAPTER TWO

EARLY DAYS

Though I have lived most of my life in Africa, I was actually born just inside England. That was at 'Hawk's Farm', near Penzance and Land's End, in 1936. I was born of staunch Anglican parents, with a strong tradition of Anglicanism running through the family.

After several trips 'down under' as a ship's surgeon, my father could not settle down to private practice in England after all the excitement of visiting places like India and Australia. Discovering that there was a need for doctors in Rhodesia, my father applied for a post in the Southern Rhodesia Medical Service. By the end of 1936, my parents and I were settled at Plumtree (western border) in the land of our choice, Southern Rhodesia. My brothers Keith (1937), Alan (1940), and Robert (1958) were all born in Rhodesia. Our extended family was small. My father left his parents behind in England, and his only brother Alan was a priest/headmaster of Adisadel College in the Gold Coast as it was then known (Ghana). He and his students built the College themselves.

A year later, in 1937, Alan became the youngest Bishop in the Anglican Communion when he was elected and consecrated as Bishop of the diocese of British Guiana (now Guyana) in South America. Georgetown, the capital, is built on the marshes and his very beautiful Cathedral was, at that time, the largest wooden Cathedral in the world. It was, in recent years, beautifully restored. (Strangely enough, almost the first church we visited after returning to England is the oldest existing wooden church in the world – 856AD – at Greenstead, Essex.) Alan's parents joined him soon afterwards in British Guiana. Grandfather Knight, a retired headmaster, was Alan's Secretary for many years, and Grandmother held sway as the Mistress of Austin House (another beautiful wooden building), the Bishop's residence. Alan and my father were both great correspondents and never a week went past without them writing to each other. So we were kept fully informed on the state of the church. We were aware that many of the priests were unmarried, and many posts unfilled, because of the shortage of finance. Despite the meagre resources that were available, one could only stand amazed at what was achieved in the development of the church's work, especially in a vast country with virtually no roads (except around Georgetown). The courage and determination of those missionaries and local church workers was brought home by the hardships and difficulties that had to be faced, for example, by weeks of travel by canoe through areas like the Rupununi in the hinterland, and far from civilisation.

Guyana is an exceedingly hot and humid country where it is commonplace to shower and change one's clothes several times a day. Despite that, Alan was a stickler for dressing 'correctly', and wore full dress (frock coat and gaiters included) whatever the weather! Nor was he ever observed to sweat or perspire!

Alan, later Archbishop of the West Indies, remained celibate all his life, strongly stressing – with a merry twinkle in those blue eyes of his – that he was married to the Church! To marry anyone else would be to commit bigamy! He died in Guyana in 1979, having served his Diocese as Bishop for forty-two years, and the Province of the West Indies as Archbishop for twenty-nine years. At his death he was the longest serving Bishop in the Anglican Communion.

When we emigrated to Rhodesia, my mother left her own mother and two younger sisters in England. Granny Jess (a most wonderful woman to us as children, always full of fun and bubbling with excitement) and Aunt Joan both emigrated – separately to Rhodesia after World War II. Joan, like my mother, was a trained state registered nurse. After a spell in a maternity unit, working for the Government at the Lady Rodwell Hospital in Bulawayo, Joan devoted most of the next thirty years of her life as a nurse to mission hospitals around Rhodesia. This included her first station at St. Patrick's Gweru. Here she was, for a long time, the only fully trained member of staff and had also to serve as an administrator as well as supervising the building of the new Hospital. She seemed to practically build the hospital single-handed, even to the extent of driving in truckloads of sand and stone in between delivering babies in the maternity unit. She also worked at Daramombe and St. David's Hospital, Bonda.

What did appal me as a youngster was the absolute pittance that Joan, and dedicated nurses like her, was given by the missionary society and the diocese. People who not only worked long hours (usually 'on-call' twenty four hours a day), but also had the responsibility for training new staff. After giving up a life of comparative luxury in secular posts, these mission employees were often expected to survive, many miles from any shopping centre, in tiny, inadequately equipped cottages, on a nominal salary of about £25 a month. Joan has since 'retired' to England and at seventy still works full-time as matron of an old peoples' home.

In addition, there were our own priests, literally living from hand to mouth because stipends were so abysmally low, with housing and furnishing conditions often a cause for much unhappiness to the families concerned. All these factors made a significant impact upon me during those impressionable teenage years. Then there was the bigotry of the Church. My parents were often ostracised and scorned because we had black people come to stay with us in our house, both priests and monks. People even walked out of the 'whites' (only?) Church if one of these black men took the service when our Rector was on leave!

But there were also the good things about the Church. Devoted priests and full-time workers – nuns, monks, doctors, nurses, teachers, administrators – who gave of their all, despite the often harsh conditions and seeming lack of care and concern from the rest of the so-called Church 'militant'! These people gave unstintingly of their love to us.

From my earliest memories life in the family revolved around the Church, the Hospital and the home. At Christmas, for instance, the day would start with attendance at a midnight service, followed by singing in the Choir or serving on Christmas morning. The rest of Christmas morning would be spent at the hospital, giving out presents and Christmas cheer to patients and staff. Very often there would be a 'party' out in the Hospital grounds for long term patients such as those from tuberculosis (TB) units.

This was particularly the case during the most impressionable years when we lived in Kadoma (Gatooma, as it was in pre-independence days, and before the word gay came to have its present connotation – the 'Gay Tomb'). At this period my father was the Medical Superintendent (Senior Government Medical Officer) for Kadoma.

Only after the patients had been looked after would we start to think of our own Christmas celebrations with the opening of Christmas presents at afternoon tea, followed by Christmas dinner – with single doctors and nurses being invited to celebrate with the family.

We were never allowed to miss a Sunday at Church. We usually got involved as servers and choristers. There were also the times of rebellion – but Dad always had the last say, and to church we went unless we could convince our own 'doctor in the house' that we were really sick. Even in the years when we lived at Filabusi (before moving to Kadoma in 1947) with no priest or church available. So Bishop Paget (later Archbishop of the newly created Church of the Province of Central Africa) agreed to the building of a lovely Church, St. Barbara-by-the-Spruit (stream), just outside our garden. It was built on the understanding that my father, a licensed Lay Reader (and later Sub Deacon) conduct Matins or Evensong on all Sundays when no Trek Priest was available – and that would only be every other month. For special festivals at Filabusi we would drive to Bulawayo. I still have vivid memories of the long drive on 'strip' roads (two parallel strips of tar, each about eighteen inches wide and far enough apart to fit the track of most vehicles) to Bulawayo on Christmas Eve to attend the Midnight

Service. My youngest brother Alan would fall asleep on the kneelers at our feet. Then came the long drive home in the early hours of Christmas morning – with an exhausted Father Christmas tip-toeing in (presuming we were asleep) to deposit batches of toys in pillow cases at the foot of our beds at first light!

Something of the splendour of our Anglican heritage was brought home to us when we returned to England for the first time for a year's sabbatical which my father decided to take in 1948-9. We saw splendid Churches and Cathedrals, and the areas we stayed in seemed to have churches that were alive and packed with people. It was during that holiday, timed to coincide with my uncle's visit from British Guiana to attend Lambeth Conference, that my two brothers and I were confirmed by my Uncle in the old family Church of St. Jude on the Hill, Hampstead, London.

What a great occasion it was for the whole family! Unlike the first day of Pentecost, we did not see tongues of fire, and neither did we hear a mighty rushing wind. Nor did we speak in tongues! But, as with so many people, we had been taught that 'those signs' were only for the new age when Christianity was brought to birth – and were no longer needed now.

So we were not taught to expect such things. What you don't expect, you don't ask for! But we were well grounded in the doctrines of the Church, and taught the importance of a good prayer life, and the need for regular Bible study, and attendance at, and support of, the church.

Probably the closest I ever came, in those earlier days, to an understanding of the possibility of a *personal* involvement with Jesus, was through my mother. Regarded by many as a saint, to me she was one of the most loving, forgiving and caring people I have ever had the joy of knowing. She was the kind of person who always looked for a person's good points and scarcely ever, to my knowledge, said an unkind thing about anyone – even against those who abused her and hurt her. I will never forget walking into the kitchen one Good Friday afternoon to catch her sobbing her heart out. I was bowled over by the sight, threw my arms around her, and asked who it was that could have hurt her so. I shall never forget her reply, possibly because it was the last thing I expected. She had just returned from the 'Three Hour' Good Friday service. Using the most vivid imagery, she began to paint a picture of what Calvary meant to her. To her, it was beyond belief that Jesus had allowed Himself to be crucified, willingly enduring the pain and suffering, the jeers and insults, in order to die on that cross and…pay the penalty for *her* sins! I found that hard to understand, taking into account the fact that Jesus died almost two thousand years before my mother lived. What *did* touch me deeply was the fact that my mother spoke of Jesus as someone who was as alive as I was – and that she loved Him as someone who lived and walked and talked with her! – and not of someone who lived immeasurably far away in heaven. It was a rare glimpse of what Jesus meant to her in her life. Although most devout and faithful in going to church and being involved in everything that was going on in the church (she was Sacristan in many churches where we had lived, making many beautiful sets of vestments and so on), the personal relationship she had with Jesus was something she rarely spoke about.

CHAPTER THREE

THE RELUCTANT PRIEST

My parents were determined, whatever the cost to themselves, we three boys should have the best education possible. More to the point, they particularly wanted a school with a good Christian Foundation. Through another family they were put in touch with a school that seemed to meet all their criteria – St. John's College in Johannesburg, South Africa. It also appealed to my parents because for many years it was built up, with the quite magnificent stone buildings it now has, by the Community of the Resurrection from Mirfield, England. As a family we had many close links with this community through their work at St. Augustine's Mission, Penhalonga, on the eastern borders of Zimbabwe.

Although I had been living mainly at boarding schools since I was five, the very fact of being left at the age of eleven in another country from where we lived, two days and a night away by train from home, where family letters took a week to reach me, was probably one of the most traumatic experiences of my early life. It took a long time, although I think I hid it well, for the heartache and loneliness to wear off. Before too long a very full life at school helped me to adjust, along with a great determination to do well academically and with a great love for all manner of sporting activities abundantly catered for at this magnificent school. I knew what a tremendous financial sacrifice it was to my parents, even to the extent of my parents continuing to maintain their wonderful 1937 vintage Hudson Terraplane as the family car during most of my nine years at St. Johns! For brief periods, when my two brothers were also at St. Johns, the cost was crippling. However Keith left after a couple of years to transfer to a more suitable technical school for him back home in Rhodesia. Alan also returned to a local school back home because he twice picked up some virus that partially, and temporarily, paralysed him. They decided that Rhodesia's climate was perhaps better for him.

'Church' played a significant part in the life of the School. Not that many seemed to take their faith very seriously, but compulsory morning and evening worship every Sunday and daily prayers during the week in the School Chapels proved a real bore to many. Some alleviated their boredom by serving at the altar, and the one position aimed for by most was that of thurifer with the chance (rather like a drum major with his mace) of executing a number of adventurous movements, including 360 degree swings with a thurible full of red hot coals and incense. To be a thurifer, as a senior boy in the school carried status! I endured much of my time in the chapels because I found pleasure singing in the choir (as treble, then alto, and finally as a bass). The choir, especially through its musical productions, enjoyed considerable prestige in Johannesburg musical circles. The Johannesburg City Orchestra played for all the Gilbert and Sullivan productions. The Choir was also invited every year to provide a special Carol Concert in the Johannesburg Cathedral over several nights each year before Christmas.

Even during those times when I was serious about my relationship with God, I was often filled with a sense of failure. There were the problems of continuing sin, the failure to pray and read the bible regularly, and the failure to worship God with any sense of reality. There was, moreover, a growing belief within me that I would never succeed in my efforts to be good enough to enter heaven. It is strange, perhaps, but of all the many sermons I had to listen to in Chapel, the one and only sermon I remember to this day was a brief comment thrown out by a visiting preacher. He simply mentioned the fact that it had been a grievous shock to him to discover that in its fifty-five year existence (nearly forty of them under a community of monks), the number of priests produced by this school could be counted on the fingers of one hand! Within three years that number was almost double!

But I did not really believe that that concerned *me* at the time. As the eldest child my dream had always been to follow in my father's footsteps. Whenever opportunity offered during school holidays I would be found in the hospital with my father, both in the wards and the operating theatre (yes, scrubbing up and all!). I not only loved the life, but was greatly excited by all that the future would hold for me.

And everything on the horizon looked wonderful – until the beginning of my last term at school. Soon my final examination would be over, and it was expected that I would enter Medical School in Capetown in the New Year.

It is difficult to convey the shock that followed. As often happened in a school like ours in the run up to major examinations, many of us would get up early on a weekday morning to attend the voluntary communion services. We hoped that God would give us extra help for doing these extra stints! It was in a quiet moment on one of those mornings when I found myself looking up at the altar (probably with no other thought than that the breakfast bell had gone and it wouldn't be more than a moment before we got out of chapel. The priest was standing there, about to give the blessing. In the moment of silence that followed I was conscious of what seemed to be a voice saying to me: 'this is what I would have you do, my son'. The first thing I remember feeling was an embarrassment that others had been disturbed by this shattering of the silence (and of course they heard nothing); and then, only secondly, came the shock that such a suggestion could be put to me! Not only because it was so contrary to the dreams and longings of my heart for the future, but even more so because I did not believe I was the kind of person God could, or would, use.

A few days later I found I just had to share this with someone. I went to see Nobby Clarke – a giant of a man (in all senses) who had been priest and headmaster of St. John's for twenty years and was on the point of retiring. I had always found it difficult to think of him as a priest, and thought he at least would tell me not to take this suggestion seriously. But I discovered new depths to him that day, and a gentleness and kindness that I did not think he had. Strangely, he understood the turmoil taking place within me. He understood my love of medicine and desire to help people who were sick. He put his finger on the fact that I could look forward to a life of relative affluence and greater acceptability in the community, and he understood my horror of a life of hardship, poverty and possible ridicule – a view that had built up over my close contact with many priests over the years. It was almost as if he could read my mind.

But he never tried to influence me in either direction. All he said was that if this was a call from God, I could not ignore it. Rather than make a quick decision, he advised me to come back to school for another year. And even here he solved my problem about the added expense for my father that immediately came to mind. Before I could say a word, he told me not to worry about this aspect, as he would arrange with the governors of the school for me to be given a scholarship covering all tuition and boarding expenses for the next year. It was a most generous gesture, and the following year would be spent much more on the 'arts' (having done nearly all science based subjects for my university entrance), taking up subjects such as Greek, and with time to wait on God.

So it was, at the end of that extra year, almost literally with my heart in my mouth, I said 'Yes'. My only request to my father was that I should do my training overseas. That was granted and there followed three years at Leeds University, and a final two years at Mirfield Theological College. Having satisfied the examiners, and earned enough money as a Rolls Royce chauffeur, to refurbish my wardrobe and meet some of the expenses of my return, I sailed home to Rhodesia – ship from Southampton to Capetown, and train from Capetown to Gweru.

Naturally there was great excitement at my return after five years, but overshadowing it all was my own feeling of inadequacy, and a fear within me that I would be unable to cope with the burden and tasks of ministry. I was really fearful of speaking in public – let alone holding forth in a pulpit. And I felt incapable of carrying on a theological argument; the only way I could was to retire to my books and write a reply! How then could God take this material –

John Knight – poor and ineffective as it was, to preach the Good News powerfully and effectively? All I knew what that I was rather like a robot being moved from one stage to another, and soon enough someone was going to discover that I was in the wrong job.

A few years previously the original Diocese of Southern Rhodesia had been divided into two Dioceses – Mashonaland and Matabeleland. My selection for ministry training had come from the poorer of the two dioceses, Matabeleland. Its first bishop was a long-standing friend of the family, James Hughes. He had been Dean of Georgetown Cathedral in British Guiana under my uncle, prior to becoming a bishop in the West Indies. On the creation of the new Diocese of Matabeleland, James was chosen as its first bishop and he was 'translated' from the West Indies. He it was who selected me for ministry training, and he also ordained me deacon in the Cathedral of St. John the Baptist, Bulawayo on the Feast of St. Michael and All Angels, September 29, 1961 and appointed me to serve my diaconate in St. Cuthbert's, Gweru (Gwelo) under the care of another long-standing friend of the family, Canon Reg Adams. A more faithful pastor and servant of God I could not have wished for as my mentor.

But 'bigamy' had begun to rear its ugly head. A few years earlier, Grandmother Knight left British Guiana after the death of her husband, and came to live with us. She was imbued with her Bishop Alan's principles, and she was delighted to come to Rhodesia and have an old friend, James Hughes, as her new bishop. James had also been a celibate for most of his life. Then came the shock. Reports came back that James, who was supposed to be attending Lambeth Conference in 1958, was frequently absent from debates. It was later discovered that he was courting – and came back to Rhodesia with a wife! Grandmother was so shocked that she took to her bed for a week and wouldn't speak to anybody. It was a long time before she could begin to accept the *fait accompli* and welcome James and his wife into our house with good grace. Not long after, Reg Adams – also a long time celibate and now in his sixties – had up and married Molly Coppock! So when I came to announce my own nuptials two years later, Grandma was resigned to the fact of declining standards! But before speaking of that, I need to speak of my first two years in Gweru.

CHAPTER FOUR

THE FIRST FALTERING STEPS

My arrival in Gweru in 1961 to serve my diaconate was not, to my mind, an auspicious one. The Church Council informed me that they had secured a room for me at a local hotel. Although very close to the Church, I soon discovered it to be the 'red light' hotel of the area. The rooms were anything but clean and my first night there was a nightmare. I woke an hour after falling asleep to find myself riddled with bites from head to foot. Bed bugs! With nothing to treat them with, I found the only way to bring relief was to spend the rest of the night in the bath. Although the bed bugs were adequately dealt with, the constant comings and goings in the rooms around me were not conducive to rest and study. I appealed to the church Council to find me a small flat or house. They regretted that the parish was finding it hard enough to pay the diocesan assessment to meet the stipend of the Rector – let alone the extra assessment for a deacon they had not asked for and couldn't really afford! Finally they relented to the extent that they gave me permission to find somewhere else to live. The condition laid down was that it was not to cost more than £17 a month – the amount they were paying for my hotel room!

I managed to find a semi-detached house of sorts. It had a bedroom with no windows, so the bedroom door had to stay open to provide air. A small sitting room completed the main part of the house. The kitchen, bathroom and toilet had been made possible by converting a small lean-to porch. The outside wall of this porch had no windows, but was covered with mosquito gauze – lovely in summer, but decidedly cold in winter. I thought the landlord had been particularly generous to this impecunious clergyman when he offered to leave a large double wardrobe in the bedroom for my use. It was only later when I came to give the room a good clean that I discovered that its real function was to cover a 3ft. by 1ft. hole in the floor! The old second-hand furniture provided by the Parish made it a little difficult to entertain. This included a bed and a mattress, one occasional chair, one dining-type chair, one table for dining purposes with a 24" x 30" top, and a small rug. Most of my social life therefore took place in the kitchenette, where we could use the stove top and sink unit for additional seating!

Eighteen months later I was able to rent, still for the same amount, a tiny prefabricated house that was without any insulation whatsoever, so it was very hot in summer and exceedingly cold in winter – but more about that later.

My early ministry got off to a shaky start. At Theological College we literally received no training in what to do and say when visiting people in the parish.

Nor were we equipped or prepared to deal with awkward customers, or with people who were chronically ill or dying. I was quite good at drinking tea, talking about the weather, and then the family, then politics, then back to weather and sport. How to talk about Jesus, or even get on to the subject – that was the problem. No one had taught me to do that, or taken me with them (like Jesus or someone like St Paul, teaching their disciples) and shown me how it was done. And what do you say to the dying apart from comforting them by saying 'Cheer up! You are going to be fine' when you know jolly well they need to prepare themselves for death? And what about the mentally ill? During my two years at Theological College we only once visited a hospital – for an hour's visit – no other institution was ever visited! Each one of us was given a bed to visit, and mine turned out to be occupied by someone who was living on another planet. But no instruction was given on what to do or say. In this first parish there were some notoriously difficult homes – so much so that I would drive around the block a few times just to gather up enough courage to go up and knock on the front door. And even then I sometimes 'chickened out'!

Of course there were also some visits I really enjoyed and looked forward to, and also more humorous moments. On one occasion I knocked on someone's front door and a very small child opened it. She took one look at me and fled down the passage shouting, 'Mummy, Mummy, God's come'! That was her understanding of the person she had seen standing in the pulpit the day before.

As a Deacon in one's first year of ministry, there are limitations on what one can do (or, should I say, could do?) Amongst other things I couldn't celebrate at a Communion service (although a 1987 report in the Church of England Newspaper on a meeting of the Anglican Evangelical Alliance indicates pressure from one part of the church for that to be changed). Nor was I allowed, in the eyes of the church, to perform marriages because I could not 'bless' the couple. Only a priest could do that! (A quarter of a century later the Church of England is in the process of changing all that, too. It is doing this so that the new permanent orders of female deacons can perform marriages. The Bishop of St. Germans is quoted as saying: "The whole thing hinges on the question of 'Can a Deacon bless?' The rule of thumb Catholic view would be that the function of absolution, presiding at the Eucharist (Communion) and blessing are preserved for priests." But the argument was advanced that blessings are in fact a form of prayer.

In the original Latin, they employ the subjunctive to enjoin God to do something. And prayer may – and should be – exercised by everyone. So

Deacons may bless and solemnise a marriage". (Andrew Brown in *The Independent* 5/11/86).

In 1961 I could do neither. Although the Church did not allow me to perform marriages, I was – in the eyes of the state – licensed to perform them as a legal marriage officer! I had only been a few months in the Parish when my Rector went off on holiday. He had arranged that a school chaplain from Guinea Fowl – a Welshman – would come in and not only take all the Communion services, but also a wedding that had already been booked. On the day before the wedding, a Friday, the stand-in priest had taken our Friday morning Communion. As the service ended, I reminded him about the wedding the next day. He replied rather petulantly, "Of course I've remembered it!" He then went across to the Parish Office and our very efficient secretary also asked if he had remembered the wedding. She was very upset afterwards because he apparently 'flew off the handle' at her for implying that he would forget something like that.

The next day, Saturday, was my day off and, as usual I went to visit friends in KweKwe about forty miles away. But because we had someone dying in hospital, I decided to cut my day short and come back and visit the old lady. It was a good thing I did. After visiting her, I came back to the Parish Office to spend the rest of the day continuing my searching through the archives for material for the History of the Church in Gweru that I was writing. Sub consciously I was aware of people arriving at the Church for the wedding, and then noted the usual lull as everyone awaited the arrival of the bride. I heard her car draw up, watched her through the Office window move into Church and heard the organist break into the Wedding march. Thinking all was well, I went on with my work. It was quite a surprise to find a harassed man knocking at the office door a few minutes later. When I opened it, (he had no knowledge of who I was because I was wearing shorts and a bright tartan shirt) he asked where he could find the priest.

Apparently the bride had arrived alongside the groom before it began to dawn on everyone that there was no priest – and the bride was taken into the vestry in floods of tears. I telephoned the priest's house at Guinea Fowl, but there was no answer and I presumed that he had broken down on the way in. I realised I had a problem on my hands if he was not to be found. Fortunately the bride had worked in the local telephone exchange. I needed to get hold of the Bishop's deputy, the bishop being away overseas, to get permission to conduct the wedding if necessary. He lived a hundred miles away in Bulawayo. I gave the girls at the exchange his name and home number, explained to the girl's their friend's problem, and said they had to find Canon Pugh wherever he was, and get permission for me to take the wedding if that was the only solution.

Meanwhile I jumped into my little Fiat 500 and roared out to Guinea Fowl ten miles away. The priest was not to be found. On my way back into town I picked up my cassock from the house to cover up the clothes I was wearing. On arriving back at the Church I heard that permission had been given for me to take the wedding on the understanding that the couple's wedding would have to be blessed by the Rector when he returned from leave.

Now came the most agonising part for me. I had never taken a wedding before – or yet been shown what to do. I had to take the services with pauses between each section, so that I could read the rubrics (instructions) in order to discover what to do next. We got through it in the end. The father of the bride was so cross he said he would never darken the doors of the Church again (we certainly hadn't ever seen anything of him before) and the priest concerned tried to tell Reg that I had failed to remind him about it. Fortunately my parish secretary was able to support me – even if Reg had doubted my word – which he didn't.

That was not the end of the story. About ten years later I was attending a reunion of pupils from one of the Gweru Schools. I just could not take my eyes off one couple. I knew that I knew them – but I couldn't 'place' them. At the end of the evening they came up to me and said that I obviously couldn't remember who they were! I agreed. They then told me with great glee that they were the first couple I had ever married, and far from carrying sad memories of the seeming calamities of that day, had had a great time dining out on the story ever since – even to the extent of relating that I had dressed in such a hurry that it was obvious I did not have a clerical collar on, for a fair bit of my tartan collar was sticking out instead!

Not surprisingly my preaching was pathetic, but then I had always been terrified of any kind of public speaking. At Theological College we had a mere two opportunities in the two years to preach the Gospel – both in local village churches, in front of tutors and fellow students. It was a devastating experience. When it came to my second time round, my Principal tried to encourage me by saying that my content had been good, but…..His advice on what to do about it? "Go and preach this next sermon into a tape recorder – and then listen to yourself!" Yes, I fell asleep! That was the sum total of my practical instruction to be a preacher of the Word of God.

Fortunately, in this first parish I had a most devoted Christian, Pam Braatvedt, wife of the Breweries Manager, to help me. A speech and drama expert, she took me in hand for over a year, underlining the parts of my sermon that should be highlighted, and encouraging me to practice preaching it until some life was brought into the words. Just before they were transferred from Gweru, Pam told me I would never really get anywhere until I threw away my written sermons (written word for word, because I didn't dare take my eyes off the script!) There was no way I was going to do that, and it would be many years before I took her advice and took the plunge.

Also in 1961, the first year of my diaconate, the great dream of bringing the whole of Central Africa together – which had seemed to be a dream fulfilled when the Federation of Rhodesia and Nyasaland was established in 1953, but which was to collapse like a pack of cards in 1963 – was now crumbling around us. Hastings Banda and Kenneth Kaunda were rising to power, and their ascendance brought with it an economic slump that bankrupted many businesses, and a rise in the number of those emigrating. St. Cuthbert's suffered a great deal during those days, but it did also, fortuitously, benefit tremendously from the changes that were instituted at the time. As I arrived in the Parish it was decided to sell the Hall, Rectory and Church (too small for the congregation) and build a grand new complex on an 'island' site that would make St. Cuthbert's a real focal point for the city. Because of the slump, the tenders for the building were ridiculously low – building firms being only concerned with keeping their work forces together to ride out the economic slump. We built a magnificent new Church to seat over 300, a Church hall, a well-equipped kitchen and store rooms, together with another large Hall that housed the Parish Office, Priest's Vestry and three other rooms that doubled as choir rooms and Sunday School classrooms. All this was built on a large 'box' plan with interconnecting covered ways. The total cost of all this was an unbelievably low figure of £40,000 and during my five years in Gwelo we paid off nearly three quarters of that debt. Yes, people would give for a building, but it was almost impossible to obtain money to pay for ministry! That Church has now become a very fitting Cathedral Church for the new Diocese of the Lundi when it was created in July, 1981.

Many fund-raising efforts were undertaken to help pay off the mortgage on the Church as quickly as possible. In the most successful fete, over £2,500 was made over one afternoon and evening. As the evening drew to a close, we decided it would not be wise to leave the money in the church safe over the long bank holiday weekend. After most people had gone home, we had a quick meeting to decide where to put the money. Finally one of my fellow organisers offered his factory cold rooms as a perfectly secure place. At the time we did not foresee the consequences of our decision. First of all we had failed to tell the Rector about what we had done, so when he came to open the safe on Tuesday morning he was stunned to find it empty! The second consequence involved the bank. Because of the weekend cold room treatment, all the coins were stuck together, and were very cold – and the notes very crispy. We were not popular – and it took some time before those girls at the bank were able to look back and laugh at the incident!

The new Church also had its drawbacks. It was almost impossible to hear most speakers because of the tremendous echo as a result of massive concrete pillars, ceilings and floors and the plastered bricks and concrete surfaces of the walls. We couldn't afford carpeting – apart from the centre aisle. We had a great time searching Bulawayo, a hundred miles away, for materials that would tone in with the paintwork of the walls and having curtains made that covered the side walls 'curtain-style'. That helped to absorb some of the echo. Acoustic tiles were almost unobtainable, cost a great deal, and would absorb dust – and repainting would mean the loss of their acoustic properties. The final effort at solving the problem was the purchase of heavy material made up like a rich, heavy curtain to completely drape the whole of the West Wall above and to the sides of the main West Doors. It was an enormous job to have all that footage made up in a small upholstery shop in Gweru. It was then erected, using scaffolding, to hang almost from the apex of the roof, and drawn back with special ties to fall free of, and down the sides of the great West Doors. All these helped a little. But we soon discovered that the best solution to the acoustic problem was a packed church – all the clothes acted as a wonderful absorbent backstop! That was proved in quick succession at the dedication service, my Ordination to the Priesthood, and my marriage.

Exactly a year after my ordination as a Deacon I was ordained to the priesthood on 29 September, 1962 with my long term friend and fellow Rhodesian Jeremy Satterthwaite, We had been through five years together at University and Theological College, as well as our year as Deacons – he in Bulawayo, and me in Gweru. The Ordination was taken by our new Bishop Kenneth Skelton.

It was about this time that I became very much aware of a young Sunday School teacher, Jill Bradbury. By mid-January 1963 we were, to the delight of our families and the parish, engaged to be married, but there were problems about the cost of a wedding, and suitable housing. Jill's Mother was a widow and still struggling to bring up a family, and there was no way that she could afford to provide a reception. This was a problem because between us – Jill a local girl, and myself as local priest – knew many of the people in Gweru, all of whom would like to be invited. We had virtually decided that the only solution was to go elsewhere and have a quiet family wedding. However many of the ladies in the two church women's organisations would not have this, and offered to provide a reception as their own special gift to us. Old family friends of Jill's from out of town – specialists in floral decorations – provided banks of flowers in the Church and for the reception. All in all, over 600 people were catered for. What amazing generosity.

The wedding day itself, Saturday 31 August 1963, was everything one could wish for – dawning bright and clear and remaining sunny and warm all day. A choir forty-strong had spent hours rehearsing special music for the occasion; at the end of the service they presented us with a taped recording of the whole service done without our being aware of it. Jill's promise to obey came over loud and clear! It was a morning wedding, with the church packed to the doors and overflowing outside. Reg Adams, as Rector and long-standing friend of the family, conducted the marriage ceremony and preached. Bishop Skelton celebrated the Sung Eucharist that followed. The wonderful luncheon reception took place in the Church grounds. Altogether a most wonderful and memorable event.

Unfortunately our housing problem was still not resolved. The tiny prefabricated house that I had recently obtained (within the £17 limit set by the Church council) would, I hoped, be an improvement for my new bride – certainly better than a house with a window-less bedroom. However my parents stayed in this prefab while we were off on our honeymoon, and decided it was so unhealthy to live in, that they rented a very nice house close to the Church. Until the Parish was fortunate to be left another house bequeathed to them some eighteen months later, my parents paid the additional rent that was needed.

We did indeed have a very difficult Church Council to deal with, even though many of the people on it *were* constructive and helpful, and some were numbered amongst our dearest friends. They, too, agonised with us at many of the decisions that were made. There was one particular group that looked upon every meeting as an opportunity to be as 'cussed' as they could – and appeared to take delight in being that way inclined. (They would probably have wanted to term it 'righteous' anger.) My Rector was a very sick man towards the end, and I believe that their attitude – their constant threats to resign over almost every issue if they didn't get their way – broke his heart and hastened him into a premature grave. Of the next two Rectors after I left, the first also died in office, and the second had a heart attack that invalided him out of the parish. The Gweru parish was known to be notoriously difficult. As with so many parishes it suffered from an acute shortage of money, literally living from one crisis to the next with an everlasting stream of jumble sales, fetes, and other fund raising events to try and makes ends meet. It was difficult not to feel like a beggar continually trying to wheedle some money out of pockets that seemed to be permanently zipped up. Not surprisingly, many complained that the Church was always asking for money.

Like so many other Christians at that time – ministers more particularly perhaps – I found contact with members of other churches quite a problem. Efforts were being made through Ministers' Fraternals to get the leaders of churches to meet together – but very often if the minister of one denomination attended, then the minister of another wouldn't. With my upbringing, only Anglicans were considered to be members of the true Church. Some of the other churches (Roman Catholics, Methodists, Presbyterians, Baptists, Dutch Reformed – for example) were all right, but….! Pentecostals however were categorised by most of the denominations as beyond the pale. 'They' were people – I had always been told – who went beserk during their services. I was so intrigued – and yet so frightened of being contaminated by their mumbo-jumbo – that one dark night I crept up to the window of one of their churches and looked in. I was disappointed! Nevertheless I still kept my distance, particularly when I discovered the feeling was mutual, and most of 'them' wouldn't come to our Fraternals because they regarded us as unsaved!

Members of the fraternal did help me over one issue with my Rector. Reg was one of the old guard who insisted that clergy should always be dressed in dark suits – preferably black (or flannels and jackets of sombre hue) a black shirt, and a dog (clerical) collar! One day I turned up in our Parish Office wearing a safari suit composed of a pair of shorts and matching short-sleeved jacket in a light cool material – ideal one would have thought for the tropics. Reg was visibly upset and told me it was totally unbecoming attire for a priest. I have a persistent streak in me, and wore it to the monthly Fraternal meeting that afternoon, where the 'suit' was greeted with delight. A few days later several other city pastors were sporting the new fashion. Reg resigned himself to the fact and just accepted that I was different. At least I still wore the regulation black shirt and dog collar. Those too also disappeared from my wardrobe some years later.

One attitude that arose in the Ministers' Fraternal did cause me deep anger for some years. Quite a number of those men had the effrontery (in my eyes) to assert that they were sure of going to heaven! The sheer arrogance of their stance – apparently believing themselves to be holy enough to go to heaven – made me very angry. Only years later was I brought to an understanding of what Scripture said about this. It was to change my life.

What a far cry so much of this seemed to be from the kind of victorious Church one reads about in the New Testament – a church that grew by leaps and bounds, was filled with enthusiasm, had a sense of purpose, and was assured of God's provision for all its needs:

"Peter made his appeal to them and with many other words he urged them saying, 'Save yourselves from the punishment coming on this wicked people!' Many of them believed his message and were baptised, and about three thousand people were added to the group that day. They spent their time in learning from the apostles, taking part in the fellowship, and sharing in the fellowship meals and the prayers. Many miracles and wonders were being done through the apostles, and everyone was filled with awe. All the believers continued together in close fellowship and shared their belongings..." (Acts 2:40-44).

There was little evidence of this in my ministry or in the ministry of the Church of the 1960's. Despite the fact that some well-known theologians of that time did not believe in miracles, I felt that there was something missing. However, more than anything else, I began to feel not only inadequate as a priest, but a real all-round failure. After visiting a person who was chronically ill and praying for him with no apparent result, the subsequent visits became more and more difficult for me because there was nothing I could do or say to help that person. We had written miracles out of normal Christian experience. So what was left?

There were also moments in our times of worship that gave me cause for concern. Would we rattle through the prayers – as we so often did – if Jesus was actually present there? Is that the way we would speak to Him? Of course we wouldn't. But we did! One priest known to me – and there were and are others like him –took pride in the fact he could get through the whole of the Communion Liturgy in seventeen minutes flat on a week day morning! It had no more meaning that listening to a machine gun set on automatic and rapid fire. The noise was there, but there was no hope of distinguishing between the individual shots. For all too many of us, the practice of our religion had become as impersonal as that.

Reg Adams died in 1965, and I was left as Acting Rector of the parish. It was a traumatic year in many ways, Ian Smith, Prime Minister of Rhodesia, – together with his full cabinet – unilaterally declared Rhodesia independent of Britain (UDI 11 November 1965). For a short time, especially as it was advocated by the Archbishop of Canterbury, we anxiously wondered if a British Task Force would fly in to try and wrest back control from the Rhodesia Front Party. Would it be a repeat of the American War of Independence (so similar in so many ways) all over again? Ministry-wise I seemed to spend a disproportionately large part of my time getting back into church those people who took exception – at one time or another – to the Archbishop's, or other Bishop's statements on the political issues of our day. From the ministry point of view, by the beginning of 1966 I had had enough, and felt that the only solution left open to me was to leave.

We did have one final blessing before leaving Gweru: the miracle birth of our son Andrew in December, 1965. Was it indeed a miracle and God's way of trying to show us that miracles still do indeed happen? Jill had been in the maternity home in Harare for some weeks with severe toxaemia before it was suddenly discovered that there was no longer a foetal heartbeat. Partly because my father was in the medical profession, there were several specialists in the operating theatre when Andrew was born. We were told later that Andrew held the record for the length of time after birth without breathing – and yet surviving. After trying everything possible, they finally injected something directly into the brain – and he started to breathe. He had a large lump there on the top of his head for nearly a year! Even that was not the end of the story. He was able to survive the next few weeks because of a special incubator which had recently arrived from the United States. It was the gift of a wealthy Harare business family who had themselves lost a child because there was no such machine in Rhodesia. Their generosity made it possible for our son Andrew to be the first child to be saved in this unit. He has gone from strength to strength from that day on,

Despite the joy and wonder of our own son, I knew that I could no longer continue in Gweru. Was it also time to look for some other kind of work?

CHAPTER FIVE

SIDESTEPPING INTO BUSINESS

With hindsight, I am sure that the main reason for my unhappiness and disillusionment in the ministry was that I was continually trying to minister in my own strength. But God, in His wonderful way, placed another person in my path who was able to help me along and rekindle within me a hope for the future. He was another friend of the family, Cecil Alderson. Cecil had been a Bishop in a number of Dioceses in South Africa, and had only recently been appointed Bishop of the neighbouring Diocese of Mashonaland. After hearing my side of the story, he suggested that it was time for me to make a move from my parish in Gweru. He offered me the tiny parish of St. Mark's, Ruwa, which had probably one of the most beautiful churches in Rhodesia, and covered the small farming areas of Bromley, Ruwa and Melfort just to the east of Harare (Salisbury). The bishop soon revealed that the parish was only somewhere for me to 'park' myself, even though it soon grew to an area of over 10 000 square miles with chapelries (Arcturus, Mrewa, Hoyuyu, Mtoko) extending to the eastern border of Zimbabwe on the main road to Malawi, and a Central Mission Station. The mission (so termed because it was not considered to have achieved the maturity of parish status) had a central church, junior and senior schools and the Shearly Cripps African Children's Home, together with eight other churches and schools on outlying stations. In addition to everything else, a priest-in-charge of a mission station was also manager of the schools.

The real purpose behind placing me at Ruwa was to make use of one of my natural gifts for the benefit of the Church. Accountancy being my special hobby, Bishop Cecil asked me to conduct audit checks on many of the mission stations in the Diocese.

As I undertook that task, I discovered that the missions and their school systems – where priests acted as managers for anything from fifteen to thirty schools – were in a terrible financial mess. Not only that, but many of the things that came to light as a result of my enquiries literally broke the heart of Bishop Cecil. He died very suddenly on a brief visit to South Africa soon afterwards.

It was my unhappy duty to welcome our new Bishop, Paul Burrough from England, with an alarming picture of gross mismanagement throughout much of our school and mission system, with many people 'on the make'. The sheaf of reports would have been enough to break the back, or heart, of most men before they even got started. Fortunately, and perhaps as a result of his incarceration in a Japanese prisoner of war camp for most of the Second World War, the new bishop was made of sterner stuff. One of his feats in the early days of his episcopacy was to walk 400 miles through the African bush during the forty days of Lent to meet the people!, a walk which included crossing rivers in flood. And he walked the legs off anyone who cared to join him for short stretches.

Soon after Bishop Paul's arrival, I was due to undertake an audit of yet another mission. I had sent a letter to the priest, advising him that he would be required to prepare all the various record books for inspection. The bishop was horrified to receive a letter threatening my life if I set foot in his mission, being very new, all the bishop could think to do was to call on the archdeacon, David Neaum, who was to accompany me that day, and ask David to take the Bishop's ring as a mark of the bishop's authority for the visit. David just laughed, handed the ring back to the bishop and said: 'You don't have to worry about John. He carries a revolver under the seat of his car!' You can imagine the Bishop's startled reaction.

The priest was not there when we arrived, and so we asked his wife to unlock the office for us so that we could start our checks. The priest arrived back later in the afternoon very much under the weather. After explaining to him that he would never get out of the mess he was in until he accepted help and advice, we finally got his co-operation for the rest of the week that we were there. Another priest was so antagonistic that he removed all the books from the office and consistently refused to let us have sight of them. The bishop eventually had to write to him and tell him that unless everything that was needed was brought to the bishop's office by Easter Sunday, he would be permanently removed from the ministry.

On another occasion I received a note from the bishop informing me that a certain mission was complaining that the previous priest-in-charge had taken the mission typewriter and duplicator away with him – would I please check it out. On being questioned about them, he said they were his own property, so I asked how he had bought them. He then explained that when he went to Mission 'X', they had neither of these essential pieces of office equipment. So with great personal initiative, he had purchased them. On being asked where the money came from, he finally agreed that he had paid for them with a mission cheque, buy argued it was his 'initiative' that had made their acquisition possible. Knowing that he didn't have a car in his latest posting, I said to him: 'If, with great initiative, you save up mission money here and finally go out and buy a car for yourself to use on the job, will it be yours when you move on to another mission?' 'Oh, no Father! That is a big thing! was the reply. One by one I loaded the typewriter and duplicator into my car and drove off.

It is important to stress that much of the blame for the financial mismanagement in the missions and schools was due to lack of training and supervision from the top. Of course it will be argued that black priests raised such a song and dance about not being given responsibility to run the missions without white overall leadership that the Church moved *too* rapidly and handed over control to priests who, by and large, were given no instruction on how to keep accounts or on how to manage their financial affairs. The result was a total disaster. Furthermore, to compound the problem, the Church had 'required' that regular financial returns be submitted to head office. When these did come in they were stacked away and never checked – so that the priest, who was at least trying, never had his mistakes picked up and corrected. Those who never sent in returns were never chased up! Bishop Alderson realised this, and for this reason asked me to undertake this job and unravel the mess that had accumulated over the previous ten to fifteen years.

We did have one priest who really did things in style. He lived far from 'civilisation', and as I found it difficult to carry out an audit while accepting the hospitality of the person one is auditing – they can usually ill afford it – I decided to take a caravan. David Neaum also accompanied me on this trip. On our first day there the priest insisted we have lunch with him. It was magnificent. Roast beef and Yorkshire Pudding – with rosella jelly and all the trimmings. The second day it was roast duck with all that you would expect a high class hotel to serve as an accompaniment. The third day was roast pork and apple sauce. And so the week went on. Just before leaving, we asked the priest if we could see his wife to thank her for the truly wonderful meals that we had eaten. He then told us that when he had important guests, his wife did not cook. Instead, he engaged the recently retired chief chef from Government House (the home of the Governor General of Rhodesia) to cook for him!

He knew matters were coming to a head when he heard I was coming, so it just so happened that his school book room – with all his unsold school supplies) burnt down ten days before our arrival. He quoted his stocks lost at about Z$5,000. Unfortunately for him, the insurance loss adjustor I had sent in was able to determine that little more than $500 of stock had gone up in smoke.

After a long round of audits, I found it unfair that one priest after another was getting away with theft and embezzlement. Bishop Cecil had clearly laid down that every layman found guilty of using funds for his own purposes was to be prosecuted in a court of law, and I had to deal with quite a few people in this way, with former employees receiving terms of imprisonment. However I was not allowed to deal with the priests in the same manner, for the bishop said that that was his responsibility. Nevertheless, when I got to this priest, I felt he should not be allowed to get away with it, so I told David Neaum that I was going to ask the priest to refund those monies that I knew he had *definitely* put in his own pocket. Earning only Z$75 a month, there was no way he could regularly afford to buy himself a brand new Land Rover as he did.

At the end of the week I showed him all the amounts that couldn't be accounted for, which amounted to just on Z$2,000. I then told him I was going to prosecute him unless he refunded the money. No two people could have been more surprised than David and I when the priest took out a cheque book and wrote me his own personal cheque for the full amount! On our long drive back to Harare we were quite sure the cheque would 'bounce'! Not a bit of it. The Bank met the cheque in full.

The overall debts of our schools system amounted to more than Z$60,000 and the Diocese of Mashonaland would have been bankrupted – and all priests given notice – if all our creditors had foreclosed on us, On being asked if I had any ideas how we might extricate ourselves from the mess we were in, I suggested a centralised system of financial control with the development of a bulk-buying system (through the operation of a tender system) to provide for all the Schools requirements, right down to the last piece of chalk used in every classroom. We needed to buy exercise books by the 'ton' – not by the gross, etc.

I was asked to draw up tentative plans to put the suggested system into operation and the outlined plans were accepted by the Diocese. Employment agencies were then approached with regard to finding a suitable administrator to undertake the multi-million dollar project. On being told that such a person would require an annual salary in excess of Z$15,000 plus expenses, the diocese decided (in view of the heavy indebtedness already incurred) to ask me if I would be willing to be seconded from the full-time ministry to take on the job….on the understanding that it would be for a limited period (so that I would not be permanently lost to the full-time ministry), and that I would still be paid my normal priest's stipend of Z$130 per month (Z$1,560 p.a.) plus house and car!
The Diocesan Standing Committee did not appear to be amused when I had the temerity to lay down two conditions before accepting the offer. First, all funds generated in the school system were to remain in the school system and the Church would have no right to 'milk' some of the profits for any other purpose; and secondly, that I alone would have the sole right of deciding who would he hired and fired. They took a month to think about that. After finally accepting the conditions, I was appointed Administrator of the Diocesan Education Office. Soon afterwards I fired all the priest school managers throughout our school system and appointed full-time professional laid managers in their place. It took quite a while before the reverberations died down!

I only lived at Ruwa for two and a half years. British sanctions were beginning to have some effect, particularly among the wealthier members of the Ruwa community who were used to drawing on large investments in the UK. The first to be affected in that connection was the Church and a number of our wealthiest members decided that their giving to the Church should be the first item to be trimmed drastically! When the allocation for my transport – in a large and sprawling rural area – was not sufficient for much more than one day's travel each month, there seemed to be little point sitting around and doing virtually nothing.

We had suffered a great heartbreak in Ruwa with the crib death of our second son, David – only a month old. It was accompanied by the usual – but quite wrong – guilt feelings that perhaps we were responsible in some way. It took a long time for the pain to diminish, and for our railing against God at the injustice of it all, to die down. At first it seemed as if nothing could take away the dreadful trauma of finding a beloved child dead in his cot, but we now know that David is with God, and through our own experience have been able to help and sympathise with others facing a similar agony. By the grace of God we finally summoned up the courage to try again, and Diana was born two and a half years later. This time, for the first time, there were no traumas whatsoever associated with he coming into the world or with those early months. She was simply a lovely blue-eyed blonde, whose radiant personality touched the lives of everyone.

Before Diana's birth we left Ruwa to live in Harare, in the Parish of St. Mary's, Highlands. During these spiritually barren yearn years – while I was Administrator of our education system – I helped out on Sundays as a priest when asked to do so by the Rector, David Neaum. I also continued the regular Sunday 'stint' started at Ruwa, of looking after those congregations I had grown to love so much out near the north-eastern border of Zimbabwe – Mrewa, Hoyuyu, and Mtoko. It was an exhausting combination. In all I motored 40,000 miles a year overseeing all our schools, much of it over the worst bush roads in the country.

For nearly seven years I was involved with administering this enormous 'business enterprise', covering many hundreds of schools. It turned out to be an enormous financial success and did wonders for the Church's relations with the Ministry of Education, parents, teachers, children and the business community. I couldn't help but wonder if I had at last found what God really wanted me to do.

In the school field, however, things were beginning to change, Under Government policy mission schools of all the denominations were being pressured into moving over under local government control. Long before this exercise was completed, David Neaum had already begun to express increasing concern about the state of my spiritual life. He began by reminding me that my secondment had been for a limited period only, which I no longer wanted to accept. Nevertheless, with David's support, Bishop Paul asked me to return to the full-time ministry because the school system's problems had been resolved. In a foreword to the *Education Newsletter* of January, 1975 (sent throughout our system) Bishop Paul said, amongst other things:

'Today probably no Anglican diocese in the world carries the responsibility for so many schools as does Mashonaland. Speaking personally, I am bound to say that when I arrived here as Bishop in 1968, one of my deepest anxieties was inevitably the poor state and indebtedness of far too many of our schools. The African Education Office from the time that Fr. John Knight was seconded to that body then wonderfully overcame the problems. Far beyond the confines of our Church, Fr. Knight has been acclaimed as something of a genius in the conduct of this Christian work. It is, of course, a priestly work when so done, but the time has come when my advisers and I are sure that we must call Fr. Knight to return to a more pastoral ministry. Inevitably this causes some dismay among our educationists….'

Reading between the lines of that statement it was obvious that they were becoming a little alarmed at the state of my spirituality, and worried that I would sell myself to the 'god' of business. They were not far wrong. In a feature article in the National Teachers' Magazine, *Forum* of April 1975 (produced by the Ministry of Education) the Editor wrote:

'John Knight could have been an accountant: he delights in manipulating figures and reads financial reports for pleasure. He could have been an architect: his working drawings for school extensions such as dormitories and staff houses have been adopted as standard by the Anglican Diocese of Mashonaland. He could have been a business man with a shrewd eye for a good buy and a better sell. He chose to be a priest….and the dog-collar doesn't chafe at all. Despite his unquestioned business acumen – testified by his outstanding success as administrator and education secretary in the African Education Office of the Diocese of Mashonaland….there has never been any conflict between it and his work as a man of God….'

How easy to pull the wool over the eyes of so many people. 'The dog-collar doesn't chafe at all'…'there has never been any conflict between it and his work as a man of God'. I worked hard at creating those impressions, because I wanted to continue in that kind of work and *not* have to return to the full-time ministry.

The true state of the affairs in my life was that, having found real happiness in a job with tremendous job satisfaction, I was not willing to entertain the bishop's idea; my answer to him was a very determined 'NO'. The bishop was, however, persistent and said he believed God was calling me to take the post of Rector of St. John's, Mutare – a city on the eastern border of Zimbabwe with Mozambique. That made me feel uncomfortable, so I laid down several 'impossible' conditions that would have to be met before I was convinced it was right for me to move on. If they were fulfilled, I would know that it was of God, and I would submit. Unbelievably all the conditions were met within the week, including finding a successor to take my place. I felt I could no longer say no, and agreed to go.

One further thing disconcerted me about the move. I kept hearing from those in the know that Reg Clark, who had been Rector of St. John's, Mutare for twenty years had in recent times begun to face problems with a rising group of charismatics in the parish. They were doing all manner of un-Anglican things and causing the parish, so they said, a great deal of grief. It was thought that a young energetic and hard-line priest would be able to deal with the 'rebellion' and bring the 'heretics' back to the true faith. And that was why I was the man chosen.

Well, I had a problem here. Having been out of the main stream of Church work for so long, I had no idea what or whom they were talking about when they spoke of 'charismatics'. Being the kind of person who doesn't like to admit he doesn't know something, he couldn't ask these informers what they meant by the term. So I visited the Christian Bookshop in Harare and, pretending I knew about the movement, I asked for any books they might have on the subject. I discovered they were as averse to them as my informants, but they said they did have a copy of Dennis Bennett's book *Nine O'Clock in the Morning.*

I took the book home and started reading it, but never got more than halfway through before I threw it into the corner of the room with the comment 'What rubbish! Intrigued, Jill pricked up her ears, retrieved it from the corner, and she too started reading it. She too could not finish it, and agreed with my assessment. At least we now thought we had some conception of who the charismatics were, and agreed on what we thought of the movement before moving off to Mutare to start our new work there. We might be filled with trepidation and misgivings about going back into the full-time ministry, but we both knew that the charismatic errors had to be firmly dealt with, and those who had 'deviated' brought back into the true fold of the Anglican Church.

What a wonderfully developed sense of humour God must have. How often He must chuckle over the antics we get up to, the hobby horses we ride – knowing that He will eventually allow the scales to fall from our eyes so that we might see how often we have been out on a limb!

I went to Mutare and received a great welcome – and, of course, played it tough for the next six months with the charismatic bunch. Mercifully small in number, I thought, thank goodness the contamination hasn't spread too far. I made a point of pretending to listen to them even though they were obviously a little 'round the bend'. I did, however, give them a fair amount of freedom to experiment with some forms of worship, just to show that their ideas didn't work out in practice.

But all through that time God was working on *me!* These people were very loving, and most persistent (I saw them as persistent troublemakers/stirrers) in their love towards me. They kept on handing me new books in the hope that, as they saw it, I would see the light. All those books irritated me as much as Dennis Bennett's had, yet for a time I read them and then returned them – usually with little or no comment because I didn't think I would be able to restrain myself from 'blowing a gasket'.

I finally made a pact with myself. If I hadn't done something, a previous ulcer condition might well soon have reared its ugly head again. So every time they offered me another book to read, I'd say 'Thank you very much', put it on one side for a fortnight, and then return it unread. If they tried to draw me on what I thought about the book, I would simply say I was still digesting what I had read! A small white lie, but essential for my continued peace of mind, I thought.

One other thing annoyed me a good deal when I arrived in Mutare. On my staff was a young priest from Ireland. I liked him instantly, and was very pleased when he agreed to stay on as my assistant priest. On the day that I was inducted as the new Rector of the Parish he, out of the kindness of his heart, gave me a little gift as a memento of the occasion. You can immediately understand the insecurity I felt in my ministry when I tell you that I was angered when I read the title of that gift. It was a book called *The Normal Christian Life* by Watchman Nee. It was almost as if he was insinuating I still needed to discover what the 'normal' Christian life was all about! But worse was to follow.

I had left the book by my bedside so that I might read it when I had a moment. A night or two later I picked it up and started to read. I found I couldn't even understand what the first page was all about! That really made me mad, so I put the book down and tried to forget about it. A few weeks later, thinking that I must have been tired the first time I tried to read it, I tried again. The result was the same! I put the book away in a drawer and decided to put it out of my mind. All this did nothing for my confidence or ego!

CHAPTER SIX

AN ASSURANCE OF A PLACE IN GOD'S KINGDOM

Soon after arriving in Mutare I was invited to attend the weekly fellowship evening of the 'charismatic' group. My immediate inclination was to decline; but on second thoughts I decided it would be far better to know what they were getting up to, and to be available to correct incorrect teachings and interpretations from the Bible. That they were 'on fire' for the Word of God was an understatement. Instead of regarding Bible Study as a duty, they sometimes spent hours every day simply enjoying and sharing the things they had discovered with one another, and they loved long exuberant periods of worship. Oh yes! I was appalled and embarrassed at such enthusiasm, and especially at all the clapping of hands and lifting up of arms! There were also informal groups where they actually seemed to enjoy spending long periods in prayer, together, on other days of the week. I often found their fellowship evening tiring and exhausting. Instead of limiting their Bible Study – like most other reasonable groups I knew – to about an hour, it was not unusual for it to continue for a good two hours and more before the refreshments were brought on!

And I had a king-sized complex about what I *thought* they were saying about me. Because they continually referred to things like 'the baptism of the Holy Spirit', and 'speaking in tongues', I believed they were in effect saying that I was not a proper Christian because without those experiences they had had, I was very much a second-class citizen.

All that only increased my anger and belligerence towards them. I began to look upon them as 'the enemy' – a group that seemed to be ridiculing the spiritual leader set over them by their bishop.

But why was it that 'the enemy' had all those things that I so longed for? They simply loved the times of worship – times which I so often regarded as a duty. When extra times of worship were imposed on me, I looked upon them – unlike these people – as an extra chore and an infringement on the time I wanted to have for myself. There was also their undoubted love for the study of God's Word. Because they spent so much time on it, they were able to quote freely from the Bible from memory, and appeared to have a thoroughly good grounding on the Bible as a whole. Even after fourteen years in the ministry, much of it squandered because I could never read the Bible with the excitement of reading a novel, as they seemed to do, I still knew so little of it and certainly did not find it easy to find a particular passage when I wanted it. Yet they seemed to do so with ease.

And they prayed out loud in public with such fluency, using their own ordinary everyday words! I had never found it easy to pray out aloud, and when I did, I used one of the beautifully written prayers from a prayer book. But it was the *personal* way in which they spoke to 'their Father' and to 'Jesus' that really surprised me, speaking to Him as if that person was right there with them. And they seemed to have no problem with expecting God to work miracles in their everyday situations. Their love for Jesus, so reminiscent of that personal love for Jesus my mother revealed when I was a child, was as real as the love one bears a dear personal friend here on earth. It seemed to bring a living reality to their faith that affected every part and every moment of their lives.

How was it, that these people, who were apparently (in much of the established Church's eyes) so off-beam as regards the 'true' teachings of the Church, had such a personal living relationship with Jesus? How was it that they radiated a joy and seemed to speak of, and experience, a power of God working in their lives that was comparable with the power and enthusiasm of the New Testament Church? How was it that they enjoyed times of prayer, worship and reading of the Bible in a way I had never found to the same extent in anyone else – and certainly not in myself? Of course there couldn't be anything in it. As soon as Biblical phrases like 'every tree is known by the fruit it bears' (Luke 6:44) began to surface in my mind, they had to be hurriedly silenced.

About two months after I arrived in Mutare an incident at one of these weekly gatherings made a very deep impression on me. A young mother gave her testimony of what God had been doing in her life, and of how members of the group had prayed for her, and she had been 'filled with the Holy Spirit' the week before. She spoke of the way Scripture had 'come alive for her that week', as if God had been speaking directly to her and her situation. More than that, she related several miracles she had prayed for – mainly for her children and for situations at home – which had all been 'provided' in wonderful ways. It was the radiant joy, happiness and peace on that person's face that made me realise that she was speaking of something that had, to her, really happened and had transformed her life.

There was another remarkable fact concerning the composition of this group. They were not apparently a group of mad individuals from the lunatic fringe of the Church. They came, by and large, from the central core of the Church's long-standing membership. Among them were people who had been deeply involved in the life and work of the Church for years – but who had always wanted something more. They had been praying for revival in the Church, and quite suddenly it had begun to happen to one after another of them. From the very outset they had tried to share 'their' experience with the leadership of the Church – and been repelled. Yet they had the tenacity not to give up or leave the Church, and continued to show love to them and pray that many others would be brought to share this experience with them.

And it seemed, surprisingly to me, to have touched people of all ages – and not just the impressionable young. There were people in the group who had been Anglicans for forty, fifty and even sixty years! There was one person we knew to be in her nineties (although she would never own up to that) praising the Lord just like the rest of them! Nothing would prevent any of them from attending their groups, and times of Sunday worship, unless it really was of the utmost importance, and then only for a reason which they believed God would undoubtedly accept as a valid one.

Their faith, and their putting of it into practice, had become the most important thing in their lives. Could these really be considered the marks of heresy?

During that first year one of our Church Councillors went overseas on holiday with his wife. Giles Wakeling was the son of a clergyman, with brothers and uncles who were bishops and clergymen. He was, therefore, well equipped to understand the kind of life a clergyman led, and the kind of pressures that are brought to bear on him – and on members of his family – and the financial difficulties that result from small and often inadequate stipends. Fortunately for us, he soon became one of our churchwardens and remained so for the rest of my time in the Parish. Jean and Giles had a good holiday overseas, but almost spoilt it, for me at least, when he turned up on his first Sunday back and said to me, 'Here's a book I picked up in England. I think you might like to read it!' Although he was not, to my knowledge, one of 'them', he appeared to be open and sympathetic to their ideas. Irritation began to rise within me as I stuffed the book in my cassock pocket and went into Church.

To this day I don't know why I broke my resolution that morning. Except, of course, God clearly intervened. After church, as I wandered across the gardens to our house, I felt the weight in my pocket, pulled the book out, and began to read it without thinking about what I was doing. I couldn't believe it! The first two or three pages were a blueprint of my own life as a priest.

An unbelievable excitement began to well up within me, and by lunchtime I had stormed through the book and my excitement had been raised to fever pitch. 'That's what I have been looking for – that's what I want'. With Jill calling the family to lunch, I only had a moment or two to kneel down and say to Jesus: 'I am wholly yours. Fill me to overflowing with your Holy Spirit, and confirm in me now an absolute assurance that I am a child of yours and that you have already guaranteed a place for me in heaven. Thank you and praise you for opening my eyes at last'.

The book? The first book written by Colin Urquart, *When the Spirit Comes.* What a debt of gratitude I owe to Colin for having the courage to reveal his failures as a priest so that I could relate to them, and for pointing the way out! And like 'them' – that is the people who had rammed so many books down my throat – I soon obtained ten copies of Colin's book and was passing them round the parish as fast as I could! I felt so sure every one would discover what I had now discovered. I was largely disappointed. For a while I failed to see that I too had not seen the truth in the past, even when it was staring me in the face. I was finally brought to understand that a 'Damascus road' experience will come to different people in different ways, and at different times. We have to accept the fact that until the Holy Spirit has completed his work of preparation in each individual, *as an individual*, there is no way that we can force that experience on anyone else.

The family could not understand why I looked like a Cheshire cat that had found an endless supply of cream. For days, I just could not contain my joy. Oh yes, I still had problems. Because of my natural reserve and embarrassment at making a spectacle of myself, there was no way that anyone was going to get me to clap or raise my hands. I still found it difficult to pray out loud – in my own words – in public. But I soon crashed through that 'sound barrier', and what a joy it brought me to gain confidence in praying openly, and more and more naturally. It became easier as I realised that I was actually speaking to someone who loved and cared for me; but even more than that – I now knew that He was intimately involved in every facet of my life and of the lives of those around me. A bumper sticker on my car rear window with the slogan 'Wherever you are, God is' was something very real to me. Instead of a relationship between a God-figure who was far away out there, and little lonely me who was here, He was in fact with me everywhere – even if I was, for example, sitting in a cinema watching an erotic X-rated film! Jesus wouldn't like that – and that put a whole new perspective on life! Although I had not intended it, it was almost as if I behaved one way in Church – because I was in the presence of God – and quite another outside the Church. No wonder the psalmist says that even if we travel to the ends of the earth, or try to hide in the dark, we can never escape from God. I knew that God was delighted when I told Him of my love and gratitude, of my cares and concerns, of my fears and anxieties, and of my hopes and disappointments. Interconnected with this was an almost ceaseless desire to sing God's praises –

which I did. Within weeks I had learnt literally dozens of 'Scripture' songs and these, together with many of the great hymns of the Church, were constantly on my lips. Suddenly verse after verse from the Bible was being imprinted on my memory through the medium of song.

Probably the greatest breakthrough at this period, and it was a specific answer to prayer, came in the area of Scripture.

CHAPTER SEVEN

A WHOLE NEW WAY OF LIFE

I have already confessed to the fact that my knowledge of Scripture, despite fourteen years in the ministry, was not as it should have been. Of course one could cover oneself by adding that no one can know everything there is to know in the Bible, and in so doing create the impression that one is as knowledgeable as a priest, for example, could expect to be! So I need to be absolutely frank and honest by admitting that I was ashamed and appalled by my lack of knowledge in this area. I was little better than the average church person who sat in most pews in most churches on a Sunday morning (although Baptists and Pentecostals seem to be better versed in their knowledge of the Bible). As a priest, I had learnt all the tricks of staying one step ahead of the average lay person in this area; and through admissions made to me, I have since discovered that it is true of quite a large number of priests and pastors. How do we do it? Simple! When floored with a difficult question, one parries it with something like this: 'Jimmy, I am glad that you brought that up and I would like to speak with you about it. Unfortunately I have to rush off to another engagement just now, but what about tomorrow…next week (the next appointment being far enough away to do the necessary research)'. Or in a group – 'That is a very important subject – but would you mind, Audrey, if I just finish this topic we've been looking at, and then we will raise it at the end of the evening'. Then you make sure the evening is filled, and at the end you say something like - 'Oh, Audrey, dear me, we almost forgot your question. I think everyone would agree it is too late to discuss it now. Let's leave it until our next meeting and I will make sure we deal with that issue first of all. But please, Audrey, if you feel it can't wait, just chat to me afterwards, or give me a ring tomorrow and we can fix an appointment'. Or one floors the questioner with some big words and an offer he can't refuse. 'Peter, I am delighted you have raised this because the whole subject of eschatology and the parousia have been in the forefront of my mind for some time. Over and over again, during my visits around the parish, I have heard similar questions asked, all showing how much people want to know more about this. So I'll let you into a little secret. I'm starting a six-week course of sermons on the subject at the Sunday morning service at the beginning of July. Will that meet your need, Peter?'

In most average congregations or parishes, in my experience, there are seldom more than one or two Bible Study groups each week. Thus it is possible for the average clergyman or pastor to keep a week or two ahead of these groups and foresee the likely difficulties that might arise. I had never had any problem doing that before, but St. John's in Mutare was a totally new scene. There were a number of gifted and enthusiastic lay leaders, and in our first year there were fourteen separate weekly Bible Study groups in operation. It would have been alright if they were all studying the same subject, but they weren't. Every group was different. Some were studying different books of the Bible, including Daniel, Revelation, Job, and John's Gospel, and others were concentrating on particular themes in the Bible. I was not leading any of them. My role? To go round occasionally to each group. That would be taxing enough, but here was the real crunch. As a group came to the end of their particular course of study, the leader would invite me round to attend the last meeting of the course and then seek answers for all the different problems the group had been unable to resolve for themselves – the 'expert' coming in to finalise it all!

I knew I was totally ill-equipped to deal with that. Up went the cry for help: 'Lord, you know how little I know about the Bible. Please give me a love for your Word and a deep desire to read and study it. And please allow the Holy Spirit to bring understanding to those passages that I find difficult, and reveal the deeper truths that lie hidden beneath the well-known and familiar passages of the Bible. May Your Word really be a lamp to guide me, and a light for my path. Lord forgive me for all the time I have wasted. You know how urgent this is. Please make time for me to catch up.'

No sooner had I prayed than God began to answer my prayer. The very next morning I woke at 3.00 a.m. – fresh and wide awake. After a time of prayer and worship, I found I just could not wait to get stuck in, and for two and a half to three hours, I studied the bible. That became the pattern of my life for a number of years, but the miracle of it all, to me, was that each time one of the groups threw me a difficult question, I would find that, without any foreknowledge on my part, the Holy Spirit had led me to study that particular issue within the previous week, so that it was fresh in my mind. How gracious our Father is! Not that I used that to protect my 'image' or to give the impression that I could be praised in any way for my abilities. Not at all. The Holy Spirit had convicted me that I had to be open and honest, and reveal to each group my lack of knowledge. I would also explain, where necessary, when God had led me to study 'their' particular issue days before having to give an answer – so that all the praise was rightly ascribed to God.

One further joy was given to me concerning this love and thirst for God's Word was a burgeoning ability to be able to find the passages that I needed, and to remember chapter and verse for a growing number of biblical quotations. That, too, was a gift from God, because I had never been able to retain more than a few verses at a time or for any period.

There was one practical issue that had to be dealt with. I was, at first, scandalised at the way some people wrote in their Bibles, underlining or high-lighting passages and so on. God soon showed me that rather than being a holy object that has to be kept in an impeccable condition, it is to be looked upon as a worship manual – still holy, but to be studied and worked through as one would a set of notes! I soon found that the actual habit of highlighting or underlining words and paragraphs, and the writing of notes and cross-references in the margin, helped to imprint those on my mind – and also helped me to find them again with greater ease.

The day I read Colin Urquart's book was the day I came to recognise as my rebirth – when I was, in the words of Scripture, 'born over again'. Not surprisingly that description causes problems to may people, particularly in the church leadership. The phrase had previously made me very angry when someone who had been a longstanding member of the Church suddenly declared that he, or she, had been born again! 'What on earth do you think you've been doing in the Church these last ten, twenty, thirty years?' I would ask with some sarcasm.

All through my life I had been struggling to be good enough for God, trying my best to please Him. All through that time I continually *hoped* that I would finally be good enough to go to heaven when I died. The chance of doing so seemed marginal. Was that why Jesus said the road to hell is so wide and many follow it – and that the road to heaven is narrow, and so very few enter God's kingdom? Added to this was another passage of Scripture that disturbed me. It was the one where Jesus seemed to be saying that, as in an examination, there is a percentage pass mark that you have to achieve if you are going to make the grade; but the pass mark laid down by Jesus seemed to be impossible for *anyone* to achieve. It was this: 'Be ye perfect, as your Father in Heaven is perfect'. I still hoped against hope that somehow I would make the grade; however, each fresh sin, and each falling into sin, would leave me with a renewed sense of hopelessness.

But would a God who loved us allow us to go all through life struggling 'to make the grade', continually striving and continually failing, continually wondering if we would ever get to Heaven? That did not smack of love! I had recently 'discovered' a verse in the Bible that I must have read literally dozens of times before realising the full impact of what it is saying. It was this (the *italics* are mine): 'These things I have written to you who believe in the name of the Son of God, *in order* that you may *know* [not hope for] that you *have* eternal life' (John

20:31 NASV). These assurances were of something that is a present certainty – not just a future hope.

Then there were the words 'Believe on the Lord Jesus Christ, and thou shalt be saved, and thy house' in Acts 16:31 (KJV). To me, everything hinged on the meaning of that word 'believe', because there is another passage of Scripture that says: 'Do you believe that there is only one God? Good! The demons also believe – and tremble with fear' (James 2:19). And no devil – even though he has an *intellectual* belief in God – is ever going to go to heaven because he 'believes' in God. So the word 'believe' in that first passage from Acts 16:31 must involve much more than an *intellectual acceptance* of God! So what does it mean?

What Colin's book was saying was that after years of struggling to be good enough for God, he had suddenly come to realise that Jesus Christ had already paid the full purchase price of all his sins and – because of what Jesus had accomplished so perfectly for him on the Cross of Calvary – he was now a *son of God!* By accepting that Jesus had already done *everything* that was necessary to restore him to a right relationship with God, he was now assured a place in God's Kingdom forever. 'All we like sheep have gone astray; we have turned everyone to his own way; and the Lord hath laid on *Him* the iniquity of us all' (Isaiah 53:6 (KJV).

For the first time I began to understand the relevance of the story of Jesus and Nicodemus for the Christian Church today. The story, in St. John's Gospel Chapter 3, is so well-known and so obviously directed against the day to day practice of the Jewish religion in Christ's day – that most of us fail to realise its significance for *the Church as it is today.*

Nicodemus was a well-known leader of the Jewish 'Church'. He had done everything a devout Jew was required to do. He had gone through all the required Initiation rites (like our baptism, confirmation and ordination) for a man who was to be set apart by God as a Pharisee and a leader of the Jews. He was one of the leading exponents of the Jewish faith, well versed in all that had to be taught to his people if they were to fulfil the requirements of God, find favour with God, and be His child forever. As a Pharisee he was recognised as more devout than any other Jewish group. He never missed 'going to church', and frequently took a leading part in it. We would not expect anything less of priests, ministers, pastors and bishops today. Yet despite his 'worthiness', despite the seeming correctness or indelibility of his 'ordination', and despite his ministry as a recognised teacher and exponent of the faith, he had a problem.

He didn't want the crowds or his fellow 'ministers' to know that he had doubts about his 'ordination'! He did not want to 'rock the boat' by letting them know that he was beginning to question whether or not he really was teaching the full truth as revealed in Scripture. So he went to see Jesus '*under cover of darkness*.' Why approach Jesus? Because this man, despite the astounding fact that he had never had any training at a recognised Jewish 'theological collage', was a man who spoke with an unchallengeable authority. Indeed, he spoke and taught and preached with the kind of authority and grasp of the Scriptures that, if one were honest enough to admit it, left the Scribes and Pharisees floundering, and made them look ridiculous in one encounter after another. More than that, whereas they had to lay down rules in order to get people 'to Church' – and most of his flock went out of a sense of duty – vast crowds simply followed Jesus wherever He went, hanging on every word, and willing to travel many miles over dusty roads to do so. But the really crucial factor was this: Nicodemus could not help but note, with astonishment, all the 'signs and wonders' that accompanied the ministry of Jesus; and certain nothing like this had happened for several hundred years within '*the church*'. It was a long time – nearly four hundred years - since there had been any prophet 'working miracles'.

But with Jesus there was an apparent never-ending stream of people being healed. Nothing could be more embarrassing for the 'established church'. There seemed to be no doubt about it: the deaf heard, the blind saw, the dumb spoke, the cripples walked, withered arms and legs were restored, lepers were healed, and even the dead – if all the stories were to be believed – were raised to life. It seemed that there was just no area of life into which Jesus did not fail to bring healing. Even epileptics were healed, and mad people and the like restored to sanity. So how come the ministry of Jesus was so power-full, and the recognised ministry of the established 'church' so power-less? All of them taught from the same Scriptures, didn't they? How was it, then, that there was such a difference between them? Nicodemus knew he had to try and find the answer.

He at least, unlike the rest of his Pharisee brothers, had the courage – albeit under cover of darkness – to go and tackle Jesus over the issue. Naturally he found it hard to broach the subject that questioned the validity of his own ministry. But he underlines the critical part of the problem when he says to Jesus, 'Rabbi, we know that you are a teacher sent from God'. Why? Because "no one could perform the *miracles* you are doing *unless* God were with him" (John 3.2).

What he wanted to say, but perhaps couldn't summon up the courage to ask, was 'Why is my ordained ministry power-less, whereas your un-ordained ministry (as the Jews saw it) is filled to overflowing with a living demonstration of God's power-filled life?' And even though Nicodemus never voiced that question, Jesus *knew* that this was at the heart of what he was 'burning him up'. I don't believe it would be stretching the biblical record too far to say that here was a Pharisee who had set out to devote his life to God, and found himself a failure – in many respects – in this area of ministry. He was, deep down broken-hearted by it. How true is that for all too many ministers and preachers of the Gospel today. It was certainly true of me.

Jesus, with those gifts of knowledge, wisdom and discernment that were so much a mark of his ministry, hits at the very heart of Nicodemus' problem by the reply that He gives (at face value seemingly totally unrelated to the question Nicodemus had posed): 'I am telling you the truth; no one can *see* the Kingdom of God *unless he is born again*'. Then there follows the seemingly facetious reply from Nicodemus: 'how can a grown man be born again? He certainly cannot enter his mother's womb and be born a second time!'

What was Nicodemus really saying? I believe it was something like this: Are you telling me that I must get in the pulpit next week and admit to all that after all my college education, 'ordination', and years of preaching, I myself have failed to understand the most important issue of all – the key to eternal life? Are you telling me that I must go back in ton the womb and start all over again? Every person understands how difficult it is to publicly admit that you have been wrong. How much more difficult for leaders to confess that they have made such a grievous error of judgement that the majority of their followers will die not knowing the truth. And that *was* the judgement of Jesus on Nicodemus (and so many of the Jewish religious hierarch). As Jesus so graphically described it, they were the blind leading the blind, and Jesus was telling Nicodemus what would be required from him if his ministry were to change for the better. He needed to eat humble pie and publicly admit he had been wrong, and to allow God to enter in and radically change his life!

Poor Nicodemus! *(Poor John Knight!)* But the problem that had developed was not entirely his fault. For over four hundred years there had not been a single word of prophecy from the Lord to Israel! The 'Church' had moved away from God and was no longer hearing Him. It was still going through all the motions it had been doing for centuries – but with no signs of miracles and wonders as in the days of the great prophets such as Elijah and Elisha.

All the initiation ceremonies were still the same. Nicodemus, like so many generations before him, simply taught and passed down to others what had been handed down to him. They tried to do all the things that the laws of the 'church' required. The initiation ceremonies were strictly adhered to; they went to 'church' when it was required of them; they gave their gifts and offerings for the work of the 'church'; some even tithed (gave one tenth) of everything they had. Just like so many people in so many churches and denominations today. But the majority – although doing everything that the 'church' required – did not have any *assurance* of eternal life, or how to receive it. For most, their religion only affected a tiny part of their lives. It had not brought them to a radical commitment of their lives to God; it was little more than a hobby.

They, like us, knew lots about God (about Jesus), but had it radically changed their lives? No, it hadn't. And what about us? All too many have never been taught that the *goal* of all the Scriptures is to bring us to that point of understanding that 'all these things have been written in order that you may *know* that you *have* eternal life' (as a present possession *now*, not just some hoped-for thing in the future after we die). And Jesus confirms this truth in John 6:47 (NASV) when he says: 'Truly, truly, I say to you, he who believes *has* [not will, or may have] eternal life,' and if we have never been taught how to appropriate that gift of eternal life here and now, then we are in the position of Nicodemus – in need of being 'born again'.

That means I stop striving to be good enough for God through my own *efforts*. No amount of 'good works' will ever make me good enough; the moment I recognise that Jesus died *in order that* I might be offered free entry to heaven; the moment I *accept* that *free* gift – then I have been 'born again'. The truth of those words finally became a living reality in my own life – and the words of this song rang through my head for months:

> It's no longer I that liveth
> But Christ that liveth in me,
> It's no longer I that liveth
> But Christ that liveth in me.
> He lives! He lives! Jesus is alive in me.
> It's no longer I that liveth
> But Christ that liveth in me!

(Composer unknown)

That newfound certainty brought a wonderful joy into my life. Christ had done it all for me already. Instead of wondering and worrying for the rest of my life about whether I would ever make it to heaven or not – I could now praise God that He had already, out of His personal love for me, made it an accomplished fact in my life.

But it also left me with a deep sorrow. A sorrow concerning the Church that had failed to teach me this truth in a way that could have stopped me striving so many years before. A sorrow, that I as a priest, had spent fourteen years in the ministry unaware of this truth, and therefore unable to communicate it to so many who were searching for the reality of the Gospel.

It has been a tremendous consolation to me to meet up with large numbers of those I had previously ministered to who have since come to an understanding of what Jesus had accomplished for them, and have accepted that gift of eternal life.

It also left me with a deep desire to teach this truth far and wide, particularly to my own brothers and sisters in the Anglican Church and in other denominations that have not been taught it, and all too often go to the grave wondering whether or not they will go to heaven, or are imbued with a false assurance of their salvation because they have been led to believe that their good works will prove sufficient. They will not!

CHAPTER EIGHT

"RECEIVE THE HOLY SPIRIT"

Having had this wonderful and totally liberating experience of knowing what it is to be 'born again' – as Jesus had commanded Nicodemus to be – there was still a great yearning within me to experience an even greater outpouring of God's power on my ministry. I remembered that it was on the day of the resurrection – as St, John records it – that Jesus 'breathed' on his disciples and said 'Receive the Holy Spirit' (John 20:22).

And yet it wasn't until fifty days later, on the day of Pentecost, that anything particularly dramatic took place in their lives. They knew that Jesus loved them, and had chosen them for himself. They had ministered in His name, going out two by two with the seventy. They had seen healings; even demons had obeyed them and gone out of people in the name of Jesus. Sometimes they had been unsuccessful, and Jesus had to tell them that some things could not be changed, except by much prayer and fasting. Even after they had deserted Him and denied Him, they had all experienced his total forgiveness. Even so, the power-filled life of Jesus was still not theirs. Yet His certain promise to them was that *when* the power of the Spirit was released in them, they would do things that Jesus did – 'and even greater things shall ye do'.

What happened at Pentecost was a fulfilment of both an order given, and a promise made by Jesus on Ascension Day – ten days before Pentecost: 'Do not leave Jerusalem, but wait for the gift I told you about, the gift my Father promised. John baptised with water, but in a few days you will be baptised with the Holy Spirit.' Furthermore, said Jesus, 'when the Spirit comes upon you, you will be filled with power' (Acts 1:4, 5, 8).

"And on the day of Pentecost there was a sound of a rushing mighty wind, and we are told that tongues of fire settled on the heads of each one of them and 'they were all filled with the Holy Spirit and began to talk in other languages as the Spirit enabled them to speak' (Acts 2,4)."

Can you imagine the scene? Jews from every part of the civilised world listened to simple, uneducated people of their own nation speaking in the languages of every nation 'about the great things that God hath done' (Acts 2, 5-11)!

And it wasn't only a once-in-a-lifetime-experience. A little later, on being threatened with death if they ever spoke again in the name of Jesus, they prayed for boldness to continue their God-given work: 'And now Lord, take notice of the threats they have made, and allow us, your servants, to speak your message with boldness. Stretch out your hand to heal, and grant that wonders and miracles may be performed through the name of your holy servant Jesus.' (It is remarkable that there was *no* direct prayer for their enemies to be dealt with!). 'When they finished praying, the place where they were meeting was shaken. They were all filled with the Holy Spirit and began to proclaim God's message with boldness' (Acts 4; 29-31).

I, too, longed to see the Church transformed in that way. And I wanted to be a part of it so that God could transform all my failings in ministry, and give me gifts that I did not naturally have, so that I might proclaim the Good News with power. I wanted to see peoples' lives transformed, renewed, healed; and because these gifts would be seen to be 'supernatural' gifts, the glory would be given to God. But how to go about receiving that release of the Spirit's power within me? That was the question I wanted answered.

I knew that that lovely man of God, Bill Burnett (Bishop of Grahamstown and later Archbishop of Capetown), had simply been praying in his own home (just before Sunday lunch!) when he had suddenly discovered that he was praying easily and fluently in another tongue. There were others I had read about who had received that mark of the Spirit's baptism when people who had already received that gift laid hands on them to receive it. We were soon to discover that God is always sovereign, and that there is no set formula that can always guarantee the gift of tongues for someone seeking that gift. Sometimes it happened through the laying-on of hands, sometimes during a person's time of prayer, and sometimes quite spontaneously. On some occasions when a person had, over a period of time, sought the gift and nothing had happened, I counselled them to stop striving to get this particular gift, and accept whatever gifts the Holy Spirit *had* given them. If the Lord wanted them to have the gift of tongues later, well and good! And all too often, sometimes within days or weeks, at a time when they were least expecting it, they would find themselves praying or singing in tongues. Sometimes it happened in the bath or the shower!

For a number of weeks and months I trusted the Lord to give me that gift in the privacy of my home! But nothing happened. I accepted that the Holy Spirit had always been present in my life convicting me 'of sin, and of righteousness and of judgement' (John 16:8). Even more importantly, I knew that no one could be brought to salvation unless the Holy Spirit was working in him or her. No one could call Jesus 'Lord' – that is, *accept* His full authority in their life – unless the

Holy Spirit was behind it. I knew that it was because of His presence in me that I, too, had experienced 'rebirth'. When I was christened as an infant, the desire of my God-fearing parents was that I should come to know Jesus and surrender my life to Him. For similar reasons they had encouraged me to be confirmed when I was thirteen, and my uncle-bishop had laid hands on me and prayed 'Receive the Holy Spirit' as Jesus had done to His disciples on the day of the Resurrection. And, as with them, there had been no manifestation of the release of the Holy Spirit's *power* in my life. Of course at the time I had been well prepared *not* to expect a Pentecost-experience because I had been told that it had only happened that way in the first days of the Church, and that such manifestations were not needed now. That was the general teaching of the Church! Perhaps that is why the Church's leadership – and so many members within the church – have found it so difficult to talk about the person and work of the Holy Spirit. It has always been relatively easy to talk and teach about the 'persons' and roles played by God the Father, God the Son, but the Holy Spirit has so often been something vague and nebulous to the mainline churches (the words 'Holy Ghost' in the English language has not helped the situation). All too often the Holy Spirit is referred to as 'it'! Oh, yes! We believe in the Trinity, but….

On a lighter level – and perhaps with more than a grain of truth – it could be said that all the mainline churches accept the Trinity but that to a casual observer, it must often be thought that for Roman Catholics and High Church Anglicans, it is Father, Son and Virgin Mary; for some Anglicans it is Father, Son, and Prayer book; and for evangelicals and protestants it is Father, Son and Holy Scripture.

And no wonder that some bishops and clergy became very 'hot under the collar' when someone at an East African Anglican Conference referred to confirmation – when we ask for the outpouring of the Holy Spirit – as 'empty hands on empty heads'! It is an acknowledged fact that the one Sunday in the year that causes the greatest difficulty 'sermon-wise' for most preachers is Trinity Sunday.

I eventually came to believe that what was needed in my life, for the *power* of the Holy Spirit to be released in me, was the laying-on of hands. This was enormously difficult for me, mainly because of my pride. Pride in my ministry as a priest, and as an ordained man of God. There is an inherent belief amongst 'the clergy' that we are expected to understand most things to do with the faith, and that we have an indelible and inherent right to minister to everyone else's needs – but at no point may the lay members of the Church minister to us! I mean it would be about as ridiculous as an Anglican or Roman Catholic priest asking a lay person to celebrate at the Holy Communion service or Mass. It was just not on! In the ordained ministry, we are taught to look upon our ordination as something that sets us apart – and in no way can the roles be reversed.

Although I looked all round Zimbabwe, I knew of no bishop or priest who had received the gift of tongues who might have been able to lay hands on me. So I made a pact with God. I would go anywhere, South Africa or wherever for this laying-on of hands. Why did I make the pact? Because I knew only too well that quite a number of my own lay people already had the gift, but there was no way that I, as a priest, was going to receive the laying-on of hands from them! I mean, amongst other things, how would they ever respect me as their spiritual leader again if I were to ask them? However, God began to show me that I had hurt these spirit-filled people over the past months. More than that, why should I travel hundreds, or thousands of my miles to receive the laying-on of hands from people who would save my dignity, when right here in Mutare there were people God had already anointed in this special way? I began to see that asking these people to do it would be a means of putting right my past judgemental and critical attitudes. It would be a way of saying sorry that would be deeply meaningful to them. Nevertheless, I found that I could not eat the humble pie! So I went on praying to God for that 'release' – but only if it happened in some other way. Nothing happened!

I went away on a clergy retreat in January 1976. There it was borne in upon me that I had been laying down conditions to God – and that in no way would God bestow gifts on me on *my* terms! It was a very painful week as I faced up to what I believed God was telling me to do. On 19 January 1976, the day after my birthday, and soon after returning from retreat, I went into the chapel (part of the main church) where quite a number of people met for prayer each morning. I began to tell them of the things I believed God had been showing me. I asked them for forgiveness for all the sorrow, hurt and pain that I had caused them, and particularly for my judgemental attitude. Then I explained that contrary to all my misgivings in the past about such ministry from lay people, I needed to ask them to lay hands on me for the full release of the Holy Spirit's power within me. Would they please do so?

There followed a truly wonderful time. There was much weeping all round the chapel as they laid hands on me and prayed for me. And what an unbelievable experience it was! (It might be of comfort to some to know that although several spiritual gifts such as wisdom and knowledge and healing etc., were discerned in my ministry over the next few years, I did not speak in tongues for some considerable time. In fact it was several years before I realised that I was *singing* in tongues before the spoken tongue followed. I have often asked myself why this was. Perhaps it was a mixture of fear of the unknown, the fear of being made to look ridiculous, and the barriers of years of *tradition* that had to be broken down).

To get back to the Chapel. There was no crowing over the one who had at last stumbled on the truth. Far from it. There was simply such a joy at what God was doing in all our lives, that I finally recognised the deep love that these people had for me, and the deep respect they held for the 'shepherd' that God had placed over them. There was also, an overwhelming excitement and anticipation at what God was now going to do in our community. There was such an urgent need for the power of God to be seen operating in our midst. The war in Zimbabwe against the 'guerrillas' or 'freedom fighters' posed a serious and daily threat to many of our lives, and Mutare was beginning to enter a period when it would be almost completely isolated from Harare and the rest of Zimbabwe – because of the fear of ambushes along the trunk routes and line of rail. We became literally a beleaguered city on the eastern border of Zimbabwe.

Not surprisingly, what had happened to me soon became common knowledge. The reverberations of that act began to take effect – usually antagonistic – among the rest of the Anglican Church around Zimbabwe. It was surprising how many Anglican priests found some excuse or other to visit our part of the country over the next few months to find out for themselves exactly what was going on. The moment I saw the interest and tried to broach the subject with them, they retreated rapidly. The only relief in the minds of some was 'thank God it has happened on the eastern border of Zimbabwe and too far away to contaminate the rest of the Church!' Nevertheless we praise God that many parishes and clergy in Zimbabwe have since experienced a similar renewal over the last twelve years.

One of the difficulties about the Holy Spirit and the Bible is that sometimes the Bible refers to the 'Person' of the Holy Spirit, and sometimes it seems to refer to the Holy Spirit as 'power'. Perhaps it is for this reason that the Holy Spirit is often referred to as 'it'. In English Bible translations the words 'Holy Spirit' are always preceded by the definite article '*the*'. That is *not* the case in the original Greek which has either '*the* Holy Spirit' or just simply 'Holy Spirit'.

The original Greek recognises two different elements. In speaking of '*The* Holy Spirit', the Greek refers to *the Person* of the Holy Spirit. In speaking of 'Holy Spirit' (without the definite article) the Greek is always referring to the *release of power* which the Holy Spirit brings about.

One example that shows this distinction appears in Luke 4:1 (The word bracketed thus: [the] does *not* appear in the original Greek): 'Jesus returned from the Jordan full of [the] Holy Spirit, *led* by *the* Spirit….' The Greek text refers to a person full of Holy Spirit *power*, being led by *the Person* of the Holy Spirit. A quick glance through a number of references to the Holy Spirit in the new Testament produces an interesting pattern that supports this supposition. For instance, the Greek New Testament obviously refers to the *Person* of the Holy Spirit when it mentions:

- the Holy Spirit as a teacher or person who speaks (Luke 2:26; 12:12; John 14:26; Acts 13:2)
- the Person who leads or directs (Matt. 4:1; Mark 1:12; Luke 4:1b)
- the Person who comes to seal a person with power (Matt. 3:16; Mark 1:10; John 1:32; 1:33a; Acts 1:8; 2:38; 19:6; Eph. 1:13; 1 Thess. 4:8)

In *all* the above examples the word 'Holy Spirit' is *always* preceded by the definite article.

But when the Greek text refers to Holy Spirit as *power*, the Greek for Holy Spirit is *never* preceded by the definite article '*the.* For example:

- when referring to people being filled with Holy Spirit power (Elizabeth Luke 1:41; Simeon Luke 2:25; Jesus Luke 4:1a; John Baptist Luke 1:15,17)
- when Mary's conception is spoken of as Holy Spirit power at work in her (Matt 1:18; 1:20 Luke 1:35)
- when a person is filled or baptised with Holy Spirit power (Acts 1:5; 2:4; 4:31; 10:38; 19:2) and when Holy Spirit power is given to those who ask for it (Luke 11:13)
- in speaking of Jesus as the one who baptises in Holy Spirit power (Matt 3:11; Mark 1:8; John 1:33b; John 20:22); and when Holy Spirit power within oneself can witness with one's own spirit (Rom 9:1).

Strangely enough I had a similar linguistic problem when I set off to preach at the prison in Mutare on one occasion. I shared this prison with a black pastor and good friend, Enrose Hwata that I was going to preach on the theme of the Holy Spirit, and that amongst other things I wanted to bring out the distinction the Bible shows between 'the Person' and 'the power' of the Holy Spirit. Enrose fortunately pointed out to me that the Shona language (used by the majority of the prison inmates) would present yet another problem. They have no definite article in their language. So, in the same way as with English translations, no distinction is made between the two different references to the Holy Spirit. Whereas English translated both 'meanings' as *the* Holy Spirt, the Shona language translated both as simply 'Holy Spirit'.

Though not perfect, it helped me to show those prisoners that the translators had overlooked something that really was quite important.

I asked those men to consider the word 'Night'. It would, I said, immediately bring to mind such thoughts as moon, stars, darkness. But if I were to add the simple prefix 'Mr' to it – Mr Night (the way most Africans invariably spelt my name!) the whole meaning would be changed. One would no longer think of moon, stars and darkness, but of a person. Such a small addition (Mr) came mean so much. And it is this subtle distinction in the original Greek New Testament that has been overlooked by nearly all translations.

For a long time I used an English translation of the Bible – at the suggestion of David Pawson – where I had systematically crossed out the word 'the' in front of 'Holy Spirit' whenever it did not appear in the Greek New Testament. It has helped my understanding of the context of those passages.

Unfortunately my 'baptism in the Spirit' caused consternation not only in the wider Anglican Church, but also in the other non-Pentecostal churches in Mutare, and particularly amongst some members of my own congregation. It caused a great deal of hurt because it was felt that I had gone over and joined 'the rebels' – despite my being sent to bring the rebels back into line again. I had gone over to 'their side'.

The immediate accusation could perhaps be summarised something like this: 'How could I betray all I stood for in the Anglican Church?'

It was a long time before I discovered that Jill had received the baptism of the Spirit – and spoke in tongues some time before I did – but never mentioned it because she thought it would upset me even more than I already was, at that time, with 'the rebels'!

How all this affected my ministry in Mutare – and particularly at St. John's – will be dealt with next.

CHAPTER NINE

THE POWER OF GOD IN TRANSFORMING ATTITUDES

When we arrived in Mutare in 1975, there was already a fair amount of ferment over the use of a recent South African experimental Liturgy, rather similar to Series One in England, which was used alternately with the Central African Prayer Book. This new Liturgy, referred to as 'the Orange Book' because of the colour of the cover, was introduced during the time of my predecessor, Canon Reg Clark. The congregation had also experienced the introduction of guitars and an African Drum, but this normally only happened at services aimed at young people. That generation of gifted musicians had, by and large, moved off to Universities and higher Colleges of Education elsewhere. Up until a short while after my arrival, the Church was packed on Sunday mornings with all the Anglican boarders from two High Schools who were obliged to attend church whether they liked it or not. Many attended with very bad grace and showed it by the way they behaved. Fortunately, unlike my predecessor, I arrived in time to see the schools alter that plan. Instead, pupils attended on a voluntary basis, or attended the special services arranged for them within their schools. When they left, it made one realise how thin the ranks really were in Church on Sunday mornings. We had to start building!

At St. John's there were essentially two main groups of people amongst the regular worshippers: those who attended the early 7 a.m. service (by and large containing a very much older age group, and much more 'traditional' in their outlook); and those who attended the 9.15 a.m. service (mostly young families, together with the majority of those who had experienced the 'baptism', 'infilling', or 'renewal' of the Holy Spirit. The 9.15 group were always much more amenable to change. There was a third much smaller group that supported the traditional Evensong, and a fourth group that consisted of those who attended the Shona-speaking afternoon service.

Canon Reg Clark and the Church Council had so arranged the use of liturgies that the Prayer Book and the 'Orange Book' alternated Sunday by Sunday at the two services so that, by changing one's time of attendance, there was always one service to cater for everyone's taste *each* Sunday. However, as many of our members did not attend every Sunday – and so could not remember which service had which liturgy on which Sunday – *every* Sunday without fail we had irritated, annoyed, or downright angered people present because they had come to the service they didn't like! This was certainly not very conducive to creating a spirit of harmony or the right attitudes for worship! I can always remember laughing at people's description of seeing smoke issuing from the ears of those who were fuming. I soon found it to be only too true. You can pick them out with ease. The 'temperature' of the congregation wanting to glorify God in the presence of even a small pocketful of resentment cools rapidly. Satan revels in that!

I therefore came into a situation that was already causing many 'prickles'. We thought we had hit on a brainwave – after a referendum in the congregation some months later – when, instead of alternating liturgies between the services on Sundays, we agreed to have the Prayer Book at the early service, and the Orange book at the 9.15. The great majority of those who came to the early service were people who loved the more traditional Prayer Book. You can never please everybody all the time and some who didn't like getting up early, but really were antagonistic to the new service, decided to leave the church. It's reminiscent of the argument over which translation of the bible should be used in Church. One great supporter of the King James, or Authorised version, was so incensed at the introduction of a twentieth century translation that he was heard to say, in defence of tradition, 'If the Authorised Bible was good enough for St. Paul, it's good enough for me'! If Paul was anything like the speaker, he would have been appalled at the Scriptures being translated from the original Hebrew and Greek! It needs to be said that though some were strongly 'traditional' or 'modern', the large part of our congregation were happy with either liturgy and many moved regularly from one service to the other.

At the height of the guerrilla war we had another invasion of school children. This time it was the girls of St. David's Secondary School, from the Anglican Mission at Bonda, forty-five miles out on the road to Nyanga. The school was moved into the empty Dominican Convent in Mutare for security reasons. The invasion of several hundred, well-disciplined girls on a Sunday morning – split between the two main services – presented the church with a seating problem. For the first time I came across a new excuse for people leaving the Church: 'The Church is too full for comfort!' They couldn't face being cheek-by-jowl with others in the pew. If the truth be known, they didn't like their church being swamped by other races, and moved to another denomination whose congregation was still all-white.

All through our time at St. John's we had a good multi-racial congregation. For most of that time we had about a third each of blacks, coloureds and whites. No coloureds seem to come to the 7.00 a.m. service, and very few blacks. Many of those who had, admitted they didn't try again because the 7.00 a.m. congregation seemed to ignore them after the service, and they didn't feel welcome. It is also true to say that the black and coloured parts of the congregation tended to prefer the more lively services. The 7.00 a.m. certainly wasn't that, although it was a worshipful service that *I* appreciated as a change. It was a deliberate policy *not* to change things at the 7.00 a.m. service. It was intended for those that liked the Prayer Book Service, preferring the more traditional hymns to those composed in the latter part of the twentieth century. These people liked the service to be conducted 'in a way it had always been done'. I promised to honour those views and practices as far as possible. It needs to be said that there was always a steady trickle of people moving from the earlier to the later service – scurrying back in shock after the first time or two – and yet eventually finding that they liked the new service and the spontaneous joy that they found expressed in the later service. By and large they were the people who had first been drawn into house groups, and had found many of their preconceived ideas, inhibitions and attitudes dealt with there.

There were two 'High Church' congregations (referred to by some as 'bells and smells' because of the use of incense and sanctus bells in the satellite towns of Sakubva and Dangamvura, but St. John's was the only Anglican church serving the city centre and its own extensive and sprawling suburbs. For this reason we had to try and cater for a wide range of churchmanship – particularly amongst the whites who had come from many different traditions within the Anglican church.

Historically the Anglican Church in Zimbabwe had always been strongly Anglo-Catholic with no provision, apart from one or two notable exceptions, for those of an Evangelical persuasion. Inevitably St. John's was unable to please all the people all the time. It is a sad reflection on us as Christians that our 'churchmanship' frequently brings out our selfishness and intolerance of others to their different, but equally deeply held, ideas about the ordering of services.

Speaking of attitudes, we had a problem at St. John's because the coloured (mixed race) people always sat at the back of the church. Only as we became more open and honest with each other did I discover the reason for this. Years before, because there was no church building for them to worship in at Florida – the area they were relegated to live in at that time – the white congregation allowed them to come to St. John's on the understanding that: 1) they sat at the back of the church and 2) (because a common chalice was used) they received their communion at the end! Just like feudal times in the West! Despite this appalling insult to them as an ethnic group, they remained faithful to the Lord.
After discovering this – and with repentance, forgiveness and healing between the two groups achieved – I was able to rib them on a Sunday morning when

they continued to pack the back rows out of habit. Despite the past indignities heaped upon them, these wonderful faithful soldiers of Christ had remained, and continue to remain faithful and devoted workers in all that the church had done, and was doing.

St. John's had on average 250 worshippers every Sunday. A quarter of these would be at the 7.00 a.m., and the majority of the remainder at 9.15. Despite the changes that came about in the lives of quite a large number as a result of the renewal, there were no dramatic changes in the format of the 9.15. The 'Orange Book' was replaced by 'Liturgy 75', approved by the bishops for a ten year period from 1975, with optional choices for various parts of the service very similar to the British Alternative Service Book (ASB) issued some years later. Changes were only introduced after a period of teaching, and then only when the congregation voluntarily implemented such change. For a number of people in the renewal, the pace of change was too slow, and sadly a percentage of them left for other more 'Pentecostal' churches. We felt it important not to empty the Church of the more traditional members, but to try and carry everyone along together.

After ten years of 'renewal', apart from much greater use of Scripture songs, the raising and clapping of hands by those wishing to do so (never more than two-thirds at any time), most people feeling free to move round the church to greet one another at the exchanging of 'the peace', and change of emphases in the service, there was no radical change in the 9.15. However the last two years saw the introduction of two distinctive features. The young people, with guitars and tambourines) were responsible for the preparation and leading of praise and worship times. The significant effects resulting from this were not so much the time spent in practising (although that is important, and they did that), but in the fact that young people saw worship as an essential part of ministry, and spent much time in the preceding week *in prayer* – for the choice of music, for the congregation, for themselves to be worthy vessels for God to use, and particularly that the worship time would help to bring people to the point of experiencing the Presence of Jesus. Not that we ever experienced the same intensity as what happened in the Temple in the time of Solomon. Yet that story does speak of the importance of *praise and worship* in breaking down the strongholds of the principalities and powers of the evil one, *so that* we might indeed enter into the Holy of Holies:

"All the priests present, regardless of the group to which they belonged, consecrated themselves....The Levites stood near the east side of the altar with cymbals and harps, and with them were a hundred and twenty priests playing trumpets. The singers were accompanied in perfect harmony by trumpets, cymbals, and other instruments, as they praised the Lord, singing:

"Praise the Lord because He is good, and His love is eternal. *As* the priests were leaving the Temple, it was suddenly filled with a cloud shining with the dazzling light of *the Lord's presence* and *they could not* continue the service of worship (2 Chron. 5:11-14)"

The second important feature was the formation of a ministry team for the 9.15. It had two regular functions. The first was to meet half an hour before the service to pray specifically for God's anointing on every part of the service – on those who would minister, for the Word of God in readings and preaching to touch the hearts of everyone, and for people in the service to be convicted of their need for Christ; they also prayed for those who were still abed, or intent on doing something else with their Sunday – that God would convict them of their need of Him and to come and worship Him! Their second function was to be available in the side Chapel to minister to anyone in need during the time that Communion was being administered. Many came forward for counselling, prayers for healing and so on. Many testified to the healings that were received, many committed their lives to Christ, and many were baptised in the Spirit.

Although *we* found it hard to observe the change that was taking place – because it seemed so slow and immeasurable – those who visited us from time to time, from out of town, were more able to measure these changes and spoke of what they saw as exciting improvements since their last visit. Almost every visitor commented on the warm welcome they received, the real sense of belonging they sensed, the obvious and demonstrable warmth and love within the congregation (across all ethnic divides), the almost tangible presence of Jesus, and the relevance of every part of the liturgy to their daily lives that they felt was achieved throughout the service.

It must be acknowledged that despite all the care that was taken not to 'rock-the-boat', peoples' feelings were sometimes hurt and feathers ruffled. We *did* often fail because we sometimes allowed our human nature to get the better of us, and we allowed our natural enthusiasms to carry us away. The actual pace of change speaks volumes for the care and concern that those in the renewal had towards those who found change difficult to accept. It has to be stressed that at no time was it felt that everyone had to fit in to the same mould, and that what *was* required was that everyone should be free to do whatever they felt was right for *them*, at any point in the worship – *as they recognised that they stood in the presence of God.* What an awesome yet wonderful privilege that is!

The more dramatic changes in patterns of worship took place in many of the House Groups. Scripture songs, quite a number composed locally, formed the bulk of the 'renewal hymnal'. Many inhibitions and former attitudes were dealt with, through teaching and study of Scripture. The most dramatic change, for dyed-in-the-wool Anglicans like myself, was the experiencing of prophecies, speaking in tongues with interpretation, singing in the Spirit, clapping and raising of hands, dancing before the Lord, ministering to one another's needs; – praying in tongues for wisdom, knowledge and discernment while doing so – and learning to discern the Holy Spirit's lead during times of worship.

Having sung in choirs all my life, probably *the* most dramatic experience for me was 'singing in tongues'. Without prior preparation of what key to sing in, what part each would sing – indeed neither notes or words are given for people to sing – people simply begin to sing 'as the Spirit gives them utterance'. Far from being a terrible cacophony of noise, or bedlam, there is not a discordant sound to be heard. I have been in a crowd with as many as 6,000 singing together in this way – with as many different 'tunes' and 'words' – and on this occasion as on many others, it turned into the most wonderful and powerful song of praise imaginable.

Yes, I initially faced many problems in these areas myself. Years of ingrained Anglican tradition made me strongly prejudiced against much of what I saw as unnecessary 'accretions' to a well-balanced, well-ordered service. Was I taking refuge in a set form of service, however carefully and wonderfully devised, because of a fear within me about those things of which I had no personal experience, and which St. Paul obviously seemed to consider to be essential if the Holy Spirit was to be sovereign in each enactment of that 'form of service'? (1 Cor. 14:26-33)

Added to that, my own British reserve made it well-nigh impossible for me to do anything that would require a public expression of my love for God in ways that are contrary to established Anglican norms and traditions. Nor can I begin to describe what it did to me the first time I heard a guitar, a trumpet, or – worst of all – a set of drums being played in Church! The sheer horror to me of such instruments left me positively longing for the ground to open up and swallow me.

When I had the courage to start voicing the horror in me, people lovingly began to point to verses of Scripture that showed me my feelings were nothing other than prejudice. Why should an organ, or at second best a piano, be 'sanctified' while other instruments are not? (Trumpets, I had thought, might just be permissible in large English Cathedrals, but....and yet isn't our worship the expression of our love for the King of Kings and Lord of Lords?) The passage from Chronicles already quoted in this chapter speaks of *a hundred* trumpeters, plus all manner of other musicians, used together with the singers to glorify God. The net result was that the place was *filled* with the glory of the Lord. Obviously God did not disapprove! One of the consequences of our modern 'sanctifying' of a single instrument is that we have denied large numbers of people their opportunity of ministering with their God-given gifts – playing their different instruments to the glory of God. Instead, as we will hear later in connection with the priestly ministry we have given the job of many to a single, 'professional' organist. References to instruments being used in worship almost always speak of large numbers of them, and a considerable variety at that, being used together to glorify God. For example, look at Psalm 150:3-5. What a joy in ministry has been denied to so many.

I could get emotionally involved in many things, and with people, but put me within the four walls of a church and I became another person, with all my British reserve coming to the fore. There was only one way of behaving in a church; hushed tones relieved by occasional brief outbursts of singing if one was that way inclined. Otherwise all movement was strictly regulated by the prayer book to sitting, standing or kneeling. All other actions (leaping for joy, dancing and the like, heaven forbid!) were carefully excluded by having the pews judiciously placed to physically restrict anyone from attempting such things! Some Baptist, Presbyterian and other churches go a stage further and place their pews even closer together so that even kneeling is ruled out. Is it not a fact that we (sometimes) consider too much enthusiasm or emotionality about the God we love and serve, and to whom we dedicate our whole lives, to be out of place in a church?

I often reveal my emotions when I attend or watch an exciting game of football, or rugby, or whatever, and indeed sometimes 'let my hair down' as I get as enthusiastic as the next person in supporting my teams and their exploits, and jubilantly jump up and down when that is appropriate. So, why *not* be allowed or able to do so when one considers the quite fantastic exploits of God all down through history, together with the miracles He performs daily in our lives? Why *not* be allowed to show special emotion when I consider what God in Jesus Christ did on the Cross for me, so that I might be forgiven, restored and given a place in His eternal Kingdom simply because He loved me so much? And why should I *not* show any emotion over the fact that He revealed that love while I was still a *sinner*? How unbelievable! Yet we have allowed a set pattern of unemotional, undemonstrative worship to be built up, and heaven help anyone who dares to break those conventions. They are withered into a state of shame by the looks that are directed at them for any infringement.

I praise God for the many loving people who released me from that kind of bondage, and for showing me that Scripture is in fact filled with examples of active, demonstrative, extravagant, and passionate praise to God. In our everyday world we often find ourselves clapping our hands to express delight or to show our appreciation or approval. What more natural thing to do as a way of expressing our joy and delight to God who does *everything* better that anyone else? It is a much-used method of praise to God in the Scriptures (Ps.47:1; Isa. 55:12). In the same way – in Scripture – it is the most natural thing in the world to express love and adoration to God by raising one's hands in praise or self-surrender. (Ps.63:4). Unfortunately our reserve often makes us fearful of following suit – not because of what God would think, let it be said, but through fear of what people around us might think!

We pray, because Jesus taught us to do so, 'Thy Kingdom come, on earth *as it is in Heaven*'. Do we rally want that? Do we want to see Heaven's pattern – of worship for instance – replace ours here on earth? In Scripture we are given a number of pictures of what worship is like in Heaven; in the well-known passage in Isaiah chapter 6 and in those wonderful passages in Revelation 4:6-11; 5:8-14; 7:9-12; 11:15-17 and 19:1 –7 for example. Powerful praise and worship indeed! However there is one thing that they do constantly which I have never seen done in a church: 'After this I looked up and there was an enormous crowd – no one could count all the people….all the Angels stood round the throne [hundreds and millions of them we learn in an earlier reference], the elders, and the four living creatures. Then they *threw themselves face downwards in front of the Throne and worshipped God….*' (Rev. 7:9-11).

Our church seating arrangements tend to make that impossible! But would we if we could? What would it do to our Sunday best, let alone what our peers might think? In Mutare we held quite a number of all-night vigils of prayer. Sometimes, being on my own in the Chapel in the 'wee small hours' I would feel the need to prostrate myself before God, yet I still often found myself looking over my shoulder in case someone walked in at the wrong(?) moment and found me like that! Was that honouring God when I was more concerned about what my peers would think? Of course not. Is it not perhaps a sign that we are not yet prepared to make that total abasement, and radical commitment of ourselves before God in the company of all our fellow believers?

What about our feet? Do we use *them* to God's glory as part of our worship? In the story of the lame man who was helped when he met with Peter and John, we are told that he immediately entered the Temple – the *place of worship* – with the disciples 'walking and leaping and praising God'. The disciples did not tell him to stop being so exuberantly excited over a miracle in a place of worship (Acts 3:8).

Dear God! Would we allow *that* in our church? Yet Scripture frequently speaks of people 'dancing' to the Lord as an expression of their joy and *excitement*. How seldom is this demonstrative joy found in any of our church services? See Psalms 30:11, 12 and 150:4 for examples.

None of this denies the fact that there is also a need, when it is right, for times of solemnity. For times of weeping and sorrow as a mark of our contrition and sadness when that is appropriate; and for something else which, though remarked upon as of great importance in Scripture, is often neglected in our times of worship: the need for periods of silent adoration in the presence of the Living God! 'When the Lamb broke open the seventh seal, there was silence in Heaven for about half an hour' (Rev. 8:1).

Of all the regular worshippers over that ten year period, including the large numbers who emigrated or were subject to company transfers to other parts of the country, probably well in excess of sixty percent discovered new joys, and found new dimensions to worship they had not experienced before. They testified to the exciting changes that it brought about in their lives.

It has taken God a long time to break down many of my past attitudes to worship, and He is continuing that work within me. The Holy Spirit's aim in doing this in me, as in all of us, is that I might eventually worship God in complete freedom, 'in Spirit and in truth'. May it be soon. Only God can do that work in us. But He also needs our willing co-operation. None of the 'over-my dead-body' attitude we so easily adopt!

CHAPTER TEN

THE POWER OF GOD IN CHANGING LIVES

Two people in a non-Anglican Church in Mutare, Harry and Sue, had also been part of the group that had experienced the baptism of the Holy Spirit before I arrived. They had been praying earnestly for renewal to take place in their own congregation. They had a young pastor who surprised me by coming to our Anglican weekday Communion services. He told me that during his training for the ministry, and whilst doing his degree at Oxford he had come to enjoy the opportunity of beginning the day around the Lord's Table at the Anglican College. He became one of our most regular attendees at those weekday services. When my life was changed so dramatically, Harry and Sue asked me to share all I had experienced with their pastor. He was searching deeply all through his short time in Mutare. We had a good relationship, but he shied away from the 'baptism of the Holy Spirit'.

On one occasion he came to me with an unusual request. One of his people had asked him to anoint her with oil 'for healing' and he didn't know how to go about it. Had I any experience in this field? He knew it to be Scriptural, because the woman had told him that she believed God had spoken to he through the book of James 5:14-16, and she wanted the elders to do this for her. She was scarcely able to walk, and the ailment had been getting progressively worse for some time.

I told him that it was a fairly regular part of our ministry, and so he asked me to carry it out on his behalf – with him observing and taking part. A number of my lay people accompanied me, and we were able to bring great joy and peace to the woman concerned. She now takes long walks without any sign of the past illness. And although the minister was getting more and more interested in what we were doing (with occasional bouts of withdrawal), he was called to serve another church before anything happened. After the interregnum, we heard that the new pastor was a mature person who had taken early retirement from his secular job, and entered the full-time ministry. We also heard, along the grapevine, that he had experienced 'renewal'. I soon found the grapevine was possibly misinformed and, as a result I found Dennis keeping his distance from me!

It was sometime later that I decided, with my Church Council, to hold a mission for the young people of our church. Through our friendship with another Pastor in Harare (Jill had been to school with his wife), we asked if members of his Youth Group – a dynamic, spirit-filled group – could come down and conduct a mission for our young people. They agreed to send their leaders down with a coach-load of young people for the weekend.

As it was going to involve youngsters from his own denomination in Harare we suggested to Dennis that he might like to bring his young people along. Without being over enthusiastic about the idea, he did finally agree that his young people could take part. The mission was a wonderful success. Many of our young people were born again. All of them, without exception were set on fire for Christ. At the end of the weekend, both Dennis and I discovered that we had been thinking the same thing – 'what a pity to break our young people back into two separate groups after all they had experienced together'! So, against all expectations, Dennis and his wife Shirley, and Jill and I became co-leaders of a combined 'YP' (Young People or Youth Praise) group.

All went well until Dennis and Shirley went on holiday. One Friday evening soon after that a number of our young people – several from Dennis' church – said they wanted to have the laying on of hands so that they could receive the baptism of the Holy Spirit. Realising that I found my self in a tricky situation, I had to mark time until Dennis returned, and so I told them that I was not prepared to do that until they had had some teaching. This, at their request, we started to do during the next couple of weeks while Dennis was still away.

However, as soon as he returned, I visited him and told him about the request and what I had done about it. Dennis immediately asked me to continue with the teaching. The next Friday night he was sitting right alongside me as I talked to the young people. And instinctively, as one usually does, I just knew that he was beginning to 'freeze'. The goodbyes that evening also lacked their usual warmth, and I knew that Dennis was having a problem over this issue. I told Jill that night that I thought that Dennis would probably tell me before next Friday's meeting that he would be withdrawing his young people from our partnership.

I was away on the Monday, and when I returned Jill said to me, 'You were right! Dennis and Shirley have asked if they can speak to us on Wednesday night, and I've promised them we will have no other engagements'! Well, at least we knew that the moment of decision had come!

As we sat in our lounge on that Wednesday evening, 23 July, 1981, I couldn't help but feel, as I quietly observed Dennis, that he was going through all the 'hell' that I had gone through during my first year in Mutare. He was greatly agitated, and constantly fidgeted with the Bible in his hands. He was obviously having some difficulty in deciding how to set about the discussion that lay ahead and suddenly, almost as if he could no longer control the perplexity and frustration and perhaps even anger within him, something went snap and he almost banged his Bible down on the occasional table alongside him and said: 'John, I just cannot go along with your teaching on the Holy Spirit!' For the next twenty minutes or so I felt as though I was riding some rather rough rapids as he poured out a stream of statements and questions that revealed all the 'doubts' that were almost literally tearing himself apart:

'I've had the distinct impression that, because I haven't experienced what you have, that you would say I was not a proper Christian.'

'Are you trying to tell me that I didn't receive the Holy Spirit when I gave my life to Christ?'

'Are you saying that I haven't been properly ordained into the ministry?'

'If it hasn't been the Holy Spirit inspiring my sermons up to now, then where do you think that inspiration came from?'

'Why do you speak about the baptism of the Holy Spirit as if it was something "extra" that everyone needs?' What was wrong with my Baptism? Confirmation?'

'What do you think the leaders and members of my church would say if these young people started talking in tongues? And in church, during a service?'

'The Bible stresses that there needs to be "order" in the church; not everyone doing their own thing!'

'It is all very well having enthusiasm, excitement and hand-clapping or waving at a YP or a Sunday school – but certainly not in Church!'

'I get the impression that all my experience of the Holy Spirit – in my life, in my ministry, in the church – are not, in your eyes, authentic because I don't speak in tongues, or that there is something wrong because I haven't had the same kind of emotional experience that some of you people have had.'

I knew where Dennis was, because I myself had been that way before. I knew the turmoil and doubt concerning my own ministry and the ministry of the Church, and my anger at them being supposedly brought into question. In the next three hours or so I was able to take Dennis step by step through the same process that I had been through.

Of course he had the Holy Spirit in him, for no one can confess "Jesus is Lord" unless the Holy Spirit enables him to do so. And if he enables you, then He also 'remains with you and is in you' (John 14:17) and will 'make you remember all that I have told you' (John 14:26), for it is 'the Spirit who reveals the truth' (John 15:26) – and 'leads you into all truth' (John 16:13). And at times like his baptism, confirmation and ordination the Holy Spirit *had* been at work. Perhaps the words 'Receive the Holy Spirit' had been said over him just as Jesus had said them over the apostles on the evening of the day of the Resurrection – and nothing had apparently happened. But we know that Jesus did *not* say those words and give nothing with it! Jesus would never have done anything like that. I explained the difference, as I saw it, between receiving the Holy Spirit as a 'Person', and seeing the *power* of the Holy Spirit released in us.

I reminded him of all the occasions when people were filled with the Holy Spirit in the Acts of the Apostles – and how something always seemed to happen that was a confirmation of that empowering. Samaria is, perhaps to some, a 'debatable case', and yet even here something happened that was so startling that 'Simon (the Sorcerer) *saw* that the Holy Spirit had been given to the believers….' and said, 'Give this power to me too….' (Acts 8:18-19). He saw something that spoke of power, and not just 'hands laid on their heads'. In the house of Cornelius 'while Peter was still speaking, the Holy Spirit came down on all those who were listening….' For they heard them speaking in strange tongues and praising God's greatness (Acts 10:44, 46) – just as had happened on the day of Pentecost!

Even Paul, then, expected the Holy Spirit to come in such a way that it would be remarked upon. Otherwise why would he have asked such a pointless question of 'the believers' he thought he had found at Corinth. 'Did you receive the Holy Spirit when you became believers?' he asked these Corinthians. And their answer was, 'We have not even heard that there is a Holy Spirit.' Paul discovered that they had only received John the Baptist's baptism – so he prepared them, baptised them in the name of Jesus, and then 'Paul placed his hands on them, and the Holy Spirit came on them'. They soon realised that they had received the Holy Spirit because immediately after Paul laid hands on them, 'they spoke in strange tongues, and also proclaimed God's message' (Acts 19:2-6).

Dennis was able to see how I understood the difference between receiving 'the person' of the Holy Spirit, and experiencing the 'release of His power' from within us. Both of us had indeed gone as far as we were able – within the limitations of what the Church had taught us. So, although we had loved Jesus all through our lives, we had only been able to 'give as much of ourselves as we could, to as much of God as we were able to understand.' at any given point in our lives, our spiritual journey. What had happened to both of us – as it does tragically enough to countless people within the Churches – was that the Holy Spirit had remained dormant, asleep, within us. Why? Simply because we had been taught *not* to expect anything else. Because of that, we had never discovered the key that would help us unlock the floodgates to a power-filled life.

The floodgates, I assured Dennis, was a good expressive word to use for it, because in St. John's Gospel (7:37-39) Jesus speaks about the streams of living water that will pour out from our hearts. Did we want those floodgates to open? "Whoever is thirsty," said Jesus, "should come to me and drink. As the Scripture says, "Whoever believes in me, streams of life-giving water will pour out from his heart." Jesus said this about the Spirit, which those who had believed in Him were going to receive. At that time the Spirit had not yet been given, because Jesus had not yet been raised to glory.'

How easy Jesus had made it for us to receive that power-filled life through the Holy Spirit. I showed Dennis that moving and descriptive passage in St. Luke's Gospel where Jesus had taught His disciples to pray the Lord's Prayer. Jesus had gone on to tell a story of a man needing bread to feed a visitor, and how he knocked-up a neighbour in the middle of the night to try and obtain that bread. He ended that part of the story with these words: 'I tell you that even if he will not get up and give you the bread because you are his friend, yet he *will* get up and give you everything you need *because* you are not ashamed *to keep on asking*. And so I say to you: Ask and you will receive, seek and you will find, knock and the door will be opened to you.' As just as a father of a child, says Jesus, will always give good things to his child – so 'much more then will the Father in Heaven *give the Holy Spirit* to those who ask Him' (Luke 11:1-13).

I gave a graphic overview of my early ministry and the almost constant sense of failure that went with it. I also pointed out how hurt I had been at what I 'thought' people were saying of my ministry – or rather, lack of ministry – and how I had discovered that in most cases it was quite untrue.

Instead of worrying what anyone thought, I showed Dennis that my only concern, after recognising that I certainly lacked the release of the Spirit in power, was that I should be ready and willing to accept anything God wanted to give me that would make my life and ministry more effective for Him. I wanted those life-giving streams of water to well up and overflow my being. I saw how effective the ministry had been in New Testament times. If the Holy Spirit could do it for those men, He could do it for us now, because God is the same yesterday, today and tomorrow. He does not change. And the state of the Church in New Testament times obviously bore little comparison to the Church of today with its present poverty, its millstone of an overbearing weight of nominal Christians, and its divisions and lack of love. And whatever the ridicule I would have to face in the Church of today, I wanted what they had – the 'baptism of the Spirit' as Jesus describes it in the first chapter of the Book of Acts. Perhaps, I said to Dennis, our mistake had been that we had not 'waited in Jerusalem' for the *release* of that power before we set out on our respective ministries. Jesus said, 'Do not leave Jerusalem, but wait for the gift of the Spirit I told you about....for when the Holy Spirit comes upon you, you will be filled with *power*'(Acts 1:4, 5, 8).

I didn't know whether I was making any sense to Dennis and Shirley, they had both been quiet for so long. It was during a pause, while I tried to think of anything else that I might say to help them to understand, that they both surprised us by going down on their knees in our sitting room and saying: 'That's what we want. Please lay hands on us for the power of the Holy Spirit to be released in us.'

Jill and I did so. Within moments tremendous joy and peace filled them both and Dennis was given a wonderful language to pray in. When I telephoned him after breakfast the next morning, he was still bubbling over with joy. He said that he had had no desire for sleep when he had got home, and had prayed all night in his new tongue!

As one can imagine, our 'joint' ministry to the young people just seemed to take off after that. The next Saturday I completed the teaching on the baptism of the Holy Spirit and quite a number of young people were baptised and given a tongue to pray in. The next week quite a few more followed. It was the week after that that a number of the young people who had conducted our youth mission the year before came down from Harare to celebrate its anniversary with us. During the afternoon we all spent time worshipping the Lord and sharing testimonies in between cooking our supper on the braai (barbecue). After supper we went over to the hall and continued with another extended time of worship. It was a lovely cloudless evening when we started.

During the course of the evening we thought a storm was getting up, for the wind seemed to be roaring all round the building. Suddenly I noticed that the girl opposite me – Susan – seemed to be in an almost trance-like state, with her arms and hands above her head, and standing quite motionless. Her lips were moving and her eyes were closed. It went on for so long that some of the girls near her – who had never experienced the working of the Holy Spirit before – thought something was wrong with her and began to lead her to the outside door. By this time I had noticed that several others were in a similar state. I went across to

Susan and realised as I reached her that she had in fact received the infilling of the Holy Spirit and was actually praising God in tongues. I explained to the friends what was happening, and we opened the doors to take her out.

It was only then that we discovered that the noise was inside the building – and that outside it was a completely clear, still night! The experience touched many lives. It was spoken of in the schools. Many mocked the believers, but from that day on there was a steady stream of youngsters pouring through our house, sharing their lives and being counselled. Many lives were wonderfully changed.

Our ministry to the young people of Mutare became a real focal point during the next six years, enriching our own lives tremendously. Saturday evenings were looked forward to with much joy, anticipation and excitement, but our most important work amongst them was training them to minister in their own right.

From the end of my first year in Mutare, my whole concept of what 'the ministry' was all about had changed radically. No longer was I to be the kingpin in the parish, responsible for most of the ministry. Instead, my function as I saw it was to train others to do the ministry. My role was simply to be 'an equipper'. As St Paul so aptly describes it in his Epistle to the Ephesians, some were appointed to be apostles, others to be prophets, some to be evangelists, and yet others to be pastors and teachers. For what purpose? Simply so that they might equip *all* God's people for the work of the church. Why? So that those who have now been specially equipped could set about building up the Body of Christ! And the end result of all this? That we might *all* come to a oneness in our faith, and a oneness in our *knowledge* of the Son of God (Ephesians 4:11-13).

The young were systematically taught to minister. Many of them, especially our own children Andrew and Diana, soon obtained guitars and taught themselves to play by ear. In a truly miraculous way the music group were able to play dozens of songs almost immediately. They were soon able to share their testimonies of what God had done in their lives, and to lead people to Christ, pray for them to be baptised in thee Holy Spirit, and pray for healing in a wide range of circumstances. What drew so many to the YP was the deep love, care and concern these young people had for one another right across the age group of teenagers, without any sign of the usual peer pressure groups developing. It was not that they wanted to be super spiritual at their YP meetings – but the games part of the evening often got crowded out because they were so hungry for the Word of God, and for their desire to meet the needs of young people. It was not unusual to find our home filled with young people almost every afternoon after school – quite often including a new person who was looking for help in his or her life, or just wanting to know more about what made this group 'tick'! Dennis was also a frequent visitor.

Regrettably Dennis and Shirley were called to another congregation in South Africa just over two years before we ourselves had to leave Zimbabwe. We were very sad to see them move away. But God's timing is always perfect even though we often have the temerity to question it. Frequently it is only when we look back on events that we are finally able to acknowledge that God's timing was right. And so it proved in our case. A matter of six weeks or so before we were 'exiled' from our home by the mob (described in Chapter 1) we had decided to bring our YP to an agreed end and hand the few we had left to another leader. Large numbers had belonged to the YP. Most of the YP members of Dennis' church had emigrated by the time Dennis and Shirley left. After that, large numbers from the Anglican part of the YP had also moved on – and almost all over a very short period. Many parents had become concerned over seriously declining Educational standards in Zimbabwe and moved their children elsewhere. We also had a large contingent who had finished their 'O' and 'A' level exams and moved on to higher places of education elsewhere. Most of them found good YP's elsewhere, and many came to play leading roles in them.

All of them were wonderfully provided for before we left Zimbabwe so unexpectedly. God clearly *knew in advance*, and they were not left high and dry!

CHAPTER ELEVEN

UNDERSTANDING THE NORMAL CHRISTIAN LIFE

It was soon after realising that I was indeed a 'son of God', as Colin Urquart so vividly describes it in *When the Spirit Comes*, that I realised I still had some unfinished business to complete. And that was the embarrassing book that my assistant priest had given me on the occasion of my Induction as Rector of Mutare – *The Normal Christian Life* by Watchman Nee. Twice I had tried to read it. The gift, to my rather sensitive conscience, had (in my mind) conveyed the impression that I still needed to discover what the 'normal' Christian life was all about. And the very fact that I had not been able to progress beyond the first page – because I was unable to really understand what it was saying – was decidedly embarrassing after fourteen years in the ministry. I now knew that I had to get to grips with that book and master the subject matter come what may!

So for the third and last time, I hoped, I retrieved the book from the bedside cupboard where it had stayed out of sight but certainly not out of mind. That would have been too much to expect after what it had done to my ego. I went over to the Church to study it, undisturbed. I was determined that this time I would not give up until I had mastered the subject matter of the whole book. Each time I found myself at a loss to understand some principle, or paragraph, I would just stop and ask the Holy Spirit to enlighten me. That always seemed to work. It was almost as if God wanted all those new doors unlocked for me. With breaks for meals and sleep, I completed the book in two days. It was an exciting revelation for me. The Scriptures were opened up by this extraordinarily gifted Chinese Christian in such a way that I 'saw' things in Scripture that I had just not seen before. For the first time I really began to understand, with a great wealth of detail, what Christ's death on the Cross had actually accomplished for *me*. For the first time I really began to understand *how* that death had satisfied God's required justice, and *how* my sin was washed away as if it had never been. And also how the working of the Holy Spirit in power can add a new dimension to the living out of the Christian faith.

I wrote detailed notes on all the major themes running through the book during that marathon two-day exercise. I wrote them in simple language that I and others could understand, drawing diagrams where necessary to help me work out how all the various threads linked together to make up the whole. It was a tremendously exciting experience. Afterwards, the notes were typed up, and many copies made by members of the congregation. This came about after hearing me speak so excitedly about it that they wanted to read the book for themselves. They used my notes and many found them helpful. Surely it is just that kind of excitement that St. Paul is speaking of in the passage from Ephesians where he says: 'We shall all come together to that oneness in our faith and in our knowledge of the Son of God' (Eph. 4:13). There is something catching about a desire to learn when the fire of enthusiasm is sparked off within us.

And that is just what happened in Mutare. Whenever we came across something exciting in Scripture we brought it along to the next daily prayer time in the chapel, or to the next meeting if that came first. Sometimes we would not be able to wait, and so we shared it over the telephone with one another. In our church, we used a new South African Lectionary that provided three readings a day from Scripture to cover every day over a two-year cycle. Each day there would be a reading from the Old Testament, one from the Gospels, and one from the rest of the New Testament. Psalms were also set for each day's use. It was surprising how much we learnt together after pooling what different people had 'seen' through the lessons and psalms for the day. Many new insights were given to us.

Another thing that happened was that we brought God into almost everything. Our prayer lives took on a totally new dimension. Apart from praying together as a group at least each week day, there were also times of praying together in pairs. If ever anyone had a need – whether for self, a member of the family or group, or someone taken into hospital, or in danger of death – we would be on the telephone to each other. Frequently, when unable to get together physically, praying was actually done while on the telephone. And occasionally, a 'freak' took place (with three people wanting to contact one another) when 'one' would be dialling 'two', and 'three' dialling 'one', all three telephones would be linked together. An engineer member of our congregation told us it was just a matter of split-second timing!

Telephone 'chains' were soon established, the 'chains' were used to pass round 'priority' and 'serious' prayer requests. The first person contacted the next two people on the list, and they in turn each contacted two people. We operated it in such a way that the prayer chains of all the denominations in Mutare were brought into operation simultaneously. Within a very short space of time we could have hundreds of people praying. And we learnt the truth of the statement 'more is wrought by prayer than this world dreams of'. During our guerrilla war that was now seriously escalating in our part of Zimbabwe that linked prayer chain was constantly in operation and we heard of many wonderful answers to prayer.

All the farming communities in our Manicaland Province – just as in other provinces – were linked to a central control in Mutare through an Agric-Alert Radio system. It also included others living in lonely outposts. It was manned twenty-four hours a day. Every day, every station was called up morning and evening to find out if all was well. If any station didn't answer their call, a security force patrol would be despatched to check out the farm. When a station came under attack from guerrillas or 'freedom fighters' (those communist-backed revolutionary groups fighting for the overthrow of the Smith Government in Rhodesia prior to Independence in 1980), they were able to press the Agric-Alert button on their set and get instant access to control. If able to do so, they would give a brief report of the size of the attack, and units would be despatched to bring help. If they were already under fire and unable to speak, the pressing of the button was enough for central control to be able to identify the call, and send in a fire-force to help them.

We had people serving on the control who were able to call up the head of the prayer chain, whatever hour day or night, and have dozens of people praying for God's protection during that particular attack while it was still in progress. I could give many instances where I believe the power of prayer worked, but I will give only one as an example.

Our control had just received news of an attack and our prayer chains were alerted to pray. It concerned two devoted Christian parents and their family who lived a hundred miles south of us near the town of Chipinge. Their home was very isolated and particularly vulnerable because it was constructed of wood. A twenty-strong guerrilla group had cut through the security fence surrounding their house late at night and approached to within twenty yards of the house. All the family were in the two front rooms with large picture windows. The gang opened up with automatic weapons and rocket grenades. Two hundred and fifty armour-piercing bullets riddled the house, and two rocket grenades exploded against it but caused no injury. A third came through the window where Lynn Alexander (the wife) lay on the floor, but got entangled in the curtain and failed to explode! Had it done so, it would certainly have killed her.

Not one member of the family was hit by the automatic fire, which literally raked the building from one end to the other at hip height, because they were all lying on the floor. But the baby was still lying in her crib along the same wall at that height. Inspection by the army next morning showed that every bullet had gone through the outer wall, and hit the inner wall of those rooms or objects within the rooms – except for three bullets that should have penetrated the cot. Only at that point had the three bullets failed to penetrate the last half-inch of wood, and the baby survived unscathed. One of the attacking groups then pulled the pin on a grenade, and presumably accidentally dropped it in the dark and couldn't find it. The blast that killed him made the rest of the gang think that Phil Alexander, the husband, was now retaliating, and nineteen of them fled away through the fence. An army major, surveying the damage the next morning, came to the conclusion that the family was only saved from death by God's intervention. At a service the next Sunday in Chipinge, Phil shared a passage of Scripture as he testified to the great things God had done. And it was this:

"I think you ought to know, dear brothers, about the hard time we went through in Asia. We were really crushed and overwhelmed, and feared we would never live through it. We felt we were doomed to die and saw how powerless we were to help ourselves; but that was good, for then we put everything into the hands of God, who alone could save us, for He can even raise the dead. And He did help us, and saved us from a terrible death; yes, and we expect him to do it again and again. *But you must help us too by praying for us.* For much praise and thanks will go to God from you who see this wonderful answer to your prayers for our safety." (2 Cor. 1:8-11. The Living Bible).

We knew that 'call to prayer' was to remind us to continue steadfast in prayer, and it was *because* we saw so many answers to prayer, that prayer became so much a part of our lives. Each new miracle increased our faith in what God could and would do. Emergency calls to prayer were always responded to, whatever the hour of the night, with groups of people in each home praying perhaps at 3 a.m. for a family under attack. Quite often 'your' children would be praying for 'their' children, some of whom would be bosom pals at school.

Apart from prayer for emergencies, there was also on-going consistent prayer for every part of Manicaland. Each prayer group in Mutare was given a sector of the province to pray for, and would pray for every person on every farm and homestead – correspondence was often entered into between the parties so that they could pray for special needs or fears.

The war gave a sense of urgency to everything we did. It was all too true that tomorrow we might be dead. People were dying almost every week in ambushes, exploding mines on the roads, attacks on farms and stores. Many would be personally known to us. Yet it was good when we saw that we 'were powerless to help ourselves', for then we did indeed – as St. Paul did – put 'everything into the hand of God. We lived 'in the valley of the shadow of death', but in no way were we cast down. Death was something we learned to live with. Nothing, however, could be more difficult than trying to minister to a family of unbelievers when a member of the family had been killed.

One of the things I came to dread was the ring of the telephone in the early hours of the morning, because it usually involved going down to army headquarters to be notified of someone's death, and then going to visit the family to break the news to them. The clergy were always given this task. When it involved unbelievers or nominal Christians, it all too often consisted of a heart-breaking scene, for they often railed against God. Sometimes they would find it impossible to accept that the loved one was dead, particularly when no recognisable body could be produced for identification; nor could they bring themselves to forgive the enemy, and so hatred would grow in them like a canker, with vengeance a foremost thought in their minds.

Where death happened amongst born-again Christian families who were certain of their place in God's Kingdom, there was a great contrast. Obviously the shock and the grief were there, but there was also forgiveness for the enemy – which was in itself a means of healing. There was the assurance that separation from the loved one was only temporary. More than that, there was the desire not to grieve for, but *rejoice* with, the loved one because he or she had now entered into the joy of the Lord for ever.

David Watson, in his book *Fear No Evil* (written while he was dying of cancer) describes the radical change that took place in his life at this time. It was 'a coming to terms' with death. He recognised that as a Christian his mental attitude had always been, 'I'm willing to die, Lord Jesus, but please – not yet!' He found that scripturally the right attitude should have been, 'Lord, I want to be with you *now* – but if you have something for me to do first, then I'm willing to wait behind and do that for you.'

St Paul describes it so perfectly. 'For what is life? To me, it is Christ. Death, then, will bring more. But if by continuing to live I can do more worthwhile work, then I am not sure which I would choose. I am pulled in two directions. *I want very much to leave this life and be with Christ, Christ is a far better thing*; but for your sake it is much better that I stay alive.' (Phil. 1:21-24). That was the kind of transformation that was taking place in many of us as Christians. We just couldn't wait to be with the Lord – and almost envied those who were called home to be with Jesus prematurely before we were!

A remarkable case that sticks forever in my mind concerns a dear friend of the family, and member of our parish, Betty. She had been an orphan and grown up with loneliness, fear and deprivation very much to the fore in her life. When she married her husband, he did almost everything for her. When we first came to know her, she had been married for over twenty years, but knew nothing of her husband's business affairs, did not have a bank account, nor did she even know how to write a cheque. Nor had she ever felt confident of her ability to cope with such things. Not long after giving her life to the Lord, she came to one of our groups and expressed startled amazement that her husband Howard had begun to show her things 'she ought to know' about their business, and where to find all the important documents, contracts and other papers he had always handled in the past. He even taught her how to keep a bank account and how to write cheques! The question in her mind was, 'Why?'

In the early hours of the morning I received one of those dreaded telephone calls. An army encampment had been mortared during the night and Howard had been killed. Would I please break the news to Betty? It must have been between 3.00 a.m. and 4.00 a.m. when I arrived at her door and tried to wake her up. As she came to the door, and opened it, she said, 'John, I know why you have come. Just tell me, is it my son, or is it Howard?' When I told her it was Howard, her very next comment was, 'All things work together for good to them that love God and are fitting into His purposes' (Rom. 8:28, Living Bible).

During the next forty-eight hours before the military funeral, she shared with all those who visited her home how God had prepared her for this moment, even to the extent of her husband sharing with her everything she ought to know. The normal roles were reversed in that house of mourning. It was Betty who consoled the hundreds of people who poured through her house. It was her courage and steadfast faith in a loving God that were a real testimony to the whole community. And there were so many others like her.

During those dark days, when most Rhodesians backed away from any suggestion of visiting our part of the country, the President made an unusual and unique presentation to Mutare – the award of the MCM (Meritorious Conduct Medal) as a mark of honour from the rest of the country for the courage and determination of the people of Mutare and the whole province of Manicaland to survive through times of great danger. The citation was as follows:

"The people of the City of Umtali (Mutare) have stood in the front line in the struggle against the forces of barbarism and tyranny since the closure of the Mozambique border in March 1976. Their steadfastness, courage and fortitude in the face of perpetual danger from terrorist attacks both within and outside Rhodesia have been magnificent and deserving of the highest admiration".

This is the first and only time that such an award has been made to a community in Zimbabwe. It was awarded on the 2nd March 1979. Mutare had already sustained several mortar and rocket attacks, both from positions just over the border and from the hills overlooking the city and it would be another year before the senseless war was brought to an end. However, the verse from Scripture that Betty quoted on her husband's death was one which was never far from our lips during those war years: 'All things' – yes! Even death, and destruction, and man's inhumanity to man – 'work together for good to them that love God and are fitting into His purposes.' Many of us thanked God for those days, in that it brought about a radical change in our relationship to God. From something half-hearted to something much more whole-hearted. Material possessions lost their importance, and the only reality was God and our present and future life with Him forever. That war situation changed our whole attitude to what the 'normal' Christian life so often ends up becoming in practice.

Colin was someone with whom I spent quite a lot of time, and a real sense of camaraderie developed between us. He had gone through very hard times with personal problems, the tragic death of a much loved son, the break up of marriage and family and tremendous financial difficulties. His faith had undoubtedly grown tremendously over those years, and there was developing within him a real personal knowledge of Jesus. Just before I left Mutare – such a wrench for all of us – he brought me a copy of something he had up on the wall of his office. I have no idea who the author is, but it expresses so closely what God did in our lives through those years:

WHAT JESUS COULD HAVE SAID TO ME

Do you really trust me?
If you do, why are you so afraid of the truth?
Have you forgotten that because I am Eternal
I am already in the future?
If you place your confidence in Me,
You will not be disappointed, for I will lead
You in My way – and love, joy, peace and power
Will be with you and in you at all times.

Only you must trust Me, even in those moments
When you are not feeling particularly religious and
When cold human logic seems more sensible than
My Way of Faith. Trust Me when everything
You treasure seems to be threatened by circumstances
And conditions over which you have no control.
Trust me in moments of loneliness when you seem
To stand without the support of your friends against overwhelming odds.

(Author Unknown)

CHAPTER TWELVE

THE POWER OF GOD IN PREACHING

It must have been the year after my experience of the baptism of the Holy Spirit that I began to be challenged in the area of preaching. For the previous eighteen months in particular, I had put a lot of work into the sermons that I prepared. Although I didn't actually write them out word for word as I had done for so many years, a large part of the content of what I would preach was down in written form so that I wouldn't 'get lost' in moving from one point to another. I still did not feel comfortable about my sermons, and began to spend more and more time 'waiting on the Lord' for inspiration and help. Nevertheless, a sense of unhappiness after a sermon, perhaps because of a lack of response from the congregation, or the 'wrong' (?) response – 'I really enjoyed your sermon this morning'! – persisted. Had I only given pleasure and entertainment?

The good thing about the Lectionary (list of readings) that we used was that it gave a theme for each of the one hundred and four Sundays and special festivals over a two year period. For each theme there was an excellent selection of three readings from the Old and New Testaments and one of the psalms. Sometimes it was quite interesting trying to discover the threads that ran through all four of them. It was also a challenge to the preacher that one or two groups in the parish used the set of lessons for their Bible Study in the week before they would be used in Church on Sunday. Some of them would be quite disappointed if you didn't pick up and mention what they had discovered! It wasn't unusual, in that case, to be pulled up short outside Church after the service, and told that you had missed the most important, or the most interesting point.

Of course it was tremendous having people in the congregation undertaking that kind of study, and they obviously drew far more out of the lessons and sermon than the average person who came virtually unprepared! At our House Groups– when a group normally met for Bible Study and Fellowship would meet once in a while for 'breaking of bread', in the home – three different people would be asked to read the three lessons set for the day between them and give a brief 'sermon' on what was meaningful and significant to them in their reading. Then there would be an opportunity for anyone else to share what they had heard the lesson saying to them. This developed even further, with a number of lay people preaching at some Sunday evening services. Interest in the preached word was growing. We had a good many who were listening for what they believed God was saying to them, and to the parish, town, community, through preaching.

I increasingly felt convinced that I wasn't really saying what *God* wanted me to say. I could read the lessons and read up what a great variety of scholars thought about each of the readings, and produce sermons that would have been acceptable to my theological college lecturers! What I really wanted to see was people convicted of sin, people challenged out of their comfortable boxes of church goers, and to see them making a radical commitment of their lives to Christ. Although I didn't expect to get the results that Peter got after his first sermon when 3,000 were saved, I longed for the day when people would be regularly saved through hearing the preaching of the Word of God.

It was another year or two later at another Clergy retreat (five blissful days of silence) that God spoke to me about this area of my ministry. It was on about the third day when I actually believe God 'spoke' to me because the message was so clear: 'You don't trust Me!' That really brought me up short. Of course I trusted Him. My whole life had radically changed in the past few years. I trusted him with my very life on almost every journey I went on. I trusted Him to protect my family through war. I trusted Him that my salvation was assured. So what did He mean when He said I didn't trust Him? It very soon dawned on me what it was. I didn't really trust Him to provide the words for my sermon. Instead, with lots of preparation and study – nothing wrong with that – I wrote down all the main points of what I would say.

It reminded me of a little girl who asked her mother what father was doing in his study. On being told that he was writing down what God wanted him to say on Sunday, the little girl said to her mother: 'Then why does he have so many crossings out?'

Many can write polished and erudite sermons that will win the applause of the people. They may well be sandwiched with superb illustrations and apposite quotations from great men over the ages, but do they change lives? Even more important, are they really the words that God would have on our lips, or are we just out to please and impress our hearers? It is interesting, isn't it, that Peter's words to the crowd at Pentecost were not the most eloquent but they were words that 1) came from the heart, 2) spoke of the apostle's *personal* experience. 3) charged the crowds with the responsibility for Jesus' death(!) and iv) challenged them to change their lives. Above all else, the bulk of what he said came direct from the Word of God in Scripture. The only response that sermon elicited from the crowd was a cry from their hearts, 'Brothers what must we do to be saved?' And three thousand joined the Church from that one event!

I knew I was back facing the challenge that Pam Braatvedt had given me all those years before. Yet how could I possibly go into the pulpit without having mapped out, in advance, all that I was going to say. Wouldn't the congregation be just so embarrassed when nothing was forthcoming and I would have to say to the congregation: 'Sorry, I don't seem to have anything for you today!' I couldn't ignore the fact that the rest of the retreat seemed to be leading me in that direction. Was I prepared to trust God to provide for me when the time came? With the largest batch of stomach 'butterflies' I think I have ever had, I left the retreat with the determination to do just that – trust God to provide the words that I would need on Sunday morning. I also knew that there would be a further price to pay – the need to spend the whole of Saturday night in prayer and waiting on God.

Saturday evening arrived and all went well until about 2.00 a.m. Then I said to God that I was just going to read through the lessons for the morning. Immediately came the response, 'You don't trust Me, do you?' With a certain amount of misery I gave in, and continued in prayer and listening to God. About an hour before I was to go and get ready to take the service, I though that at last I could look up the theme for the day and quickly glance through the set lessons. Again came the challenge, 'You still don't trust Me, do you'? I remained obedient and kept the book closed, but when I started that service, I felt like a lump of lead. After the hymn and opening prayers, the Old and New Testament lessons were read by people from the congregation. Then we had another hymn. I still couldn't piece together the theme because I hadn't yet read the Gospel lesson for the day. Up into the pulpit I went – more unwillingly than any schoolboy trudging off to school, but grateful once more for the high wooden sides of the pulpit that hid my shaking legs! I called out the page and reference for the Gospel, and read it.

The moment had arrived – the sermon. I literally hadn't a thought in my mind. Help! 'Lord I am now trusting you – so over to you.'

I remember little about that sermon, and have often wished I had recorded it. One thing I *do* know is that I believed that everything in that sermon was directed at me, with God challenging me in almost every area of my life. I do remember thinking at one stage that it was perhaps a little unfair of God to use the sermon-time to talk about *my* life – instead of a sermon that would have helped the whole congregation! Yet all through the sermon I noticed that the cold terror that had flooded my being rapidly drained away and I was filled with a tremendous warmth. Despite those areas in which I was being convicted, I had a joyful knowledge of God's love and concern for me. As I stepped down from the pulpit to continue the service, I was surprised to see that I had preached for nearly thirty minutes – without a note!

It was after the service that I was really brought up sharp, for one person after another left the church visibly moved, and several had tears in their eyes. Some asked how I could 'possibly know that about me – you have been such an answer to prayer for me'. Almost everyone said something that they revealed that they thought I was looking *only* at them during the sermon, and that I had touched on things they didn't think anyone knew about them.

All I could do was to go back to the Chapel, praising and thanking God that I could indeed trust Him. Despite the experience of this Sunday, I knew it was not God's intention that I stop studying the Scriptures for each Sunday, or just go 'empty' into the pulpit, but He showed me a new way that I have used ever since. If the words of my parishioners in my last year in Mutare are to be believed, the sermons have had a greater and more telling effect as time has gone by.

The Lord showed me after that Sunday service that in future – some time after the Sunday services and before going to bed – I should read through, and mull over, all three lessons for the following Sunday. I would also try and understand the connection of the theme in each of the lessons, and of any other themes I noticed. Then I would 'put it all to bed' in my mind and heart for the rest of the week. On the Monday or Tuesday I would look up a wide spectrum of commentaries on the texts, from traditional Anglican through Evangelical to Pentecostal ones. (One begins to gather very interesting insights when one studies a passage looked at from the different angles and perspectives of scholars from such varied churchmanship). All through the week the material would be kept in mind, often sub-consciously, with the themes being related to the events and situations of the week, and to their relevance and effectiveness for family, church, community and country. Ideas that came to mind would be committed to prayer, not paper.

By Saturday evening I would usually have a picture of the main thrust for the sermon, and of the Scriptures that would be underlined to draw out the relevance of that thrust to God's Word and our daily situations. I would always end the evening by reading through the lessons for a final time before going to sleep. As a result the readings were subconsciously running through my head as I slept. Many is the time when I have been woken up in the early hours with either a totally new angle on those Scriptures that I had not seen before, or with a crystal clear illustration from real life that would vividly bring to life what I believed God was wanting me to say to us through those Scriptures. However good my material appeared to be, I never wrote it down, for I still knew that I had to go into that pulpit on a Sunday morning with an open mind.

Sometimes it was only while I was actually reading the Gospel – or listening to the other two readings – that a verse or a word would almost seem to light up like a neon sign, and the whole direction and thrust of the sermon that had been in my mind all week would be radically altered.

It was still an uncanny feeling to have to put away – at the last minute – what one had thought of using, but I began to experience a real excitement within me whenever it happened – as with the sermon in the Cathedral on the day that it would later be invaded by a rampaging mob! And there was a joy and a delight in somehow knowing that this was of God, and not me, because I had never had the natural ability or confidence to speak like this.

Something seemingly insignificant at first, which led to a tremendous growth in my faith and consequent confidence in preaching, was the knowledge that God had been there before. I need to explain what I mean by that statement. During the war years (and subsequently) we had many 'special' services. National Days of Prayer for an end to the war, for 'solutions' acceptable to the warring factions; for thanksgivings for various deliverances from mortar attacks and the like; and even events like national or community days to pray for rain during a crippling drought.

Never once, for any of those 'special events' did I ever have to search for an appropriate selection of readings for the occasion. We never once changed the ordinary lessons that were set down for that day in our Lectionary.

The lessons for each day over a recurring two-year cycle had been drawn up some years before. When thinking of Lectionaries and how they came into being, one sometimes has a vision of boffins sitting with damp towels around their heads, trying to put together an orderly pattern of lessons that will take account of the church's year, the set pattern of festivals and feasts, and the need to read systematically through all the books of the Bible in that two-year period!! Yet those 'boffins' could not, by any stretch of the imagination, know that in three or five or eight years' time there would be a 'special service' for this or that in Mutare, or in Zimbabwe!

Yet for every special service we ever had (and remember that in most cases we had nothing to do with the choosing of the day) the lessons set down in out Lectionary for that very day were the most appropriate – and usually the most devastatingly pertinent – that one could hope to find. And at every one of these services, I used the sermon to draw attention to this fact. After a while, people began to sit up and take notice. We were dealing with a God to whom nothing was impossible. God *knows* the end from the beginning. He had been there before us – and years before, without their realising it, inspiration and direction had been given to those 'boffins', those compilers, to select exactly what was right for 'that' day for us in our situation!

My own ministry in preaching has moved away from a kind of distant, impersonal and rather theoretical preaching of the Good News to a more personalised sharing of myself and God's day-to-day dealings with us as a body seen through the Scriptures. Some of St Paul's words have meant a great deal to me in recent years:

'I can be proud of my service for God. I will be bold and speak ONLY *about what Christ has done through me* to lead the Gentiles to obey God. He has done this by means of words and deeds, by the power of miracles and wonders, and by the power of the Spirit of God' (Rom. 15:17b-19a).

I was led to be more and more open in baring my soul before my congregation. The more honest I was in sharing my fears, failings and lack of knowledge – and the great things that God was doing to rectify my life – the more the congregation was able to identify with me and be encouraged in their own struggles. I spoke frequently of actual miracles that had taken place in the lives of individuals during the previous week, which brought many to an understanding that God was indeed very much alive and active in our midst. They would sometimes return home from the service with 'goose bumps' running up and down the middle of their spines. That was how real God was to us. And still is!

CHAPTER THIRTEEN

THE POWER OF GOD IN WARFARE

Terrorism and guerrilla warfare in the twentieth century will go down in history as one of the most brutal, cowardly and sadistic forms of warfare, in which disproportionately small numbers have been able to hold virtually whole nations to ransom. Tiny groups of men and women – for the most part indistinguishable from the rest of the people – can render nations virtually powerless because 'the enemy' adopts cowardly hit and run attacks on soft targets, lays landmines without any concern as to who will be blown up, and terrorises the population because it never knows where the unseen 'enemy' will attack next. This warfare is worse than any plague in history and has Africa in particular (and Afghanistan in the twenty first century) by the jugular; and it is slowly but surely destroying whole nations (Sudan, Ethiopia, the Congo, Zimbabwe et al).

Neither side is ever 'holier than thou' – the uncontrollable and more sadistic element on either side going to any barbaric lengths to achieve their ends, or ostensibly 'pay back' the other side for what they have done to them. Those who have won 'freedom' for their people have regrettably, all too often, 'sanctified' a vicious and evil form of warfare that is now used by black opponents to oust former liberators *ad infinitum.* The black leaders now in power are appalled that their own countrymen should use the tactics of guerrilla warfare against them, and (the kettle calling the pot 'black') brand it as 'barbaric' and 'unacceptable' to mankind, and its perpetrators as 'murderers' who must be brought to justice. Africa is over-run by a never ending, and bloody, tug-of-war for final supremacy. This is the case in so many countries in Africa where a very small but vociferous group has got into power and civil war has continued unabated ever since. The war in Zimbabwe (Rhodesia at that time) has brought much the same results. The whites entering Rhodesia just before the end of the nineteenth century brought to an end a seemingly ceaseless war. The warlike Matabele plundered, pillaged and decimated the Shona people at will. The latter lived in perpetual fear of these marauders. Seventy years later these two 'nations' joined forces to win back their former sovereignty from the whites, although for the most part under separate commanders – Robert Mugabe and Joshua Nkomo.. Today 'the shoe' is on the other foot, and the Shona are oppressing the Ndebele people. In the 1990's Mugabe sent in his notorious 5th Brigade, trained by the North Koreans into Matabelend, and, as has now come to light, killed twenty thousand Ndebele to ensure they posed no problem to the Shona. Their bodies were later discovered thrown into old mine shafts.

There is no doubt whatsoever that Ian Smith's Unilateral Declaration of Independence on 11 November, 1965 was the final act of 'throwing down the gauntlet to the African nationalists. Ian Smith's 'no African rule in a thousand years' or 'in my life time' only added more fuel to the fire of determination to win freedom from white domination at any price. As with any guerrilla war, terrible deeds were committed on both sides. Innocent villagers were interrogated and tortured – many of them suffering at the hands of both sides – if interrogators thought that the villagers had aided or abetted the 'other' side.

It was not surprising that many villagers were embittered. All too frequently, when a guerrilla group met up with a security force patrol, a group of villagers would be in between and would take the main brunt of the crossfire. It was only after the war that we came to realise how much we had been brainwashed by 'propaganda material' through the government-controlled media. Partly as a result of that, hostilities continued for over ten weary years, and the loss of much life, before Independence under an African Government came to the new Zimbabwe.

In some ways it was scarcely a war at all. At no time did the guerrillas use tactics, which could have totally paralysed the country, although apparently having the manpower and explosives to bring that about. Relationships between the vast majority of whites and blacks in the towns, on the surface at any rate, continued as normal. Many black and white groups prayed together throughout the war for a solution to be found, and for an end to the conflict. We prayed with many blacks who were devastated when their children were abducted (or went voluntarily) over the borders to fight with the 'freedom fighters'. We prayed for their safety and for God's protection over them.

In the country the most obvious change was that the guerrillas brought about the closure or destruction of large numbers of schools, churches, hospitals and clinics – and the determined efforts of the freedom fighters' were used to stop all government programmes in the Tribal Trust Lands – whether it be birth control, health education or correct agricultural practices (dipping to prevent tick infestation, land measures to prevent soil erosion, etc.) Again, it was the villagers in those rural communities who suffered the most. Almost all church life stopped in some areas, with people being forced to close up or destroy churches, to burn their Christian literature, including any Bibles, prayer books or hymn books, and 'being persuaded' to stop all church services and to go back to the ancestral worship of their forebears.

In some ways it was perhaps the best thing that could have happened to the Church – particularly the Anglican Church which is the only one that I know most about. We were over-burdened with a large number of nominal Christians. Many became members of a Church if it would enable them to enter the next stage of schooling in a local church school. Far too many 'members' were churchgoers when it suited them, but had no inhibitions or scruples about consulting the local witchdoctor when that was deemed necessary. In a research project that I undertook just before the war really got a grip on the country – and which shook the Bishop to the core when I presented my findings – I discovered that our Easter Communicant numbers stayed virtually static at about 28,000 over a ten year period despite the Bishop confirming as many as 6,000 new communicant members every year!

Large numbers of these nominal church people quickly fell away during the war – with guerrillas telling them this was purely a white man's religion! It was largely the truly committed who remained faithful through this 'persecution'. God is still dealing with a number who have remained for one reason or another, but still have reason to consult the witchdoctor and their 'ancestral spirits' on all the important family matters. Fortunately, much of the top leadership of the 'black' part of the Church has made a strong stand on this issue, and shown up those things that are incompatible with Christianity.

The very first mortar attack in Mutare took place in 1976 in the early hours of the morning, and the residents of the suburb of Greenside (where my brother Keith and his family lived) took the brunt of the attack which came from Machipanda, just over the border in Mozambique. Despite a large number of mortars being fired no one, quite miraculously, was killed. One person had a slight stomach wound from a 'splinter' after a mortar shell hit a heavy fencing post. Our son Andrew, about eleven at the time, was probably the only person in Mutare who slept right through the whole attack!

Another attack on Mutare that came from Machipanda again involved a whole series of rockets just after 5.00 p.m. one Wednesday afternoon. It was early closing day, so most businesses had closed at 4.00 pm and the business and shopping centre were virtually deserted. We later discovered that the prime target was the central police station – because as soon as an alert sounded, every able-bodied man in the city, serving in the police reserve, would report to that building for duty. One direct hit on that building could have killed, wounded or immobilised a large part of the city's defence manpower. Our leaders quickly learn from that, and from then on had the men meet at a number of different points.

On this occasion, all the rockets came from the same rocket launcher. The first landed in a stream, the second in one of the Senior Girls' Playing Fields, and so on. Another one, from its trajectory and line of flight – should have gone into the tallest high-rise block of flats (narrowly missing Police Headquarters), curved round the building and landed in the road beyond, a few yards from a petrol station and about a hundred yards from our house and Police HQ. It ploughed deep into the pavement between a number of stationary cars containing a number of garage employee wives! (Garages did not observe early closing days and closed at 5.30 p.m.). This was the only rocket that failed to explode! The next day, it took the bomb squad eight hours to gingerly dig it out, and take it elsewhere to be detonated.

At the time of that rocket attack, I was about to conduct the blessing of a civil marriage, and a number of Christian friends had come around to lend support. Our garden was filled with all our small children, aged from three to fifteen. They had been so well trained at School as to what to do in the event of an attack, that as soon as they heard the first rocket explode, without any panic at all they all formed up 'crocodile' fashion and the older children led them into our basement. It took us, in the Church, a little longer to realise what was happening; when I ran out into the garden, the children were already safe! Soon all of us were in Church singing God's praises and thanking Him for His protection. In no time several coloured families and quite a large number of local black employees from neighbouring properties arrived in a state of shock – no doubt drawn by the singing – and joined in. A wonderful spirit of family fellowship developed as we prayed for release from fear, and our young children filled the place with their songs of praise. The couple who had wanted their marriage blessed never did turn up!

A t-shirt was produced after the next rocket attack – this attack coming from the mountains to the north, and overlooking, the city – with a slogan printed on it inviting people to come to Mutare because its golf course had more 'bunkers' than any other golf course in the country! This attack took place just before a major golf championship match. Although those firing the rockets had a perfect view of the whole city below them, most of the mortars landed instead all over the golf course. Special rules were introduced for that tournament – because there had not been time to deal with the 'unapproved' bunkers – for golfers to take their golf balls out of these 'bunkers' without being penalised. Again no one was hurt in this rocket attack, although school boarding hostels and the hospital itself survived near misses.

One of the special blessings of the Agric-Alert system, which I have already mentioned, was that farmers were given a running commentary on what was going on in Mutare, and parents were quickly given assurance that their children in the boarding hostels were safe. It can be imagined what untold agony was saved when farmers twenty and thirty miles away were woken by the explosions and knew they were coming from the direction of Mutare. The residents of Mutare were also helped by the Security Forces. The latter took over the local waveband on the radio as soon as an attack started and we were given a running commentary on all that was taking place. Through every attack, each household moved into a safe area in the house away from all windows. Whatever hour of the night, we would make tea, serve biscuits, and have a time of prayer for the city's protection – while listening to the radio as it gave us up to the minute information.

After the first mortar attack on the city, a large battery of guns was bedded down in a valley just the other side of a range of hills to the south of Mutare. In the event of further attacks from Machipanda in Mozambique, they could 'neutralise' that very quickly. And so it proved after the rocket attack on the police station. Machipanda was quickly 'knocked out'.

When the next rocket attack came from the hills to the north of the city, the security chiefs decided that the guns to the south should also protect the hill range on our northern flank. This entailed turning the guns around and shooting over the hills just south of the city, right across the whole valley in which the city was spread out, and 'homing-in' on the top of the range north of us. This had to be very accurate, because if too short, the shells would hit the houses on the southern flank of that range, and if too long, would go over the range and hit the township and farms on the other side! So they decided it would be important to have some target practice in daylight to ensure that they had got the elevation right for the guns.

The city was warned that on a certain afternoon at 4.00 p.m. this would take place Right on four, the first shot screamed over the city and landed right on the ridge of the hills. Seconds later, there was a massive explosion right in the centre of the city.

The guerrillas had also learnt about the exercise and arranged for a bomb to be placed in the City Centre timed to go off at 4.00 p.m. They had even gone one better. They informed *The Star* Newspaper in Johannesburg – minutes before the event – which a bomb was about to go off in the Main Street of Mutare. While one of *The Star* reporters was on the telephone asking our *Manica Post* if they knew anything about it (and the local editor was telling the Johannesburg reporter that only a military bombing practice was taking place) the bomb went off, shaking the whole city's morale.

It was sometime before we learnt that it was a bomb, and not 'a short shot from one of our guns' that caused the explosion. Bombs in shops were a nerve racking experience for several years, and it was thanks to the tight security and the indignity of personal body searches and the searching of bags over a period of years, that we only suffered two major bomb explosions in Mutare – the only casualty being the women who carried a bomb into Meikles Department Store, where it went off prematurely.

It was quite a remarkable fact that during the many mortar and rocket attacks on Mutare, considering the compact nature of the city in a bowl surrounded by hills, that the city suffered no fatalities, and very few injuries. It was a reminder of something that many of us had seen just before one of these attacks. Nearly seventy of us had been away for a long weekend of 'renewal'. We had taken over a hotel up in the Nyanga Mountains. It was a very moving weekend for all of us. On the drive down to Mutare quite a large number of people, travelling in a number of different cars, all saw the same phenomenon. Just a single cloud, in the form of an enormous hand, seemingly placed directly over Mutare. All were given an absolute assurance that it was God's protection over our city. We carried that picture with us all through the guerrilla war, and praised God that despite our unworthiness and many failures in bringing about a just solution to the war, His hand was over us, assuring us of His love, His care and His protection.

One night an army vehicle arrived at Mutare Hospital with quite a number of wounded men. They had survived an ambush on the tar road just south of Mutare. The driver, realising how seriously hurt some of the men were, didn't stop but drove straight to the hospital. It was only after the wounded had been attended to – and the driver was climbing back into his cab – that he noticed an unexploded rocket precariously lodged in the bodywork of the cab immediately behind where he was sitting. With all the subsequent jolting – in bringing the vehicle in from the point of ambush – it was a miracle the rocket hadn't detonated. The driver literally turned white as a sheet when he realised how close to death he had been, and gave thanks to God for their miraculous escape.

Armed convoys used to escort vehicles from one part of the country to another and became a regular part of our way of life. Major convoy routes covered the two main roads south from a) Harare via Masvingo to Beit Bridge on the South African border; and b) from Bulawayo to Beit Bridge.

A further major convoy route was from Mutare via Birchenough Bridge to Masvingo, and there to join the Masvingo-Beit Bridge convoy route. Other convoy routes operated south of Mutare to two large centres at Chipinge and

Chimanimani.- and joined or left the main convoy route from Mutare through to Masvingo. Only one or two convoys a day ran on most of these routes and the majority of these roads were recommended no-go areas to the general public at other times. Convoys were usually protected by Landrovers armed with Browning machine guns mounted on a central swivel in the back of the vehicle – with a rudimentary seat attached so that the gunner could swing, with his gun, round a 360 degree radius. For the most part, none of these gunners had any protection from enemy fire. Many had miraculous escapes during ambushes. Max Shepherd, a member of our congregation, was one of the police reservists manning such vehicles. In one ambush he was subjected to a hail of bullets from both sides of the road and not only survived totally unscathed, but was able to drive them off with his return fire. On rough roads, the gunner's position was precarious indeed – with only a strap round him and the central mounting to protect him falling off – and with a vehicle bucking up and down and rocking from side to side at high speed, it was incredible that they could shoot at all when the unexpected attack came.. In cold weather they nearly froze to death because they had no protection from the elements. No fun being driven at 60 mph in such conditions.

On one occasion we were travelling back from a conference in South Africa, and our truck/caravan combination was too slow for the convoy. We were detached by the Convoy Commander (whose word was law, and who had to consider the safety of the greatest number) at the Bubye River, and we had to travel the next 160-mile stretch on our own. It is quite an eerie experience when you have a good three hours to worry about the safety of your family. And then, once again after Masvingo, we found we had to travel the next 195 miles to Mutare also without convoy protection for the same reason. We were considerably relieved to reach home in one piece.

One Christian woman who greatly endeared herself to all of Mutare by her tremendous courage, determination and radiant cheerfulness was Ceylonia Joubert, whose vehicle had been blown practically to smithereens by a boosted landmine. For week after week she lay in our hospital severely crippled and in great pain, not knowing for sure if she would ever walk again. All of us as Pastors used her at one time or another to speak to other patients who were often better off than she was, but who were distraught or who had lost hope for one reason or another. Ceylonia had a real Florence Nightingale ministry in that hospital. Praise God, many, many months later she finally walked again. She was one of the very last people I saw before leaving Zimbabwe in 1986 (six years after the war ended) – still having to struggle to walk with any degree of ease, and always with pain – but still as radiantly cheerful as ever. Her story speaks of the courage of so many country folk driving dangerous farm roads during those days.

Another teenager was not so lucky. In another landmine incident, in the same area, she was made a quadriplegic for life. Two of our national airline planes were shot down with ground to air missiles while taking off from Lake Kariba, a holiday resort, filled with tourists. The first crashed with the loss of everyone on board. In the second, the pilot, in a quite outstanding feat, got the plane down in practically one piece in the bush and far from help. As many of the passengers thanked God for a truly miraculous escape the fittest and strongest set off to get help. Not long after a group of terrorists arrived on the scene and massacred all those who were still there in cold blood. Such barbarity defies explanation.

Of course, in all probability no two groups of guerrillas were the same. One of our friends in the Cashel area – half way between Mutare and Chipinge – had just brought his children back to school for the new term. Their youngest daughter was too young for boarding school and lived with us since Sarah and Diana were in the same class at school. Sue, the wife, went on to Harare to collect their 'new' second hand car while Tim returned to Cashel. Before reaching home, he stopped to chat to local MP, Des, who was inspecting his own lands. They spent some time chatting, and it was almost dark when they realised they must get home. Tim was the first to drive off and, at the first bend in the road, ram into a hail of bullets from an ambush. He tried to return fire with his FN, only to find that practically the first bullet must have hit his weapon and jammed it. Lying there with serious wounds mainly in the area of his buttocks, he realised that this was probably the end. At any moment someone would come up and finish him off.

But Des, with incredible courage, grabbed his FN from his vehicle and ran up the road firing at Tim's attackers (I can't remember the exact number now, but there were about six of them). When he ran out ammunition, he ran back to his vehicle to reload and return. But by now the guerrillas decided to run off. Tim was rushed into Mutare Hospital where, for a while, it was thought all would be well. Later on, though, they decided that they might be able to provide better facilities in Harare, and they put him on a plane to fly him there. It was a terrible shock to hear that he died in the plane en route to Harare. Sue, with quite incredible courage, returned to the farm and kept it operating! But the most extraordinary event happened soon afterwards when she actually received a letter of apology from the guerrilla group saying they had never had any intention of hurting Tim. They thought that the first vehicle to have driven off was Des' vehicle, and it was him – one of Ian Smith's MPs – that they were intent on killing.

A very strange war indeed. It was also to affect Diana. To know that Sarah's Daddy had died as a result of an ambush really put a terrible fear in her heart every time I drove out of town. She would weep every time I went away, wondering if that would be the last she would ever see of *her* Daddy. She was only seven.

CHAPTER FOURTEEN

THE POWER OF GOD IN SEEMING TRAGEDY

Probably the most horrific and barbaric of all the atrocities committed in the war – and there were many – affected our community in Manicaland most of all. It concerned the Elim Pentecostal Church and their missionaries. They had run a large mission station to the north of Nyanga – a very remote area – for a good many years. During the war, with their dirt roads being continually mined, and since many threats were being made against them, they decided to take over an abandoned school in the Vumba Mountains on the southern edge of Mutare. Although continually urged to do so by the security forces, they refused to carry arms for their own protection. Late one night a guerrilla group moved into their school and, apparently without any of the black pupils being aware of what was going on, gathered together all the white missionaries – men, women, children and a babe in arms – took them out on to the dark hillside on a bitterly cold winter's night, and cold bloodedly butchered them all to death with axes.

Only one woman did not instantly die that night, but crawled away into some bushes more dead than alive. She was not discovered at first the next morning, but when she was, she was unconscious. She died a few days later in hospital. Nothing was more harrowing than the mass funeral in the Queens Hall in Mutare. The city's pastors were asked to carry the coffins, and I carried the casket of the baby. The only people of that Elim group to escape the massacre were the pastor/headmaster and his wife, Peter and Brenda 'G', who were away in England on furlough at the time, and the children, of those butchered to death, who were away at boarding school. These children were flown home to relatives in England.

Twelve people died a martyr's death that night. A plaque has been erected in the Vumba Mountains overlooking that hillside with words that ran something like this: "Father, we do not understand, but we trust You".

The words on the plaque were written by Mother Basilea of the Darmstadt Sisters in Germany. For the Christians, a note of victory ran through the funeral service, for we knew that the blood of the martyrs is something very precious to God, and that it is never spilled in vain. The first 'miracle' that came out of the massacre was the result of the schools being closed down. There were many strong born-again and 'spirit-filled' Christians in the school. They were divided up and fed into other schools where, in some cases, their Christian witness had a remarkable effect on improving the Christian witness amongst pupils who were only nominal Christians. But how does one ever forgive the callous and brutal murderers? We knew at the funeral we had to pray for their forgiveness, and for their salvation. Jesus could forgive his murderers while hanging on the Cross. We had to do likewise.

Peter, leader of the Elim Mission in Zimbabwe at the time of the massacre, was on furlough in England but he flew out for the mass funeral. Later, on his return to Zimbabwe, he heard many persistent rumours circulating about the gang that had committed the crime. As he said, there is a need for Christians to beware of sensational rumours: 'the Bible teaches us to prove all things" and then to "hold on to that which is good".' The Elim Mission Director in England, Brian Edwards, had also heard these rumours and asked Peter to investigate them. 'And very reluctantly I did', says Peter.

He heard that the leader of the gang was training for the ministry at a Pentecostal Bible College in Harare, Zimbabwe. The Canadian principle of the college was a friend of Peter's. When Peter asked Glen the truth concerning 'this man', Glen invited Peter to come and speak to the College, meet with this former guerrilla afterwards – and then make his own assessment. After speaking to the college, Peter was left in the Principal's office with the man responsible for the killing of all his former colleagues and members of their families. Gavin, about twenty-eight years of age, told his story to Peter.

In 1974 he had become Senior Student of the top African Secondary School in Zimbabwe, but he ran away and made his way north through the bush, across the Zambezi, into Zambia to join the liberation struggle and be trained as an insurgent. This very bright lad was quickly singled out for his intelligence and leadership, and spent six months training as a political commissar. Then he was appointed as a platoon commander with sixteen other men under his command. After re-entering Zimbabwe, this time from Mozambique, he found himself, in June 1978, operating in the Vumba area south of Mutare, and close to the Elim Mission School. He decided to close down the school and, if necessary, kill the missionaries.

There were a number of reason for this, and these included; 1) His determination to lower white morale in the country, and 2) by closing down all possible institutions in the area in order to create a more effective infiltration route for other groups entering the country.

A message was sent to the missionaries to leave the mission or else be killed. This was relayed to the Mission Board in England, and it was agreed that steps should be taken that would enable the missionaries to leave the area during the hours of darkness. Within days of sending the threat, the gang moved into the school on the night of 23 June, 1978 because the missionaries had not acted with the swiftness that was required. The only point at which Peter interrupted the story was as Gavin began to describe what happened as they led the men, women and children out to their deaths. Peter asked, 'What did the missionaries do when they knew they were going to die?'

Gavin replied that they did something the gang found very strange – they prayed. First, in their prayer, they said they were there, not because they wanted to be there, but because God allowed them to be there. The next two things that stuck in Gavin's mind were that the missionaries prayed a collective prayer for their murderers – that God would have MERCY on them, and that God would SAVE them. It was the words mercy and save that had struck him. Then they killed those people with axes and left them scattered over the hillside.

Gavin's gang continued their activities. A week later two of his men were killed. A little later two were captured. That left thirteen of them – and most survived until the end of the war eighteen months later.

Some time after the war ended, they were stationed in an army camp at Entumbane near Bulawayo, in the south west of the country. They were sitting together one Sunday reading a Sunday newspaper and their eyes caught the headline of an article which read 'Dear Comrade….' (All revolutionaries and combatants called themselves 'comrade'). They read the article with interest, and it went on to say 'God loves you, Jesus died for you, comrade.' It went on to tell the story of a Cuban revolutionary Marxist called Raphael, and as they read the story of his conversion to Christ, they became enraged and infuriated. The advertisement, for that is what it was, went on to say that if the reader wanted to know more about this, they were to write to Margaret 'L' at Box….Bulawayo.

They discussed this, and it was finally agreed that Gavin should write a letter to Margaret expressing their great interest, and inviting her to come out to the camp to answer their questions. Having lured her to the camp, they intended taking her out of sight and killing her. Gavin wrote the letter and put it in the thigh pocket of his drill trousers and set off for the mailing point at the camp. When he got there, he couldn't find the letter. So he scribbled another hurried note to Margaret and asked her to send further information. By return came a little Gospel of John, a booklet explaining how to give one's life to Christ and Margaret's own testimony of how she came to Christ.

(Postscript 2011: Margaret L. happened to come across my book two or three years after it was published, contacted me, and complained that I had got her name wrong. I had to explain that quite a number of names in the book were changed because the people concerned, like Margaret, were still in Zimbabwe and might be 'targeted' if it was discovered what they had done).

Gavin read it all. He obtained a Bible and began to study the Scriptures; at weekends he visited various churches and listened to the preached Word of God. Although it made sense, and all sounded very wonderful, he knew that he had sinned so deeply, and been such a terrible man (he had given his life to the devil) that there was no hope for him. Yet he kept on reading and thinking.

One evening a number of them were gathered in the barracks when suddenly they had a vision. He was not hallucinating, nor was it something in his mind – but an objective reality out there 'because we all saw it'. They saw a vision of a Cross, and then it was as if the hand of God came out of this vision upon them in judgement. He cried out that God would have *mercy* on him, and *save* him. (The very words that the missionaries had prayed for them before being killed). God met with him and gave him an assurance of his forgiveness and salvation. Then there developed within him a burning desire to share this startling discovery with the former members of his platoon who had survived. He began to teach them, and minister to them. He prayed with them and, in turn, he led seven others (and this is perhaps the most incredible part of the story) to Christ. They all, eight of them, decided to train for the ministry so that they could preach the Good News to others. The other seven had passports, and so hurriedly got out of the country (some to East, and some to West, Africa and enrolled at Bible Colleges. But Gavin had no passport and had to stay in Zimbabwe. He too left the army and entered this Pentecostal Bile College in Harare.

After hearing his story (and probably still in a state of numbed shock) Peter prayed for him. This man who had been the leader in the brutal massacre of God's people, people Peter had known and worked with, was now a brother in Christ!

After Peter got home, he told his wife that he just wanted a period of quiet so that he could accurately record the facts of a conversation he had just had. When he returned to the sitting room he found a visitor sitting there, a young man called 'C' who was a law student at the University. Peter told him that he had just had the most incredible experience, and related all he had heard. After he had finished, 'C' said, 'describe the man'. Peter did. When he had finished, 'C' said, 'that is the man! Don't you remember him? I was a student at Elim at the time of the massacre. The man you describe is the man who called the whole school together and gave us a political lecture that night.'

Eight full-time missionaries had been massacred that night. Now exactly eight of those who had done the terrible deed had given their lives to Christ and were in training for full-time ministry for the Lord.

Another pastor in Zimbabwe was able to clear up another 'rumour' for Peter. Pastor 'K' had been ministering at a military nursing home at Nyanga (Troutbeck), where seriously wounded men were rehabilitated, the home run by a Captain who had himself become a Christian. He invited Pastors to come in and minister to the men. As Pastor 'K' was preaching, a paraplegic man in a wheelchair screamed and cried out for *'mercy'*. After quietly closing the meeting, Pastor 'K' went over to minister to this man and listened to his story. He was one of the group of guerrillas who had massacred the Elim Missionaries. 'I led him to faith', said Pastor 'K', and he is now being helped further in his walk with Christ.

Jesus prayed that His murderers would be forgiven. Those hardened and callous Roman soldiers, to whom the putting to death of yet one more man would mean nothing, were brought to faith by what they saw and heard. The centurion summed it all up when he said, 'Truly, this man was the Son of God'. Stephen, the first Christian martyr, also prayed for forgiveness for his murderers as they stoned him to death. The worst of them all was their leader Saul, a Pharisee, 'breathing out murderous threats against the Church,' yet he, too, came to faith when he saw a vision of Christ on the road to Damascus and became, probably, one of the greatest missionaries of all time.

The Elim massacre was diabolically brutal. Those murderers had been prayed for, that God would have *mercy* on them and *save* them. God not only answered the prayer of Jesus, but also the prayer of Stephen, and the prayers of those missionaries out on that cold hillside as they faced death. Out of the total group of seventeen that committed the dreadful deed, nine are known to have repented of their deed and committed their lives to Christ. Eight of those men set out to train for the ministry. Gavin, we know for certain, completed his training and is now part of an evangelistic team preaching the Good News of Jesus Christ in Zambia.

As Peter said, 'There is no sin that is so deep that the love of God is not deeper. The only thing that God cannot forgive is the wilful rejection of Jesus Christ.'

Most surely 'all things' do indeed 'work together for good to them that love God and are fitting into His purposes' (Rom. 8:28). God helped to put this kind of prayer on our lips throughout all the atrocities we heard about, perpetrated by either side. 'Father God, we don't understand why you permit such terrible things to happen, but we know that you bring good out of even the most terrible things engineered by the devil, and we praise you for the good that *will* come out of this. Amen.'

CHAPTER FIFTEEN

THE POWER OF GOD SEEN THROUGH ANGELS

There was a real flap on. Military intelligence had learnt that the largest guerrilla force to enter Zimbabwe was about to cross into the country in our area – a densely forested and mountainous area. Many small 'details' or 'sticks' of men were out searching for signs of this group. A young Christian we know, and his friend, formed a two-man stick, with radio, and were searching through their allotted section. They came over a hill and were well down the slope before realising that the thick undergrowth of the valley floor was 'crawling' with men. They had unexpectedly walked into the hideout of nearly a thousand guerrillas who had with them a small mountain of war *materiel.*

At the same moment they too were spotted and a battle royal ensued. Our two friends could only do one thing – dive into a small contour on the hillside, and start returning fire. They started praying. Their radio was not picking up any friends. In moments, the three or four magazines they each had for their FNs were expended. They knew that only God could help them now. All of a sudden, they realised that all the shooting had stopped. Looking carefully out of their meagre hiding place, they were scarcely able to believe what met their eyes. The large group were moving swiftly back towards the border, leaving much of the heaviest material behind. In subsequent follow-up operations, one man was caught and interrogated. Amongst other things, they asked why the group had run off down the valley. The guerrilla explained that when they saw the whole hillside 'alive' with soldiers in white uniforms, they knew that they were heavily outnumbered, and so made a run for it!

Escaping unscathed, our young Christian friend could scarcely believe that he was still alive! Then, a few days later, he fell off his horse during a period of 'R & R' (a period of rest and refreshment granted to service men so that they could return home). As a result, he was hospitalised with a severe fracture of the leg, and was given a glorious opportunity to tell many people of God's wondrous 'doings' in his life.

On another occasion when three 'soldiers in white' appeared, they brought protection to an elderly couple living in a lonely homestead. Feeling a bit more nervous this particular evening, the couple knelt down to pray as usual before going to bed, and asked that God's angels would protect them from danger. In the early hours of the following morning a guerrilla band attacked a neighbouring homestead a couple of miles away, and met with more than they bargained for. It was occupied by a security force patrol. In the battle that followed, the security forces took, as prisoner, one of the men they wounded. In the debriefing that followed, the guerrilla explained that they had decided to attack the neighbouring farmstead, but when they got there, they found it surrounded and heavily guarded by 'soldiers in white', so they abandoned their first plan and moved against the homestead that – unknown to them – was actually occupied by the security forces!

A nurse who had been stationed at Nyanga also tells of an elderly man living on a farm nearby who was worried that it wasn't safe for him to remain on his land. However, he said that he would stay as he had a great belief in prayer. His servants told him that the guerrillas hadn't attacked his house because they were afraid of the figure in white guarding it!

Although angels are mentioned in the Bible – and my parents had taught me, as a small child, to believe that they stood guard round my bed while I slept – I had never really considered them a reality in my life. Can one really believe in them to actually protect one? I had not really consciously thought so. And yet, angels in white – defending God's saints – have been reported in many wars in many continents all over the world. It was only as I came upon one incident after another in our 'own' war that I seriously began to question what I really did believe about angels. There was no doubt whatever, in Scripture that we are told of a ceaseless battle going on in the spiritual world between God's angels, and the fallen angels who come under Satan's banner.

Angels are often used as God's messengers – as they were to Zechariah, Mary, Joseph and many others. In the Bible, they are also seen as guardian angels, but I never really thought of them, consciously, as playing an important part in *my* life – until various incidents in the war taught me otherwise.

Although no convoys operated on the Mutare/Harare road, for much of the war it was recommended that certain sections not be used after 4.00 p.m. Travelling as I regularly did to meetings in Harare, I didn't think it dangerous enough to take note of these suggested restrictions. It saved so much time on the 320-mile round trip if I got there and back in the same day! However, because Jill finally asked me very specifically not to travel back in the evening after dark, I then waited over and returned the next morning and often left Mutare in the early hours so as to get to Harare before breakfast.

On one occasion I left home soon after 3.30 a.m. As I approached the timber estates outside Macheke, I passed two large Swift trucks going in the opposite direction. Seconds later, a few minutes after 5.00 a.m., I entered the wooded section and, rounding a long bend, saw the road covered in logs. No way would the little Toyota get over those. Braking hard, I was able to stop in time and – imagining a lorry ahead must have dropped them on the road – jumped out and threw enough logs off the road to allow me to proceed. Without further thought about the matter, I travelled on to Harare.

Early the following morning I set off for home. I stopped at the Macheke garage to fill up with fuel because an old friend going through hard times with the loss of traffic on this road owned the garage. He greeted me outside and told me of a heavy attack they had sustained the night before last in the village with rockets and mortars. The police station had been attacked, and at 5.00 a.m. the guerrillas had fired rockets at two Swift lorries at a roadblock they had built just near the edge of the plantations! I must have missed them by minutes – or perhaps they didn't see me?

On another occasion, also very early and long before most people are around, I was travelling very fast with the wind against me. Probably for that reason the group never heard me coming until it was too late, but near the line of hills close to Nyazura I was surprised to see a group of men off-loading bread and food from a very dilapidated van. Quite a number started to run back into the bush – but I didn't really think about it too much at the time. That night, a guerrilla gang attacked Nyazura – from somewhere close by where they had obviously been hiding up – and tried to destroy the garage and petrol station. Coincidence? Maybe!

The only time someone in one of our prayer groups tried to stop me travelling, was when I was due to take a funeral service at Chimanimani, about sixty miles south of Mutare through the mountains. There had been a number of ambushes on this road and a Catholic Priest, much loved in the area, had been killed in one of these. At our prayer meeting that morning, I was told that someone believed my life was in great danger and that I shouldn't travel along this road. We tried once more for an armed escort to take us, but there was a shortage of men and vehicles. The funeral had to go on. So with further prayers for protection, the undertaker and I – as we quite often did, set off with me 'riding shotgun' in the hearse. He carried a revolver, and I had an Uzi (sub-machine gun), which I always carried, out of town. As we approached the bottom of one particular pass, I had a tremendous sense of the presence of evil – and prayed for our protection.

Nothing happened, but on our way back, we found that the store at the bottom of that pass had been shot up and gutted by fire. Security force personnel on the scene were sure, considering the time lag, that those men must have already been in their ambush position when we passed by the first time!

Twice in my life I have nearly written myself off in a car…but for the grace of God. On each occasion, I was travelling close to a 100 miles an hour in the dark – I used to travel far too fast – and about to breast the brow of a hill, when some sixth sense (or guardian angel?) made me brake furiously just as I crested it. On the first occasion I stopped within feet of the first of a herd of cattle that had strayed on to the road. The second time I stopped within a few feet of a van that had hit an ox head-on, and vehicle and animal covered the whole roadway. Whatever it was that warned me, I was sure that they were signs of God's protection over me. But angels…?

To my mind the matter was finally cleared up with the visit of a well-known international speaker and leader. It had been arranged that after his visit to Harare he would hire a car and drive himself down to carry out the next part of his visit in Mutare. The scaremongers had obviously got to him in Harare, for he telephoned and suggested that his Mutare Conferences be postponed until some future occasion. I said that if he were a little anxious about driving himself to Mutare, I would come and fetch him myself. It was obviously an offer he felt he couldn't refuse!

We therefore arranged for him to meet me at a well-known hotel in Harare the next day – but I warned him about the curfew on our road to Mutare, and that we would need to leave before 2.00 p.m. He was delayed by almost two hours, and it was nearly 4.00 p.m. before we finally left Harare. At Macheke, which we reached at about 5.30 p.m.., I showed him the large board advising motorists not to travel on this next section after 4.00 p.m. I told him I was quite happy to continue through myself, but if he was anxious and concerned, we could turn back and stop the night with friends in Macheke. 'I'm not worried at all', he said, 'You keep right on.'

About fifteen minutes later, just as it was getting dark, we entered an area that we jokingly called 'ambush alley' – a particularly appropriate name for a thirty mile stretch of winding road through a great belt of rocky outcrops and hills. Apparently our guest then began to repent before God for unnecessarily putting our lives at risk, and started asking God for special protection over our car. He believed he heard God say that I WAS protected. On asking what that meant, our visitor was told to look out the window of the car and above it. He was shown the most enormous angel spread out over the car with a flaming sword stretched out ahead. This, he was told, was how I was always protected!

But the international speaker never told us! He did however relate the whole story to a group in Harare on his return, where we had a number of friends! We believe that there was a very special purpose behind those facts being revealed to us. You will remember little Diana's deep concern, nay even real fear, over my travelling out of town – particularly when she knew I was not travelling with an armed escort or in convoy? Well, after this incident, everything was wonderfully resolved. I only had to remind Diana of the angel, and his flaming sword stretched out over my car, providing me with all the protection I needed, and she became all smiles again. All her pent-up fear for her Daddy was taken away. How merciful God is!

CHAPTER SIXTEEN

THE POWER OF GOD IN LITTLE THINGS

I had been a very heavy smoker for most of my life. When I arrived in Mutare I was smoking sixty cigarettes a day. Oh yes! I hated it often, but there was apparently no way out of the hold that it had on me. I had smoked roughly fifty a day (a typical Rhodesian box held fifty) for over twenty years and was well and truly hooked. As a good Anglican, one of the things I had tried giving up ' for Lent' for a number of years was this dreadful – and for me a very expensive item on my budget. That Lenten penance was purgatory, but gave me a real sense of achievement and the wistful belief that, if I really wanted to, I could give it up anytime. That wasn't true. After a number of Lents without cigarettes, Jill and the children asked me *not* to do that any more, because living out their lives with me during those periods was unbearable! It was too much of a Lenten Penance for *them*! And the last time I had given it up, I put on 40 lbs in six weeks, so I too was convinced that it was not a good idea to try that again.

In those days, my smoking and the charismatic group in Mutare hadn't seemed to go together. For a start, none of them smoked and they never had any ashtrays, but in no way were they going to get me to stop. (I would make my own temporary ashtray out of the silver paper in the cigarette box!). I saw no reason to stop smoking – except for actual prayer times – while the Bible study was going on. I had a feeling that that irritated them, although they never said so, but I wasn't going to give them the satisfaction of stopping. Of course, if the truth be known, I had such a craving that I couldn't get through an evening without cigarettes. Totally without my knowledge, half-a-dozen of them made a pact to pray for me to be weaned from my addiction. They agreed to pray for me daily until the habit was taken away. Each time they met they would ask each other if there were any signs that I had stopped. They prayed that God would take away every desire for the need for nicotine in my body, and that I would have such an aversion to cigarettes and smoke that I would feel positively nauseous in the presence of anyone smoking! Of course, I knew none of this at the time.

One night when we returned from one of 'their' groups, Jill and I were retiring to bed as usual. Jill was bathing next door, it was after midnight, but I still followed a new practice I had started of listening to teaching tapes before going to sleep. The tape recorder lay on the bed, and I was sitting up against the headboard thoroughly enjoying one of the last cigarettes of the day. The particular tape was one of a series by David Pawson, delivered on successive nights at a Conference, over a period of about a week. As this particular tape started, David referred to something that had happened as he was leaving the Hall the previous evening.

'By the way', he said, 'as I was leaving here last night someone came up to me and asked if it was sinful to smoke.' (Don't you dare, I said out loud, taking a deep drag on my cigarette!). David continued on the tape, 'I can't tell you if it is sinful to smoke or not. (Thank goodness for that!) 'All you can do is ask yourself a question – "Is it of the flesh, or is it of the spirit".' (Dear God!).

I knew the answer to that without a second's hesitation. Quite deliberately I lent over and stubbed out my cigarette. The unfinished packet lay by my bedside for over a fortnight – untouched! Although my very first waking act had always been the lighting of a cigarette as I rolled out of bed, I had no desire whatever for one the following morning. To this day I have never wanted to smoke another cigarette. [PS 2011 – I haven't smoked for nearly forty years now]. What is more, I cannot bear to sit in an enclosed space with anyone who smokes. It makes me positively ill. Nor can I 'stomach' going into a room permeated with stale smoke and uncleaned ashtrays.

I had started listening to David Pawson's tapes because I had learnt that he was an exceptionally good expositor of the Bible, and I had already asked God to help me learn more about it. I didn't feel threatened by David Pawson because I knew him to be non-charismatic! (Only later did he himself start speaking in tongues and then amended his teachings on the work of the Holy Spirit). Although I had problems with miracles – simply because many modern theologians and Church leaders not believe in them – I knew that here was a real miracle. Only God have taken away, so instantaneously, that craving (and my body's need for nicotine) in this way. But what really convinced me was this. Jill did not hear the initial start of that tape, because she was still bathing. Jill knew nothing of my instant decision to stop smoking. Remember, I was not worth living with whenever I had previously been deprived of cigarettes.

Ten whole days later, after a dinner party in our house, Jill was handing out coffee to our guests. As she went past, a lady offered me a cigarette. I said, 'No thank you very much'. Jill literally stopped dead in her tracks and said, 'I don't believe it! I've never heard you refuse a cigarette before! Are you sure you are alright?' When I told her I had stopped ten days earlier, she was totally disbelieving, yet all through those days she hadn't noticed anything! She hadn't noticed that all the ashtrays around the house remained clean! She hadn't noticed that the smell of stale smoke, and the ghastly smell that comes from filled ashtrays left overnight, had gone! She hadn't even noticed that I hadn't been smoking in all that time! None of the children noticed I had stopped! I put on no extra weight this time as a result of God taking away my desire to smoke, and I had no 'withdrawal symptoms' as a result of coming off nicotine! Only God could have done all that.

Now I also have the perfect answer to anyone who asks the question, 'Is it sinful to smoke, drink, flirt or whatever?' I can't tell you whether it is sinful. You simply have to ask yourself the question, "Is it of the flesh, or the spirit?" " Is this something God would approve of, or is it the satisfaction of a human craving, and over indulgence, or a lust within you that would in fact be displeasing to God?" No one can escape the consequences of that. I have had much cause to be grateful to those women who prayed so faithfully for me over that period of time, for David Pawson's timely question, and most of all for the Holy Spirit's miraculous work within me in response to those prayers that made it all possible.

To return to my spouse, Jill had undergone a really traumatic shock when her father suffered a heart attack, and died. Jill was only twelve at the time and the eldest of three children. The family faced tremendous financial difficulties with the unexpected death of the breadwinner of the family. It was not helped by the fact that soon after her father's death – whether as a consequence of the traumatic shock or not, who knows – Jill began to experience epileptic fits. For a time it was thought that it was *petit mal* and that she would soon outgrow it, but it was later diagnosed as *grand mal*. The situation was not improved by the fact that many combinations of drugs used to try and control the situation had dreadful side effects. Some caused a tremendous depression, and others left her with the feeling of being perpetually 'drugged' or 'under the weather'. But as soon as she came to terms with her epileptic condition (and how difficult that is for anyone, let alone a petite, blond extrovert 'bombshell' wanting to enjoy life to the full), and the right combination of medicines was found to keep the seizures at bay with the minimum side effects and without depression, we began to see positive improvement.

It was after we arrived in Mutare, after we had been 'born again' and we had begun to experience a number of miracles in our lives, that Jill's attitude really changed and we began to believe God could and would heal her completely. On numerous occasions special prayers for healing were said for her, including prayers and laying on of hands by those visiting the town and known to have a ministry of healing. Naturally, when there were signs that she was not totally healed (experiencing a seizure a month or two after believing she was healed), great disappointment would follow. We can never understand why, in some cases, conditions are not apparently healed after believing prayer. Ours is not to question why, but to trust that God knows best. Tremendous benefits have flowed from Jill's condition, not least my own understanding of the kind of traumas families undergo when an epileptic is discovered in the family. If on hand at the time, I can arrest the seizure and save Jill from all kind of damage that so often happens during one of these attacks. And I was able to show families what to do in such circumstances.

We praise God for the tremendous amount of healing that *has* already taken place. Having experienced anything of up to one or more seizures a month, Jill has only had two in the last five years, and we thank God for the ministry to epileptics and their families that it has brought us. (Postscript 2011. A year after coming to England in 1986, Jill was able to see a specialist who dealt in epilepsy. Because they were able to measure these things in England in a way that was not possible in Zimbabwe, they discovered Jill had far too heavy a dose of medicine. They changed one of the drugs that she had taken before, and then over a period of months – with constant scientific checking – found the exact balance of drugs needed. Everything in her life changed dramatically for the best after that. And as a result of those tests and altering of drugs and dosages, Jill has not had another seizure in the last twenty-five years. Praise the Lord!)

St Paul tells us: "But to keep me from being puffed up with pride because of the many wonderful things that I saw, I was given a painful *physical ailment* which acts as Satan's messenger to beat me and keep me from being proud. Three times I prayed to the Lord about this and asked Him to take it away. But his answer was, 'My grace is all you need, for my power is strongest when you are weak'. I am most happy, then, to be proud of my weaknesses, in order to feel the protection of Christ's power over me. I am content with weaknesses, insults, hardships, persecutions, and difficulties for Christ's sake. (The opposite of everything preachers of the modern Prosperity Gospel would have us expect?) For when I am weak, then I am strong.' (2 Cor. 12:7-10).

Some contend that this remark, by Paul, had nothing to do with an *illness* not being healed, that we can and should expect healing of every illness and deformity. I also believe God created us to be perfect, and that He wants us to be whole. Yet sometimes *complete* healing is delayed, perhaps even beyond the grave, if that will be to His greater glory, because He *is* Sovereign. A perfect example of this is seen in the story of Lazarus. He was sick unto death. His sisters, and probably Lazarus, had absolute faith in Jesus' power to heal. But He didn't heal him when he got that urgent message. He could have healed even from a distance, as he did with the Centurion's servant and on other occasions. But He didn't. Despite the faith to believe for healing, Lazarus was allowed to die and was buried.

But much later, in an action that brought far greater glory to God and far more people to faith, Lazarus was raised from the dead and his sisters and friends received him back alive. Sometimes, for those called to wait, there is even greater glory to be experienced.

We have been privileged to experience God's healing power in all kinds of situations, but perhaps the one area that surprised us most – why it should have done I now find hard to understand – was in the simple everyday things. A headache, a cold, a migraine, menstrual pains and the like. How easy to just accept that because they are so 'normal' and common, that God wouldn't want to be troubled with things like that! But He is. He made us perfect. He loves us, more than anyone else does. And just as a parent 'aches' for a little child with an earache, or headache, or when burning up with a fever, so our Father in heaven is just as moved when He sees us screwed up with pain.

But we need to ask! Scripture tells us that in all too many situations in life we do not receive, because we do not ask. And added to all this is the care and concern that we have for one another. It is said that a problem shared is a problem halved. The same applies to our little illnesses as well. Just to have someone show loving concern for us brings a measure of healing in itself. And to know that they care enough to ask if they may pray for God's healing there and then shows how much they care. Many are even prepared to ask God to allow them to take the pain upon themselves – and so 'free' the person they love.

On many occasions I have seen people deeply disappointed when someone has heard of their illness – promised to pray for them – and then walked off without doing anything about it there and then. Why? All too often because the person is shy or embarrassed at praying openly for the sick in public or out loud! What a tragedy to miss such a golden opportunity of really showing that you love and care for that person. Believe it or not, it is a fault most commonly found in priests and ministers dealing with members of their own flock! If you ever say, 'I'll pray for you' – do it there and then!

Did you know that God can also 'heal' mechanical objects? Because Jill only ever had epileptic fits first thing in the morning, the medical profession never put any pressure on her to stop driving. So what could a mere husband do? Nothing! In my previous education job I was away from home so much of the time that we always had a second car. When we moved to Mutare, Jill kept it. It was a very special car for us. It was a real bargain for it had belonged to a little old lady who scarcely ever used it. When we bought it from her, it was six years old and had only done about 20,000 miles.

Once in Mutare, I found myself continuing on our Diocesan Standing Committee in Harare and having to travel the round trip of 350 miles two, and sometimes three, times a month for that and other committees on which I served. The obvious choice was to use Jill's Toyota because we got an incredible 65 miles to the gallon out of it. With petrol rationing through the war getting more and more acute, it was a boon.

On one of those trips, with a car load of people who were as newly excited by their faith as I was, the car began to falter and then go slower and slower as the engine ceased to 'fire'. I asked everyone to start praising God in song for what He was going to do to put this right! Just before it came to a complete stop it fired once more and on we went! We continued to sing God's praises. On the way back from Harare it happened on three occasions and, each time, started up again as we broke into praises to our God. We had decided by this time that there was clearly a fuel blockage somewhere, or dirt in the carburettor somewhere, and I resolved to get the car serviced and checked out after we got home. A service was long overdue!

However, rushing off to work next morning in my own car, I never gave it another thought. Sometime later I had to go to Harare again. It was only when we were well on the way that I remembered that I had failed to have it checked out. I confessed this before God and asked Him to take care of us until we got home and I could get it done. I know that God has a sense of humour! The car failed four or five times each way, and each time songs of praise to God got it working again! We got home safely.

The next morning I remembered my promise. As I sat in the car, I thanked God for bringing us home safely on each occasion, started it up and drove it round to the garage. The foreman was a good Pentecostal friend of ours. I told him what had happened on each trip, and the 'remedy' that had kept us going, and asked him to check it out and give it a good service.

About half an hour later he asked me to come round. When I arrived he called one of the mechanics over and asked me repeat my story. He said the mechanic hadn't believed it when he had told him the story. As I finished, the mechanic produced the 'points' from the distributor. He asked how I had got the car to the garage, because they had tried to move the car into the garage, and the engine wouldn't 'fire' – and they had had to push it in. The points, quite unbelievably to the mechanic, and to us, had literally no points at all. Each end had the plastic non-conductor sheet to which the points are normally fixed, but was otherwise 'clean as a whistle'! I don't understand how it works, but the facts spoke for themselves and there was no dirt in the carburettor, or blockage along the fuel line!

Jill also believed the car was capable of running on empty. We really could not afford to run this second car, hence the infrequency of servicing, and we could afford very little for petrol. Jill believes that for at least a week, at the end of each month before payday, it seemed to run on empty. She never did any unnecessary journeys but would ask God to just keep it going until the next pay cheque arrived. However, as soon as I gave her the money for petrol, if she tried to do one more trip before going to the garage, she *always* ran out and would be upset because she would have to telephone me to fetch a can of petrol and come to her rescue. The very fact that the car averaged 65 miles to the gallon overall over a month I believe speaks for itself. I never found another Toyota Corolla 1968 model owner who ever got as much as that. When we sold it, it was snapped up by one of our local garage employees!

One of the great joys of living in Mutare was the never-ending stream of people who poured into our home seeking help. There were people who wanted help in family disputes and difficulties. People in a financial mess. People who just wanted a shoulder to cry on. Women unable to cope with running the family business because the husband had to spend so many spells away from home each year on police or army reserve duties. People wanting help because their fear for loved ones serving in the bush became intolerable and every parting more and more traumatic. Even a woman suffering hideous nightmares every time her husband was away on call-up. People trying to come to terms with grief. People needing healing. The break-up of so many marriages. The horrific growth of alcoholism as all too many lived on their nerves at 'the sharp end', where every turn in the road could produce an ambush or an unseen boosted landmine. (Were those pieces of cow dung on the road put there by guerrillas to cover holes dug through the tar for landmines?)

Men who came to us because in a military mix-up between different units, one group of men had ambushed another, and killed or wounded their own people. Because of the kind of guerrilla war that it was, men were shooting life-long friends in their own 'stick' during 'hairy' situations on dark nights. That is hard to live with – and even harder when you face the widow and children who are as close to you as your own family, and meet always daily.

There were still other apparent tragedies. There was the day a young woman was brought into our house in a terrible state. She had developed German measles at the most critical time in her pregnancy, and the doctors feared the chances of abnormality in the baby very high. Naturally, she was beside herself with anguish.

Would there be any point in praying for her, she wondered? We began to tell her of many miracles of healing that had taken place in answer to prayer, and asked if she had faith to believe in it for herself. She said she did. Both Jill and I, together with a Christian friend of ours who had brought her to us, began to pray for absolute protection of the embryo from any effects of the German measles. As we prayed I was given an assurance in my spirit that she would be delivered of a perfectly normal baby. However, there was one thing that was required of the couple. Each night, her husband was to pray with her and, with his hand on her stomach, they were to praise and thank God for this perfect baby God had given them.

I always found that kind of forward prognosis hard to give! It was very much like laying my own faith on the line! But the eventual birth of a very healthy baby was the special bonus. With God, nothing is impossible.

Our third child to survive, Lynne, was a 'shock' to all concerned – especially the parents! We had long since given away all our nursery furniture. But what a blessing she has been – a real *laat lammertjie* (late lamb). She grew up in a home that was scarcely ever our own. She was used to seeing people being prayed for and ministered to. All too many poured out their hearts and tears. And Lynne knew what to do for the latter. Because we had no paper hankies in Zimbabwe, the next best thing was toilet paper, and away Lynne would fly to the toilet when she saw someone begin to cry.

On one occasion, Jill had gone out and only Lynne and Leah – our domestic – were in the house. A young woman came to the front door. Lynne, only three at the time, invited her in because she looked so upset, and sat her down in the lounge. She then ran through to the toilet to fetch some toilet paper and returned and gave it to the lady, who was now really crying – imagining that Jill was being called!

As if she did this everyday, Lynne sat down in the chair next to her and asked her if she was very sad. On being told that she was not feeling at all well, Lynne came across to her, put her hands on the young woman's lap, and said to her, 'Can we pray to Jesus to heal you?' Totally overcome, the woman said 'Yes!' So, without further ado, Lynne shut her eyes and prayed, 'Jesus please make this lady better. Amen'. Apparently the young woman just felt all the pain draining out of her. Lynne had total faith in Jesus' ability to heal! The woman left soon afterwards on 'cloud nine' and told us about it later. And that 'joy in Jesus' that has been such a mark in Lynne's life has continued. (Postscript 2011: It is still there today as she runs the Charity 'Family Impact' in Zimbabwe).

When we were in 'exile' in Harare after the attack on our Cathedral, Lynne expressed a desire to be able to 'pray in tongues'. A friend laid hands on her, at the age of five and a half, and she was immediately given a most lovely prayer language in tongues. And it was during those dark days that she got a friend to write a letter to us, at her dictation, to tell Mummy and Daddy not to worry about anything, because everything was going to be all right! Out of the mouths of babes and sucklings..!

CHAPTER SEVENTEEN

THE POWER OF GOD IN SEEMINGLY IMPOSSIBLE REALMS

In order to speak of miracles that touched my mother's life, I need to go back in time. In 1963 my father had retired from the ministry as SGMO (Senior Government Medical Officer or Superintendent) of Mutare General Hospital. He and my mother had been very distressed at the break-up of the Federation of Rhodesia and Nyasaland and decided to emigrate to New Zealand, where he had been offered a post in North Island. It was quite a wrench after nearly twenty-eight years in Rhodesia. Before leaving, they had joined with Jill and me at our wedding in Gweru at the end of August. Unknown to us, they had stopped off in Harare on the way down because they had been concerned about my mother's health for some time and visited a specialist physician. My parents decided not to say anything about this; for fear that it would spoil our wedding.

Three weeks into our honeymoon, we were called back to Harare because Granny Jess had had a severe fall and was dying in hospital. As we arrived at the hospital, my father called me aside and broke down as he told me the news about my mother. She had leukaemia, her condition was critical, and they had cancelled their move to New Zealand. My mother's great anxiety was for my youngest brother, twenty-two years younger than I was, and only six at the time of our marriage, when this leukaemia was discovered. Who would look after him, as Dad's life as a doctor would not make Robert's upbringing easy.

As we faced the situation and committed it to prayer, I will always remember my mother's prayer: 'Lord, if it is possible let me live long enough to take care of Robert, until he can take care of himself.'

When she survived that first major assault of leukaemia Gordon Brander, her physician, told us that in seven years we would face the same crisis point. He himself had recently lost his first wife to leukaemia. He had brought her through the first attack, but not the second. Treatment over that entire period kept Mum's condition stable – but right on time – seven years later, she began to go downhill fast. Through all those anxious days there were many prayers for healing sent up. She was anointed with oil, and prayed for, in Harare Cathedral. Miraculously she came through that a second time. Medically speaking, I am told that very very few have ever survived that second attack. Over the next seven years her blood count was checked regularly, and careful adjustments made to the medication to try and keep her stable.

Mum developed a new and wonderful gift. Painting. Our homes were soon filled with watercolours and magnificent oils of the countryside and mountains she loved so much. Every day she lived had become an unexpected bonus for her. Daily, she rejoiced that Robert was growing up and now nearing the end of his High School education. By now, my father had retired once more – this time from his private practice in Harare which my brother Alan had taken over – and they were living in their cottage in the Nyanga Mountains in the Eastern Highlands above Mutare. We had arrived in Mutare ourselves at this juncture.

By 1976 her condition was again very unstable and she was weakening all the time. Gordon Brander that wonderful physician and friend did everything he knew to try and restore her blood count to some semblance of normality, but with out success. It must have been early in 1976 my father brought her down to Mutare for her weekly blood count. Even that forty-five mile journey was too much for her and she arrived exhausted.

We spoke of the fact that we had, at that time, a special healing service in our Church one Sunday a month – and the next one was in two days' time. I saw the look of hope rekindled in her eyes, and she said that they would come.

My father telephoned the blood count results through to Gordon Brander in Harare just before they left for home. Gordon said he very much regretted that he just had no further suggestions to make. It would now be simply a matter of weeks at the most. By the time they left for home, Mum changed her mind and said that she just couldn't face another journey down, and asked that we just pray for her by proxy instead on Sunday. But even though Mum knew the end was so very close, she refused to give up. On Sunday evening they both surprised us by turning up just before the service. My Mum said she felt certain God was telling her to be there, and so she summoned up the strength to face another bone-shattering journey (to someone so frail) down from Bonda. As I anointed her with oil and we laid hands on her and prayed for her healing, there was such a peace in her face.

There was no dramatic change to see, but all through that next week she began to feel stronger and stronger. They came down on the Friday and there was a miraculous turn-around in her blood count. Gordon wrote to her afterwards and said that she must know that this time his medication had nothing whatever to do with the change, and that God alone had intervened! How we praised God for His goodness to us.

During the next three years she continued to run her home, painted many more oils, even visited England on holiday – the first time for thirty years, and only her second visit since emigrating from England in 1936 – and generally astounded us all by her cheerfulness and renewed zest for life.

Because of the severe shortage of doctors during the war, Dad allowed himself to be pressed back into Government service yet again – running the hospital at Nyanga, and later helping at Gweru General Hospital. It was from Gweru that they came to visit us on their way to South Africa on holiday, and mother was taken ill in our house. They decided that after this holiday, Dad would finally retire again and they would come to live in Mutare. The cottage and property at Nyanga were now unsafe to live in. Several neighbours had been killed in attacks on their homes, and many had experienced lucky escapes, and the general situation precipitated the withdrawal of all their friends to the security of the towns. (One farmer had an incredible escape. He and his wife were on their way to bed, when he slipped back into the lounge to read something. Being a man of habit, his wife expressed surprise that he was not sitting in 'his' chair! Moments later, a rocket smashed through the glass window and ploughed straight through the centre back of 'his' normal chair!)

Feeling a lot better the next day, Mum took Dad out and helped him to choose, and buy, a small house not very far from us. A day later Mum was in Hospital. People who die from Leukaemia often die slowly and painfully. Mum 'knew' her time had come. A few days later, with her agreement, I prayed with her for release into the hands of Jesus. Within a matter of hours of praying with her, we were called to the hospital in the early hours, and she slipped peacefully into the hands of someone she had always loved and served – and who loved her. It was 19 July, 1979.

Her initial prayer to Jesus had been honoured. She had lived long enough to see Robert complete his national service and able to earn his living. God certainly answers our prayers! And her length of survival as a leukaemia patient set something of a medical record – living as she did for sixteen years after having been given only weeks to live! Thank you Jesus!

Old 'Pop' Coventry was one of the grand old men of Mutare, having been there from its earliest days. He was not a churchgoer, and probably hadn't darkened the doors of a church for many years, but his daughter Merry, and granddaughter Ning, were Christians and deeply concerned that he did not know the Lord Jesus. They were anxious that he should be brought face to face with Jesus before he died so that he could, as Jesus required of Nicodemus, be 'born again' and assured of a place in heaven. Try as we might, we seemed to make no impression on him.

He was well into his nineties when he was rushed into hospital in a deep coma. Ning asked me to come and pray for him. Here I was back in one of those difficult situations that I had so dreaded in my early ministry, but I had recently read that people in a coma – and how often we hurt them by saying things in their presence without recognising this fact – can frequently actually hear, even though they are not able to respond in any way. So although Pop was seemingly unable to hear or respond, I began to tell him about Jesus and what He had done for Pop. Furthermore, I explained that even now he could put his life right with God by committing his life to Jesus. If he wanted to do that, I would pray for repentance for him and pray the prayer of commitment for him as well. If he had understood all that I had said to him, and he really wanted to do this, I asked him to give us a sign by raising his right hand and arm.

It was an exhilarating experience to see him painfully raise his right arm and hand straight up, with such a look of gentleness in his face. That story, which I related at the funeral, moved many hearts and just underlined once again how good and merciful God is, and that nothing is impossible for our God. That experience has helped me in ministering much more confidently to others who are in a coma and seemingly unable to hear or respond.

It was Maureen Bailey who told me how much my prayers, readings from Scripture and regular words of encouragement had meant to her, when she was in a coma, after being blown up in a landmine on a convoy to South Africa. What had particularly excited her was that I had told her that she had escaped with scarcely a mark on her. Her sister Wendy, confined to a wheelchair and deteriorating fast from multiple sclerosis, was mercifully killed outright in the same explosion. The miracle was that Maureen and her parents survived virtually unscathed! The car was so totally disintegrated by the boosted landmine that no one bothered to bring the bits back to Mutare – yet with Maureen practically unmarked!

Tookie de Meyer, only recently arrived in our parish, arrived on our doorstep one afternoon in a very distressed state. It appeared that she had just had news from her mother in Johannesburg, that her much younger and deeply loved sister (Gwinnie) had epilepsy!

Probably the best therapy she could have at this point was to discover straight away that Jill – who looked so well and healthy and perfectly normal – was also an epileptic. For many months we prayed with Tookie through the ups and downs of her sister's illness. We even had the joy of finally meeting Gwen when she came up to visit Tookie, and of praying with her. That period of time resulted in a close friendship between Tookie and ourselves.

Naturally we were deeply concerned when Tookie herself took ill and was rushed into hospital with a suspected growth in her left side. She was operated on, but quickly sewn up again, because there seemed to be no way of tackling what turned out to be an enormous growth totally surrounding the kidneys themselves. Over the next few days tests revealed that one kidney had already been severely damaged and was no longer functioning – and the second kidney was beginning to fail. Her physician and her surgeon held out little hope for Tookie, the Medical Superintendent, Bill McGowan. Bill had become a great friend of ours and was a spirit-filled member of the Roman Catholic Charismatic group in Mutare.

All our prayer chains were alerted and everyone was asked to pray for a miracle. Tookie herself was fully briefed on all that had been discovered and her chances of survival. Her deepest anxiety was for her adopted son. Tookie and her husband had adopted Ralph as a baby after both his own parents had died. Since that time, Ralph's stepfather had died, and only Tookie was left. Ralph himself was still in Junior School. As Tookie and I prayed together, acknowledging that Jesus was sovereign in this situation, her special prayer to Jesus was that He would let her live long enough to allow Ralph to be able to take care of himself. She found it such a special comfort to know that people all round the city were praying for her. Next morning, with her condition still critical, they decided they had to risk another operation to save the one kidney if there was to be any hope for her, and to see how much of the growth could be safely removed. An hour after leaving for surgery, Tookie was back in her bed in the Ward. With such a quick turn around, I could only imagine the worst. Unbelievably as it may seem, they found the growth had completely disappeared and *both* kidneys appeared to be functioning normally!!! Further tests proved both kidneys were in perfect condition. Bill McGowan was filled with wonder and amazement at what he had seen with his own eyes. And, of course, it gave Tookie a completely new outlook on life, just to know that God had loved her enough to allow her to experience a miracle of such proportions.

Quite a few years later we were about to leave for South Africa on holiday. Tookie came to us and asked if we would allow her to follow us down in her own car, as she was a little nervous of the long stretches to the border. It was a particularly hot summer, and we heard that the area through the low-veldt to the border was experiencing temperatures of between 120 and 130 degrees Fahrenheit. To try and avoid that, we left home at midnight with the intention of arriving at the border before mid-morning. Unfortunately we had mechanical trouble and we were delayed at Masvingo for nearly seven hours. We left there at noon to drive the 200 miles to the border. About halfway, I was surprised not to see Tookie's car follow me over a slow rise. We went straight back and, being unable to find her car, began to search the bush. We discovered that she had presumably fallend asleep at the wheel, gone over the edge of a small bridge, and the car had then bounced back under the bridge and out of sight.

But Tookie and her Aunt had been killed instantly. It was a very sad time for all of us. Our own car was marooned because I was unable to get it going again. Jill and the children were given a lift back to Masvingo by a passing motorist, with the bodies of Tookie and her Aunt following in a police vehicle.

I had to sit there in the 130-degree heat for four hours before a tow vehicle took me back to Masvingo – and there we had to stay. However, Tookie's prayer, when in hospital and facing death all those years before, had been answered exactly. Ralph had just started work with an electrical firm in Mutare!

Because this had been the answered prayer of both Tookie and my mother, I realised at that point that we need to be very careful about what we are praying for, because we sometimes we get precisely what we ask for!

Tookie, like my mother, was ready to meet with Jesus, and our one comfort at the time of her death was that she already had the assurance that Jesus had bought a place in heaven for her. She had also told us on more than one occasion that she was now ready to go when Jesus called her.

His ways are indeed past understanding! And there is scarcely a better promise in the Bible than 'Behold', says God, 'I have always loved you, so I continue to show you my constant love' (Jeremiah 31:3).

CHAPTER EIGHTEEN

THE POWER OF GOD IN PERSONAL GIVING

'Give to others, and God will give to you. Indeed, you will receive a full measure, a generous helping, poured into your hands – ALL that you can hold.' In fact the same Scripture passage goes on to say, 'The measure *you* use for others *is the one that God will use for you*' (Luke 6:38).

Although I had realised the Bible had much to say on the subject of giving, I felt that the Church had already done my duty for me by paying me less than a living wage! As a result, I use to feel doubly good when I did actually give an average of £2 a month towards the Planned Giving or Sustentation Offerings in the Church! And yes, our salaries were acknowledged to be scandalously low. When I was ordained in 1961 the stipend of a single priest was £43 a month. When I got married, our salary scales laid down that a wife was worth £12 a month. Each child was 'worth' another £4 a month. For the next *twenty years* that salary scale remained virtually *unchanged*, despite the enormous increase in the cost of living over that period. From the very beginning, we struggled to make ends meet. Admittedly we were provided with accommodation (pitiful indeed as it was in our first parish in Gweru, and heavily subsidised by my parents later), and with light and water, and with some form of transport (or subsidies towards it).

We only survived our first few years of marriage financially because Jill continued to work full-time in secular employment, but after Andrew's birth, when Jill was so ill, she was unable to look after, or hold Andrew, for several months – let alone try and go out to work.

Of course the free 'perks' did increase in value as the years went by, but the cash stipend that provided food, clothing and other essentials, didn't. For quite a long period we were using nearly a quarter of our stipend on drugs for Jill, until free hospital medication was eventually provided – and most gratefully received,

It was an article on 'Christian Giving' by our Bishop, which appeared shortly after we arrived at Ruwa, in 1966 that gave us pause for thought. Since Andrew's birth, Jill had not been working, and our salary was so pitiful that we just couldn't make ends meet. What Bishop Alderson was saying was this: because the state now performed many of the functions formerly dealt with by the Church, God's people were no longer expected to tithe since their taxes (we did not come into the tax bracket!) already provided many of the community service programs previously provided by the Church. So his recommendation was that churchgoers should give – not one tenth (a tithe) – but a twentieth! Even that shook us rigid. We couldn't afford that, yet because we were desperate, we decided to try! Over the next few months our financial situation seemed to become even more critical.

The only thing that saved us was an unexpectedly large 'Easter Offering'. (In those days, the Rector was entitled to receive the Easter offerings of his congregation). The offering was larger than we had ever received before, because as a Curate one only got the Whitsun Offering). We failed to see at the time that it was a return on our 'planting' of seeds of faith. By carefully husbanding that 'windfall' we were able to augment our monthly stipend a little, as well as take a short holiday with our family, but the ugly spectre of school fees and school uniforms was also beginning to loom large on the horizon. How would we cope with that?

It was about this time that we attended David Neaum's church in Highlands for a Sunday Evensong. David Neaum's sermon was far more challenging on giving than the Bishop's article. He is a great believer in a number of fundamental teachings from the Bible. One of those is the necessity for God's people to tithe! However 'hard' his teachings on this subject, we found a ring of truth in them. No way could we find any Biblical argument to contradict the fundamental truth of what he was saying.

What was also important, David told his congregation, was that you should give your tenth to the work of God immediately you received your salary, and it had to be a tenth of your GROSS salary – and not of the net figure after tax and other deductions had been made – (The tax didn't worry us – we had never yet had to pay any). It had, said David, to be a 'stepping out in faith'.

Jill and I had a very traumatic time after that sermon, for both of us felt totally convicted of the truth of what David was saying. But how could we ever do it? we asked ourselves and both knelt down and committed the question to God. At the beginning of the next month we would step up our giving from £3 a month to £6.60, and we would pay it before we did anything else! Surprisingly to us, we survived, but only just. Each annual Easter Offering (after being tithed) was carefully put aside to provide a little holiday and the remainder went towards a monthly addition to our stipend – but it was still a struggle, and we never had anything to spare. Remarkably we managed to keep it up for the next seven years until we went to Mutare.

(The Easter and Whitsun Offerings was never a fair system for augmenting a poor stipend. Priests in wealthy parishes did well – those in the poorest parishes might get next to nothing. The unfair system is no longer used.)

But in Mutare, through much sharing at Bible Study Groups, we reeled from one shock to another. We discovered that the Jews were never absolved from tithing, however high Roman taxes were running. Jesus said, 'Pay the Emperor what belongs to the Emperor, and pay God what belongs to God' (Mark 12:17). Under the Romans, those taxes were considered crippling. The tithes or freewill offerings of a good practising Jew would be not less than twenty percent of his income. Furthermore, despite Roman taxes, Jesus not only endorsed the law about tithing, but stressed it was simply *a minimum:*

'How terrible for you, teachers of the Law and Pharisees! You hypocrites! You give to God a tenth even of your seasoning herbs, such as mint, dill and cumin, but you neglect to obey the really important teachings of the Law, such as justice, mercy and honesty. These [justice, mercy and honesty, etc.] you should practice, *without neglecting the others* [tithing of everything, yes, even the leaves in the herb garden!] (Matt. 23:23 – such an easy reference to memorise!)

If taxation and other expenses provided no excuse for the Jew from tithing everything he had, then such considerations provide no excuse for the Christian either.

The truth that finally 'blew our minds' – revealed by a friend in a statement made at one of our Bible Studies – was that we had never properly tithed at all! All that we had tithed was our salary – but we had never tithed our free 'perks'. We began to see that our accommodation, light, water, and telephone bills paid by the church, and the provision of a car, were all part of our income even though we never saw it in the form of cash! How could we assess that? Light, water and telephone were relatively simple. The Income Tax Department assessed what part of those was for personal use, and what part for Church business. They could also put a value on the rentable value of the house which the open market could be expected to provide. We could argue that on our kind of income we would never be able to rent that kind of house which was used by both Church and clergy family – but that was really a red herring. We loved our house! And income tax also assessed the value of the private motoring we did in our official car. It can be imagined what all that added up to, and what a hole it would make in our cash income when we tithed it! Yet we were absolutely convinced that that was what we had to do if we were to be obedient to God:

"I am the Lord, and I do not change. And so you, the descendents of Jacob, are not yet completely lost. You, like your ancestors before you, have turned away from my laws and have not kept them. Turn back to me, and I will turn to you. But you ask, 'what must we do to turn back to you?' I ask you, is it right for a person to cheat God? Of course not, *yet you are cheating me*. 'How?' you ask. In the matter of tithes and offerings. A curse is on all of you because the whole nation is cheating me. Bring the full amount of your tithes to the Temple, *so that* there will be plenty of food there. *Put me to the test and you will see that I will open the windows of heaven and pour out on you in abundance all kind of good things*" (Malachi 3:6-10)."

But God tells us something very important in this passage – something that explains why our money never stretches as far as we would like it to, and why we experience breakages, and heavy unexpected bills. God says to us:

"Then I will rebuke the devourer, so that it may not destroy…" (Malachi 3:11, NASV). What a wonderfully descriptive word, 'the devourer' is to describe the way things break, or wear out, or are destroyed by pests. It was an eye-opener to discover God could nullify those problems! It is startling what God can achieve in making everything stretch so much further. A remarkable example of this is found in the Bible when God's people had no other source of supply to turn to. Not only did he provide quail and manna to eat, and water to drink – most people know of those astounding facts, but are unaware of something else concerning that period – but, 'for forty years the Lord led you through the desert, *and your clothes and sandals never wore out*' (Deut. 29:5).

It is not without reason that Jesus speaks more of the essential need to get our money matters right with God than he does about any other single subject! And we do tend to worry more about money, or the lack of it, than about almost anything else. Yet, when we tried tithing everything we ever received, it worked miraculously. We have not often had luxuries, but we have never had to do without anything that was needed. Even more surprisingly, perhaps, we learnt that we did not even begin to give *anything* away until after we had tithed. Tithing was not *giving*. It was a return to God of what Scripture reminds us is rightfully His due. He gives us everything we have. None of it is ours. It is given to us in trust, and we show our thanks by returning one tenth of all that we receive as an acknowledgement that it is His anyway, and as a token 'thank-you' to Him for that gift.

We only start to give to God or any charity *after* we have paid our tithe to God. That is why Scripture talks about tithes *and* freewill offerings. Jill and I learnt in our own life that God expected a lot more of us in the realm of giving than just returning Him His tithe. The more we have been lavish in giving in this way, the more He has given us to handle on His behalf! We even tithed and gave freewill offerings of what we might have considered ours – such as, in later years, a tax rebate.

When God made it clear to Jill that she was not to drive any more, we sold the car we no longer needed. Before doing so, both of us felt convinced that we were to give away all the money we received to a particularly deserving cause that God had laid on our hearts. When we sold the car, we were astounded at the price that we were offered. It was considerably more than we had paid for it some seven years earlier! There was even a temporary temptation to keep 'the profit' for our use! Nevertheless we felt it was some small 'compensation' for all the tithes we had not paid in the past – and it was surprising (probably quite the wrong word to use?) how abundantly we were blessed as a family.

We shared with our children all that we did about tithing and freewill offerings. We shared the miracles of God's provision whenever it was seen. They saw that it worked. When they decided to tithe their birthday money, they were delighted to find that much more arrived the next week. Should they tithe that as well, because if they didn't, they could buy something they wanted? Again, they decided the tithe came first. The next week, the same happened again, and they tithed without a moment's hesitation. They nearly fainted when the following week they both received a totally unexpected gift for their Savings Bank of $150! They thankfully gave God His share of that as well.

Probably the most incredible experience of God's provision followed very soon after Jill and I made the decision to tithe everything – even our free 'perks'. It must have been about three months later when we saw an advertisement about the first enormous Renewal Conference that was to be held in Johannesburg, South Africa. There were two very large stumbling blocks to our going. The first was that only those who were sent an invitation could go, and we knew nothing of the organisers nearly 2,000 miles away in East London, South Africa. The second was the cost of the conference, the obligatory five-star hotel accommodation (the only kind of hotel blacks could stay in South Africa, and part of the obligatory conditions laid down by their government for any multi-racial gathering), and the cost of travel to and from South Africa.

We had nothing in savings! Both Jill and I felt convinced (wishful thinking?) that we were meant to be there, but that we were to trust God for everything. We committed those two problems to prayer, and decided that if we were really to trust the Lord, we must tell no one about the conference, or our wish to be there. The following morning we received an invitation through the post from someone we had never heard of in East London! The letter had been well on the way when we prayed – but what about the money that was needed? That was far more difficult.

Two days later there was a knock on our front door. One of our parishioners stood there looking a little embarrassed. She said, 'I don't know how to say this, and perhaps you will think me a bit of a crank. But in my prayer time I felt absolutely convinced that you are to attend a conference in Johannesburg that I was reading about last night, and I believe the Lord has told me to come and say to you that I am to provide all the money you would need! When we shared what we had prayed about, she too was overcome! 'Please, you must let me know then, as soon as you are able, how much you will need'. With that, she left. Three weeks later we needed to send off our deposits. The lady in question arrived at our door again and reminded us that we still had not let her know the cost. But here is $70 to go on with.' Within a few cents it was the Rand conversion we required for our deposits.

I could not bring myself to tell our helper how much money we needed; it was something I just could not do. Jill said we had to! Driving round to her house, Jill and I had such a furious argument over this issue that she insisted I stop the car. She got out and walked off! We both finally arrived at the ladies' house in a fairly 'steamy state' – but I was adamant. I could not ask for money. So the evening was spent talking about everything else but….A day later, we had to post off the rest of our conference and hotel fees. Our donor arrived on the doorstep at exactly the right moment again. 'John, you still haven't told me how much you need, but I think there is enough in this envelope to cover most things. If you need more, please, you only have to ask'. I thanked her very much. The amount was again accurate to within a few dollars, and we posted it off.

When another family heard that we were going, they thought we should make a holiday of it as well – with our children – and offered us their caravan. Another person then offered their truck to tow it. A few days before we were to leave we realised that we would have to refuse the offer of these vehicles. The petrol for the much heavier combination would cost us an extra $60 we didn't have. We decided that we would telephone the two people concerned the next morning, thank them for their generous offer, and say we had decided it would be less tiring to go in our own small car.

Somehow we got involved in several things the next morning and overlooked the telephone calls. So during lunch I finally went to make the calls and found a sealed white envelope on the cradle of the telephone. It had exactly $60 in it!

Our God *can* provide everything He believes we need. How we praised His name on this occasion….and many times since.

Jesus went on to say, 'and so I tell you: make friends for yourselves with worldly wealth, so that when it gives out, you will be welcomed in the eternal home. Whoever is faithful in small matters will be faithful in large ones. If, then, you have not been faithful in handling worldly wealth, how can you be trusted with true wealth?' (Luke 16:9-11). If we are faithful in the use of money, *then* God will give us true riches – a new wisdom and understanding and power and authority in Christ Jesus.

What God does through tithing is to draw us out of ourselves. By obeying His laws about very natural things like money, He not only shows us what miracles can happen with things that we can see and understand, but through that He leads us on to understand the part of His Kingdom we could not see – the miracles of faith.

How often have we heard this argument? Do you believe the Bible speaks about the need to tithe? Yes! Do you believe the Bible to be the Word of God? Yes! Do you believe in God's will for your life? Yes! Are you ready then to start tithing? No!

Why is that? Surely there is no other reason than that we are not willing to start. Not willing, as God outs it in Malachi, 'to put God to the test'. Now if I am not willing to start with the least that I have (money), then why is God going to give me responsibility over more important riches? So Jesus tells us to get that right and all the rest will follow.

It was James Duff in his book *Flashes of Truth'* who said,

'There are three kinds of givers – the flint, the sponge, and the honeycomb. To get anything out of a flint, you must hammer it, and then you only get chips and sparks. To get water out of a sponge you must squeeze it, and the more you squeeze it, the more you get. But the honeycomb just overflows with its own sweetness. Some people are stingy and hard as flint; they give nothing away if they can help it. Others are good natured; they yield to pressure, and the more they are pressed, the more they will give. But, thank God, there are still others who delight in giving without being asked, and it's the givers of this kind – cheerful givers – that the Lord loves.'

Whether we are offering ourselves or our possessions to God, there's no question about the kind of attitude that is most pleasing to Him. He loves cheerful 'honeycomb' givers who overflow for His glory and the good of others.

CHAPTER NINETEEN

THE POWER OF GOD IN CHURCH GIVING

Members of the Church have failed to support God's work as laid down in His Word. It shouldn't surprise us, then, that the world does not respect us. It is said that an ardent communist will give everything he can to forward the spread of his ideology by giving every spare moment, by giving all he can of his income (considerably more than the 'tithers' in the Christian Church), and by being willing to sacrifice all – even wife and family – so that his communist principles and efforts will help to convert the world. Most members of the Christian Church have no such dedication. Many have regarded it as little more than a social club. Very few indeed are concerned that not only most of the world, but also most of their relations and neighbours have no idea of the salvation that Jesus offers them, or tells them how they can receive the gift of eternal life. The reason? Perhaps most of them have not been born again themselves?

Nothing gives the Church a worse image than when it is seen to be continually pleading for more money, or when large placards greet the visitor at some place of worship explaining that it costs £XXX per day to keep the place open, and that everyone entering this 'House of God' is expected to pay an entrance fee to come in and look at it. And why should the world respect us when we ourselves, as Christians, do not respect God or His way? How true it is to realise that we show how much we care *by how much we give*!

If our belief in Christianity has not yet touched our pockets, our wallets, our purses or our cheque books deeply and spontaneously – as honeycomb givers who do not have to be asked – then does our religion really hold much value for us?

When I moved to Mutare, and had to accept the fact that I was once more being called back into full-time ministry, I was determined that the things that had previously got me down (and made me want to leave the ministry) would have to change; if not, those things would break me.

For instance, I cannot imagine Jesus standing by and congratulating church members who run church bazaars, fetes, cake sales, jumble sales and the like to subsidise insufficient giving by their members (themselves included?)! Nor can I see Jesus being delighted with a Church Council that requires the vicar to sit outside the church all day for a 'Day of Giving' to balance the budget, or to raise funds to repair the steeple!

In Matthew 21, verses twelve and thirteen we hear 'Jesus went into the Temple and drove out all those who were buying and selling there. He overturned the tables of the moneychangers and the stools of those who sold pigeons, and said to them, "It is written in the Scriptures that God said, 'My House shall be called a House of Prayer' ". Their dishonest and unlawful practices (without any Scriptural approval whatever) must be classed as theft, for in verse 13 Jesus said, 'You are making it a hideout for thieves'. There was no need for the Temple to hold such sales, or to make a quick 'buck' by insisting that people only put 'temple money' in the plate. If the Jews gave as the Scriptures required of them, not only would the tithes provide all that was necessary to pay for the priestly ministry, but with all the 'freewill offerings' added to them, the 'Church' could more than meet the needs of the widows and orphans, the needy strangers in their midst, and all the other social welfare programmes they should be undertaking.

But the leaders of the Temple were greedy. They wanted more, and so creamed off the profit of those who bought and sold in the Temple. And it became more and more necessary to devise other sources of income as more and more Jews, seeing the ungodly fund-raising efforts of the church and the hypocrisy of their leaders, saw no reason to continue paying their tithes and freewill offerings as Scripture required.

"I ask you", says the Lord, "is it right for a person to cheat God? Of course not, yet you are cheating me. 'How?' you ask. In the matter of tithes and offerings. A curse is on all of you because the whole nation (God's people) is cheating me. Bring the full amount of your tithes to the Temple.....*and put me to the test* and you will see that I will open the windows of heaven and pour out on you *in abundance* all kinds of good things (Mal. 3:8-10)."

Does that speak in support of a Church 'scrounging' for money? It certainly does not. But it does show us where to look for, and how to remedy, the problem. The 'thieves and robbers' in the Church need to recognise themselves for what they are. Uncomfortable? Yes, indeed! But then Jesus never did have any inhibitions about dealing with that particular sin in peoples' lives – publicly! He pricked the pompous bubble of those who grandly or ostentatiously threw their £5, £10, £20 or £50 notes or bundles thereof into the Temple treasury by showing that their giving was utterly worthless in the sight of God. He said this about them because they only gave *what they had to spare anyway*! It really didn't cost them anything in terms of sacrificial giving! Only the poor widow, who put in everything she had (a total sacrifice), was praised by Jesus as doing something that was pleasing to God.

On 22 June, 1979, a very interesting article appeared in the *Church Times* in England on the subject of giving:

'Church people in the Diocese of York are being urged to give at least two pence of every pound of their *net* income (after payment of taxes and national insurance) to their local church. This, it is claimed, will bring in enough money to meet needs at local and diocesan level.' 'At present,' said Reverend Alan Bill, their Stewardship Advisor, 'people were giving a halfpenny in the pound. The 2p standard was a minimum duty level of giving. It could be achieved *without sacrifice.* But those who can, are being encouraged to give up to 5p in the £1' (£1 for every £1,000 of income suggested by the Church Commissioners) '...General Synod last November asked dioceses to commend this to their parishes. But it was criticised at a recent York Stewardship Conference as an inflexible standard...it was also said to be *unrealistic*, asking for a five-fold increase in the giving level; and it would give the Church *more than it needed....*' (The emphasis is mine).

I wrote to the *Church Times* on the subject of that article, and my letter was published as follows:

'Sir, An article.....entitled 'Flexible standards of Giving' has just been brought to our attention. It intrigued us for a number of reasons. 1) The recommendation was for an increase of giving to a level of *two pence in the pound* of net income; and 2) It would give the church far more than it needed'. With regards to 1), we would be interested to know what Scriptural basis was found for this decision? And with 2), we must accept we live a long way from England and have no right to make any judgements on what we read, but *is* the Diocese of York really raising sufficient funds to a) pay all their clergy a living stipend/pension; b) maintain all their church/cathedral buildings in good repair; c) have sufficient funds to provide for new Churches, etc. in developing areas; d) evangelise and re-convert England to Christianity; e) assist the work of evangelism/missionary outreach elsewhere in the church? '

'Perhaps in this last connection it is of interest to you and your readers to note that this Diocese of Mashonaland – with no endowments from the past – is self-supporting, despite the war that has been raging here for some time. This Parish of Umtali (Mutare) now has a total membership of 560 families; many of these are nominal, but about half of these contribute something to the budget. We have a totally multiracial membership. We pay an assessment to the Diocese of

$678 per month. This pays a percentage of the diocesan overheads, together with the stipends of three priests working in Missionary areas of our Diocese. Umtali is a town on the Easter Border of Zimbabwe/Rhodesia and one of the hardest hit by the war. In November last year, instead of visiting or canvassing our parishioners, we decided to send out a statement of what we believed God's Word was saying to us about giving.

But of course, 'promises' of an increase of thirty-one percent are one thing; what results in actual practice is often a sad reflection of things promised. But God has blessed us mightily (full statistics accompanied the letter). The results are staggering in any context, but in a war torn land the results can only be termed miraculous – because God alone could have made it possible. We prayed that God's Word would convict our hearts; we can testify that He has been gracious…

To explain what happened, I need to go back to a period about a year after I arrived in Mutare. With all the changes that had been taking place in my own life, I found that I now had to make my new position clear to members of our church Council – that I would no longer approve most forms of fund-raising. As far as I was concerned there could be no fetes, bazaars cake sales, jumble sales or anything else of that nature *to augment* Church funds. Yes, we had difficulty in balancing our budget from the income that was coming in, but instead of begging for money, we agreed to make every effort to acquaint parishioners with the principles of giving laid down in the Bible. From then on, we issued a special brochure each year that set out to do three things; first, it gave the income and expenditure of the past year on a large diagrammatic chart; second, it set out what the Church Council thought would be required in terms of expenditure for the coming year (income was never guessed at!); thirdly, and most important of all, the rest of the brochure concentrated on teaching the principles of Scriptural giving.

No appeals were made; it was simply left to the Word of God in those teachings – together with much prayer that went into the brochure's preparation and over it as it was sent out – to convict people about their need to give to God's work, and at what level. One Sunday a year, 'Budget-Offering' Sunday, the preaching was also geared to teaching those principles of giving.

There was something further that we did. Instead of following normal past practice of waiting until the year end to see 'if we had any to spare to give away' to charities and other needy causes, we decided to be good stewards of what was given to us each month, and to give away a minimum of a tenth of our monthly income. It was very clear to many of us that 'the measure we used in giving money away' as a Church, would be the measure God would use in giving to us! And that has proved true over and over again. The better stewards we proved to be in this connection, the more money God entrusted to us – because He knew that we would not use it selfishly for our own needs, but for the extension of the Kingdom and those in need. Rather than building up greater reserves 'for ourselves for rainy days', we had to trust Him to take care of tomorrow's needs.

Later on we were able to go a stage further. Giving away a tenth of what one receives each month does not involve any measure of real faith! So God showed us that when an urgent appeal came to us – and we believed God was expecting us to provide for that need – we did not wait until the end of the month to determine what the tenth would be and then give that! Instead we would, in faith, immediately send off what we believed was required of us, and trust God 'to make up' what we would now need to pay our monthly accounts at the month's end. It was not unusual, when we took such a step of faith (oh, yes! it did cause anxiety to some who were used to looking at finances from worldly 'accountancy criteria') we would be wonderfully overwhelmed to find that our income would often increase, and totally unexpectedly, five or six times more than the average month.

The net result was that we not only had enough to meet our expenses, but even more money to give away again!

The reverse was also true! Whenever we found ourselves unable to meet our expenses, a quick check always revealed that we had 'overlooked' giving money away during the previous month or two. Even though to do so would threaten us with an even more serious shortfall, we knew first of all we had to give away whatever we had – to make up for what we had omitted to give away – and, hey presto! – in no time at all our income would rise again and our creditors would be paid!

These changes didn't happen overnight. Despite all the teaching that was undertaken in this field, many are still not convicted in this area of giving as Scripture requires. It was not uncommon also, for someone to come and see me after receiving the annual Budget Offering Brochure and, pointing to an article on tithing, say to me, 'John, why haven't you ever taught us this truth before?' When I was able to pull out brochures from previous years and show them the same principles had been taught year on year, they would be amazed and have to admit that they had just never 'seen' this truth before. As with Jesus saying of people 'they will hear, but not understand,' so is it also true that people will often read, and yet not have that spiritual truth convict them in their heart' until such time as the Holy Spirit opens their spiritual eyes! Sometimes it is just plain 'cussedness' on our part, because we do not want to face the consequences of what total obedience to God will entail in our lives!

SUMMARY OF PLANNED GIVING, GIVERS AND TOTALS

	Church Plate Offerings	Number of Planned Giving Families $1 to $4 p.m.	$5–$9 p.m.	$10–$50 p.m.	$ TOTAL	% of TOTAL
1975	$2 300				2 300	17
		106			3 246	23
			43		3 132	22
				34	5 334	38
				1975 TOTAL	$14 040	
				$10–$100 p.m.		
1978	3 060				3 060	17
		69			2 070	12
			32		2 220	13
				39	10 332	58
				1978 TOTAL	$17 682	
1981	4 500				4 500	17.7
			55		3 198	12.6
				54	17 688	69.7
				1981 TOTAL	$25 386	
				$10–$150 p.m.		
1983	4 500				4 500	13.9
			42		1 980	6.1
				60	25 800	80
				1983 TOTAL	$32 280	
				$10–$2 000 p.m.		
1985	5 000				5 000	6.9
			58		4 000	5.5
				64	63 000	87.6
				1985 TOTAL	$72 000	

SUMMARY OF TOTAL GIVING FROM PLANNED GIVING AND CHURCH PLATE OFFERINGS WITH COMPARATIVE NUMBER OF FAMILIES ON PARISH ROLL

YEAR	FAMILIES ON PARISH ROLL	$ TOTAL GIVING	NOTES
1975	800	$14 040	Large exodus during latter part of the war
1978	580	17 682	
1979	560	25 080	
1980	510	26 388	End of war: Independence of Zimbabwe
1981	480	25 386	
1983	450	32 262	
1985	430	72 000	

They say that actions speak louder than words. Financial figures can have the same effect (see the accompanying table of figures). It is staggering to see what God can do with a little group of people in one parish. There is still a very long way to go. My own estimate is that there were still only about thirty families tithing their income in 1985. However, given the tremendous number of people who emigrated during the war and after Independence and the substantial numbers who transferred to other places in Zimbabwe, we lost an average of five or six 'tithers' a year from 1976 onwards.

We also experienced a very painful fracture in the Church. Although I was seen to join 'the rebels' when I joined 'the charismatic' – for want of a better word – I felt that God called me, however difficult the circumstances for myself, to remain within the Anglican Church. What was more, I knew I had to bend over backwards in trying to meet the needs and aspirations of the more 'traditional' members of the congregation, and to apply brakes on our enthusiasm and desire to change modes of worship too quickly. The net result was I seemed to displease some. And so came the most painful parting with many whom I loved very dearly, who felt that the Church (as they saw it) was remaining static. And shedding tears they left for churches they believed were more open to the 'leading of the Spirit'. In terms of financial loss it was also staggering, because they formed the bulk of those who tithed at that time.

However God provided many others to take their place, with scarcely more than a hiccup, and those who did leave have been wonderfully used in dynamic leadership in building up other parts of the Body of Christ. In addition, many of those who left later returned to the congregation.

About three years ago we estimated what income the parish would handle if everyone were to tithe their income – the minimum laid down in Scripture. It worked out at a staggering figure of about $75,0000 per annum. And that only included those who were already 'planned givers'! Can we begin to imagine what a force Christianity would be to reckon with if that kind of resource were available to provide for many more full-time workers and equipment for the extension of the Kingdom of God?

One of the reasons for the extraordinary increase in parish giving came about, I believe, because of our commitment to give money away. We never, in fact, gave away as little as ten percent of our income. In the first five years it averaged out at about thirty percent, and the highest figure overall, in any one year since the scheme was put into operation, was forty seven percent of our income. It is *the principle* that is important. The more lavish we were in providing funds for the needy and for the extension of the Kingdom elsewhere – often through denominations and organisations outside the Anglican Church – the more money God entrusted into our hands. Be 'stingy' or 'hard as flint', or selfish as a Church, and that Church will always be begging for money. 'Give', Jesus said, 'and it shall be given unto you.' And the principle God always adopts is that *we* have to take the first step and *give in faith*; and it is only as we show God the liberality of 'our measure' that He then responds even more liberally!

One of our members had run a business for many years. It always seemed to stay 'just in the red'. Every year-end statement, after taking into account things such as depreciation, consistently showed that the business was not making money. Once the owner gave her life to the Lord, this problem gave her some concern. After several of us discussed it, we decided the difficulty seemed to rest with the fact that the income of the business was not tithed to God – even though the business had been dedicated to Him. Tithing in this area was impossible because her husband was, if anything, a little antagonistic to Christianity at this time – and he held the purse strings. Even after he gave his life to the Lord, he would get a little 'hot-under-the-collar' if his wife suggested tithing the business income. His argument, understandably from the human standpoint, was that the Bank Manager would never go along with such a principle while they still owed the Bank a considerable overdraft! His argument seemed perfectly reasonable: 'You can't rob Peter' – the Bank Manager – 'to pay Paul'- God!

However, as the husband's own commitment deepened, he finally agreed that they should tithe the income of the shop to God, as provided for in the Scriptures. The result was in their eyes unbelievable. Nothing happened overnight, but in a matter of a few months they were out of overdraft, and the business went from strength to strength.

God's ways *are* past understanding; but the principles are His – and they work!

The same happened to a farmer and his wife. Soon after purchasing the farm, they ran into deep financial trouble. They made a deep commitment of their lives to God and heard about tithing at one of our Bible Study groups. They started to tithe everything that came off their farm. Very soon, although the farm fell in the rain-shadow of the mountains and often-experienced difficulties with irrigation, the farm was being described as 'the green oasis' in that belt of country. On one occasion they were so short of cash that they could not provide insecticide to deal with a great invasion of pests, which threatened to wipe out their crops. The couple turned the problem over to God in prayer. Within a few days their neighbours hired aircraft to come in and spray their own crops. What happened? All the birds from the neighbouring farms were driven onto the farm of the Christian couple, and they rid the farm of pests without a drop of insecticide being sprayed!

On another occasion the drought was so severe that the area which farmers could irrigate was severely limited. This young couple planted two crops, which they desperately needed to service their loans. The one lot was irrigated, the other was not. The one that was not irrigated was called 'the Lord's crop'. All through the season the rain was very meagre indeed, and they wondered if the irrigation water supply would even hold out for the land they were allowed to irrigate. As it turned out, the Lord's crop – which had no irrigation whatever – turned out to be the best crop of sorghum they had ever had on the farm.

The same principles worked miraculously for us in the Parish. We never had to hold any 'sales', or use any 'gimmicks' to raise money – even for the major expense of maintaining a large number of properties, all of which were regularly attended to on a planned five-year cycle. In 1985 we already had two full-time priests working in the parish. At short notice, and without having budgeted for it, we were able to offer an additional full time post to one of our laymen. His salary, the cost of an extra house and vehicle to be provided for, was beyond what was available monthly at the time we engaged him. However, we believed we were doing what God wanted us to do, so no appeals were made to the parish to step up their giving. Not only were we able to meet all the additional costs, but our level of 'giving money away' was still maintained at over thirty percent of the total for that year. God indeed takes care of the 'things of tomorrow'!

CHAPTER TWENTY

THE POWER OF GOD IN EQUIPPING THE SAINTS

In 1977 ours was the first Anglican Parish in Southern Africa to experience a Lay Witness Mission. Lay Witness Missions (LWMs) are run with the support and guidance of 'Africa Enterprise', an organisation set up under the leadership of Michael Cassidy and Bishop Festo Kivengere (It was this Michael who later kindly agreed to write the Foreword to this book).

Their primary concern, as an organisation, is to carry the Good News throughout Africa. An LWM takes place in a parish or congregation after six months of intensive preparation within that congregation. Then a group of lay witnesses from many different Churches and Church backgrounds (after suitable training by Africa Enterprise LWM staff) arrive for the weekend. One important principle governing such witnesses is that they must meet their own travel expenses when taking part in such weekends. It is a mark of their commitment to share the Good News with others. One such group recently went all the way from Zimbabwe to Australia to conduct two LWMs, and another group travelled (yes still at their own expense!) from South Africa to Canada.

After the arrival of the Lay witnesses, large meetings of the whole congregation are held on both Friday and Saturday evenings around a communal fellowship meal, with a number of witnesses sharing their testimonies of what God has done to change their lives. Then the whole crowd is divided into small groups under the leadership of the visiting witnesses, and people are brought to a deeper understanding of what the Gospel is all about, and their need to respond to it. 'Coffee Groups' are held in peoples' houses on the Saturday morning and these are followed by 'women's only' and 'men's only' lunches.

The Mission ends with a time of worship on the Sunday morning, and a personal testimony and challenge given at that time by the Leader of the LWM, himself or herself a lay person. He makes a call for every person in the congregation *'to give as much of himself as he can, to as much of God as he understands at that point of time'.* Our LWM was an outstanding success, with many lives radically changed for God. Because of its success, and the large influx of new faces in the congregation, a second LWM was held just two years later.

That first LWM was ably organised by Chris Sewell, who had been appointed as a full-time lay minister in our congregation when my assistant priest, Leslie

Crampton, was appointed Rector of Masvingo. We worked well together. Chris had been a member of the CID in the Police. He was such a 'hard nut' in the eyes of a former colleague of his – a Pentecostal Pastor – that Chris was placed at the bottom of that man's list of possible 'converts' because he considered that it was unlikely that Chris would *ever* change. With God, fortunately, nothing is impossible! Chris gave his life to the Lord in fairly dramatic style, was baptised in the Holy Spirit, and became a leading light amongst that renewed group that I found at St. John's on my arrival in 1975. It was soon after my own life-changing experience that Chris felt the call of God to resign from the police and work full-time for the Lord.

Such a ministry, that of a layman, has its drawbacks. In the Anglican Church any Lay ministry is limited in what it can undertake. The lay minister can never carry out functions that are 'reserved' for the ordained priest. So although the task of the Church is to train *all* its members for ministry (Eph. 4:12), the dichotomy remains. A layman, however well trained, however richly endowed in gifts of the Spirit and gifts of ministry must always remain a 'lay' person unless he is willing to be ordained. Only then can he 'break bread' at the Lord's Table for the family of God. But the roles can never remain interchangeable. Once the die is cast and he is ordained, he finds himself automatically separated from what tends to be regarded as a second-class ministry within a layman's group.

The Church is all the poorer for this attitude. Very early on in the Church's life – certainly by the second or third century – this led to the establishment of a 'separatist' professional ministry. Soon afterwards, it was expected to do almost all the work of ministry within the Church, with the lay person bowing out of ministry almost altogether, and surrendering his God-given talents and responsibilities. This group eventually became to be little more than pew warmers on a Sunday morning. Satan had indeed won a dramatic victory! Instead of having to work against a whole congregation mobilised for ministry and equipped for evangelistic outreach, he was now able to concentrate all his efforts against 'the one-man ministry' in each congregation.

As Anglicans, there were problems over believers' baptism, and Chris and his wife Helga felt totally convinced that God was calling them to take this step. This made it impossible for Chris to continue serving in ministry while the Bishop's licence remained an essential requirement for him to be able to do so. So Chris had to leave, and we were really thrilled when he was appointed as the leader of Africa Enterprise in Zimbabwe with a much wider, fuller and, in many ways, more satisfying ministry.

One of the most important effects of the LWM was the desire born in many hearts to share their faith with others as the visiting lay witnesses had done. As a result, training weekends were started for those members of our congregation who wanted to become witnesses with the LWM Team. The majority of these people are still actively witnessing whenever able to do so. They witness in Churches of all denominations when called upon to do so by the LWM organisation. They have shared their faith with members of many different denominations, and with unbelievers, in cities, towns and villages across the length and breadth of Zimbabwe, and even further afield – all at their own expense. They have seen many lives changed, and that has done much to encourage them.

One Scriptural principle I took very much to heart very early on in my 'renewed' ministry in Mutare was that my two primary roles in the ministry were to a) bring people to a knowledge of the saving power of the Gospel and b) to equip the *whole* Body of Christ for ministry.

"And He (Jesus) gave some as apostles, and some as prophets, and some as evangelists, and some as pastors and teachers, for the *equipping* of the saints *for the work of service*, to the *building up* of the Body of Christ; until we *all* attain to the unity of the faith, and of the knowledge of the Son of God, to a *mature* man, to the *measure* of the stature which belongs to the fullness of Christ." Then, St Paul tells us, "the *whole* body, being fitted and held together by that which *every* joint supplies, according to the proper working of *each individual part*, causes the *growth* of the body for the building up of itself in love" (Eph. 4:11-13, 16 NASB).

There was one complaint that we seemed to be continually bringing before the Lord. Why did He take away all those we trained almost as fast as we trained them? With the large exodus from the country during the war and immediately afterwards – coupled with Zimbabwe's ever present problem of a large part of the population being liable to transfers around the country on promotion – we seemed to spend our time continually training new leaders to train others. Some did not leave us and began to feel the pressure of continually training new leaders. People like Jean and Giles Wakeling, Bill and Liz Reynolds (Bill being the second full-time lay minister in the congregation), Gwynne Palframan, Barbara Shepherd, my wife Jill – and so many others. God soon showed us there was a purpose. We were to think of ourselves as a 'Maternity Unit'! Our task was to continue training people as witnesses, evangelists, Bible Study leaders, and equippers so that they might be sent out all over Zimbabwe and further afield to serve the Lord in His Church – whether in the Anglican or the wider Church.

The excitement of having people trained as witnesses led us on a further step, to something the Anglican Church is not particularly noted for – training lay evangelists fully equipped to a) share the Gospel with unbelievers; b) bring those people to commit their lives to Christ; and c) train those new converts into becoming not only soul winners, but trainers of yet more soul winners for Christ.

While continuing to build up the Body of Christ, God had already given us (using a number of courses devised by ourselves and others), much prayer and thought was given to how we might train evangelists who would carry out these functions. In this connection, Gwynne Palframan returned from a holiday in South Africa bearing a book she had found entitled *Evangelism Explosion.*

Although excited by it, we felt it was too American. I adapted our own training course to the principles laid down in this manual. It was, my trainees told me, the best course we ever did. I believe it was the excitement of presenting the Gospel to someone – with results – that did us a power of good! We had actually achieved a breakthrough in something almost all us find difficult to do – sharing our faith *effectively* with others.

Later on I was able to attend an Evangelism Explosion Clinic and have myself 'certified' (wonderful American terminology for certificated) as an EE Trainer. Before long I was helping with EE Clinics (a five-day concentrated course equipping pastors and their leaders to start seventeen-week courses in their own congregations) in Soweto, in South Africa, and in Bulawayo in Zimbabwe. And I was in due course accredited as a Clinic Teacher.

To my own base in Mutare I was able to bring in clergy and pastors, as well as their lay leaders from Mozambique, Malawi, Zambia and Zaire – as well as from all over Zimbabwe – to be trained and equipped for evangelism. I also had the privilege of visiting Zambia on a number of occasions to encourage the work of evangelism.

The most exciting field to me personally, was our own city. After we had trained about twenty people in our own congregation, word began to get about the city that the Anglicans were doing very 'un-Anglican' things. Regular teams were visiting unbelievers in their homes, sharing the Gospel, and bringing people to Christ. As a result of this, two members of a Pentecostal Church came and asked if I would train them! I agreed to do so subject to the approval of their pastor. Before very long we had pastors and lay people from almost every denomination in the city training under our leaders.

The richness and joy of our fellowship was one of the most memorable aspects of it all. When one shares so much of oneself with a member of another Church for seventeen weeks of concentrated study, checking of homework, much praying together and visiting together in teams to share the truths of the Gospel with unbelievers – tremendous bonds of fellowship develop. For quite a long time we had a unique experiment in progress. Teams of three (the usual EE practice so that 'trainees' get broken-in slowly – and learn to do it by following the example of a leader, just as Jesus taught his disciples) would be drawn up on a multi denominational basis. When one of these teams brought a person to the point of making a commitment to Christ, you might well imagine that the team would have a problem in deciding which church this person should join. In fact we left it to God to lead that person to a Church of his own choosing, and the team would simply try and 'nourish' that person's development until members of the 'new' Church took over the responsibility.

Probably one of the many well-worn excuses used by so many when challenged with the Gospel message is, 'How can I know which Church is the right one? You are all so divided!' This excuse quickly fell away when the person visited discovered that the group was representative of a number of different Churches and, even more important, able to show that all the Churches taking part in this exercise were in agreement on all the most important aspects affecting the proclamation of the Gospel of Salvation!

I have to admit that I had never been trained to actually lead anyone to Christ. Certainly not at Theological College, nor with anyone with whom I had worked in ministry. I had taught lots about the Gospel, about Jesus. But to actually sit down with an unbeliever, or with a member of the church who was unclear about his salvation and be able, in a concise form, to present the Gospel of Salvation in such a way that would convince the hearer of his need to repent, and point the way clearly to what he had to do to get his life permanently right with God – that was something I had not known how to do.

The greatest moment of my life came when, after nearly sixteen years in the ministry, I was able to sit down with an unbeliever I didn't know from Adam and, in a couple of hours, share the Gospel in such a way that he committed his life to Jesus Christ! Obviously the work was done by the Holy Spirit, but I had been given such clarity concerning the Good news Jesus had to offer the listener, that he was entirely convinced. The indescribable joy of that moment brought home to me in a new way that Christ never intended us to 'hug our faith to ourselves'. 'Go in to all the world,' Jesus said and share your faith, St Paul says much the same when he tells us that we need to be able to give a reason for 'the hope that is in us'. It is nothing very difficult, he says. You don't require university or theological degrees before you can be set loose on the world. Far from it. All you have to be able to do is to tell of the great things that God has done in *your* life. And the most important is how Jesus came to give you new life with Him forever – starting right here in this life, living a transformed life by the power of the Holy Spirit! (Rom: 15: 18,19).

Of course we had some difficult moments over sharing the Gospel with strangers. There were times when we were abused and ridiculed, and had door slammed in our faces, but they were rare indeed. One of the remarkable features about Africa today is that 'the fields are white unto harvest', and Jesus is sending forth His labourers into the harvest He spoke about, in order to reap it. In our own experience in Mutare over a seven-year period, and in all our clinics in Zimbabwe (and the ones I attended in South Africa), over fifty percent of the people who heard the Gospel presented to them made a commitment to the Lord Jesus. That is a staggering, but exciting, fact!

There was one thing that we learnt very clearly. The Gospel has the power to change lives in every strata of society. God is no respecter of a person's wealth, educational ability, or status – or lack of any one or more of them. The 'same' Gospel has the power to convert both the academically brilliant and the humblest person from the slums.

My wife tends to have a persistent streak in her at times. One night as our groups were getting ready to go out on our evangelism visiting programme – and all the visits had already been decided upon – Jill suddenly said, 'I believe God wants us to visit Mr. X'. A shocked silence followed. One could almost feel the response of the group leaders – 'Well I am not offering for that impossible assignment. Anyway, I already have a visit lined up!' I was foremost among them, for the man was a well-known leader in the community, a great intellectual, and known to be somewhat antagonistic towards the Christian community. So I told Jill, that as no one offered, God obviously did not want us to cancel one of our other visits and go there that night! Jill does not give up easily. The following week the same thing happened. Again no one volunteered.

Believe it or not, knowing that she was probably antagonising me by doing it, but convinced in her own mind that God had laid this person on her heart, Jill then brought it up for the third week running. Following my natural human instinct, I was angry with her because it seemed to show me up as a coward who was not willing to tackle this tough case. But of course she was absolutely right! In my anger, and to silence her persistence and any suggestion that I wasn't brave enough to tackle this assignment, I said – with a fair degree of bad grace – 'All right! I'll go!'

I faced some bad moments before I reached that house and, after entering it. And we did have a very hard time of it. For two hours and more every intellectual argument he could think of, all his scoffing at the hypocritical types that went to Church, were thrown at us. Eventually I was able to make a presentation of the Gospel to him, and to share what Christ had to offer him as an individual, someone Jesus died for and still loved. Obviously we had an enormous back-up of prayer going on through all our support groups at the time. They knew where we were, and no one was under any illusions as to the difficulties they knew we would be experiencing. But God is fantastic. That man's heart was changed. 'I will remove your heart of stone, and give you a heart of flesh' (Ezek. 11:19).

He was, deep down within himself, looking for something that would really satisfy him. He gave his life to Christ that night as we prayed together, kneeling on the carpet in his lounge. And what peace and joy filled that room as we talked together afterwards over a rather late cup of tea. How we praised God as a Christian community later still that night! And how grateful I was for Jill's persistence!

On another occasion one of our teams arrived at the home of one of our black doctors. They got a very warm welcome, but the hearts of the evangelists began to 'freeze' as they heard this man relate his story. He had spent fifteen years in Russia training to be, and practising, as a doctor. He had been thoroughly indoctrinated by the communists. What a challenge! Despite the apparent obstacles, and with their 'hearts in their mouths' at times, they went ahead and shared with him the things that had radically changed their own lives for the better, and which had given them something to live for. They shared what the Gospel of Salvation had to offer. The man admitted that communism and all the other ideologies that he had tried had never satisfied him. Hearing the Gospel presented that night, so clearly outlining what God had prepared for those who loved Him, convinced him that he had at last found what he was looking for. He surrendered his life to Christ that night.

Stranger than fiction, perhaps, but a week later he was rushed into hospital, very ill. By the time they discovered the very unusual complaint he was suffering from, it was too late to save his life. Yet he died with the certain knowledge – something he had not had ten days before – that he would be with Jesus in Heaven forever! We seldom realise how short someone's time might be, so no wonder St Paul reminds us, however much we might 'ruffle someone's feathers' in doing so, to preach the Gospel 'in season and out of season' (2 Tim. 4:2).

Another visit that really challenged one of our teams took place one night as they were undertaking door-to-door evangelism in a block of flats. One door was opened by a young person who immediately invited the team in. As soon as they got inside they realised that here was someone who was very much a supporter of the new Independent Zimbabwe. The walls were covered with the new Zimbabwe flag together with great big posters of Robert Mugabe our prime minister. They congratulated him on his enthusiasm for our lovely country. It turned out that this man had spent much time outside the country during the war, and had returned as a political commissar. As such, he had responsibility for indoctrinating the proletariat (us, the people) with communist ideology, and the Marxist-Leninist doctrines adopted by our new government. Nothing daunted, the Gospel was presented. Perhaps not so surprisingly, the person concerned revealed that he had become a little disenchanted with the 'earthly paradise' that had been promised and which showed little sign of materialising. In contrast, the Gospel, and what it had to offer in both his life and in the next, really made an impression on him, and he decided to give his life to Jesus.

Over the seven years that the evangelism programme was in operation (until we left the country) a great many of our people – together with pastors and leaders from many other Churches both within and outside Mutare – had a tremendous sense of achievement in being equipped to share God's Good News with others effectively. There can be no greater joy, in obedience to Jesus' direct command, than in seeing someone brought into the Kingdom.

CHAPTER TWENTY-ONE

THE POWER OF GOD IN SPREADING THE GOOD NEWS

I have been told on good authority that a great preacher, with a recognised prophetic ministry, prophesied in Rhodesia just after the Second World War that 'many years hence' a revival would sweep through Rhodesia and that it would begin in the little border town of Mutare. In 1972 a small group of Christians were meeting together in that same town. Barbara Shepherd, a long-time member of our congregation, told me that it was about the time that people began to be 'baptised in the Spirit' and 'speak with tongues'. The small group had little experience of the prophetic ministry – particularly the kind when someone stands up and says, 'Thus says the Lord….'

A stranger walked into their group that night and spent the evening with them. In the middle of the meeting he was given a prophecy – and he shared it with them: 'In ten years a light will go out from this city that will transform this nation and the nations round about'. Ten years ahead seemed far, far away, but Barbara, being that kind of person, recorded the prophecy. For a number of years it was virtually forgotten.

In 1982, all the Churches in Mutare joined together in a mammoth citywide campaign called 'Mutare for Jesus', or 'Mutare kuna Jesu' in the Shona language. After months and months of preparation, an enormous Africa Enterprise team, nearly forty strong, flew into Mutare under the leadership of Michael Cassidy. They represented eight nations including Kenya, Uganda, Tanzania, England and the USA. For three weeks every party of our community in Mutare and the outlying districts was contacted. Many people gave their lives to Christ as teams visited schools, businesses, industry, farms, the police force, and churches. A quite incredible outreach was also started amongst the various army encampments in the area. This was a very sensitive area indeed, with the government doing its utmost to mould together three former armies that had, until a short while before, been in confrontation with one another – the ZANLA, ZIPRA and Rhodesian armies. Many thousands of Bibles were distributed in these camps (and elsewhere) at public meetings where, to obtain one, the men had to stand up in front of their peers! Quite a number committed their lives to Christ.

During the main week of the campaign, when major rallies took place nightly in three separate sections of the city, *six thousand people committed their lives to Christ!* The majority of these were first time commitments!

Both city and province were dramatically affected by that campaign. It was so well publicised that almost no one in the province was unaware that it was taking place. At one night's meeting in the suburb of Sakubva, almost the entire crowd of nearly two thousand responded to the 'call'. The speaker immediately recognised that they could never cope with such numbers. Amongst other things, he noticed that most of those sent in by the various churches to act as counsellors – obviously only nominal Christians themselves – also came forward to give their lives to Christ! The only thing he could do was to spell out exactly what a really radical commitment to Christ would entail – including renouncing trust in all charms, visits to witchdoctors and the like. The number that finally responded to that radical challenge was still large, but more manageable.

Great care had been taken by our Shona pastors to decide exactly what Shona word should be used in our mission title. '*Mutare kuna Jesu*' was finally chosen as being closer in meaning to 'Mutare *for* Jesus'. There are many different dialects amongst the Shona people, so it is all too easy to use a word that will mean something entirely different to one of the Shona groups. Despite all the care that was taken, this happened over the Shona title! A group in a remote area about a hundred miles south of Mutare really caused the local pastors a hard time. To that group of Shona people 'Mutare kuna Jesu' meant that Jesus was going to be physically present in Mutare, and hundreds were pestering church leaders for personal appointments with Jesus in Mutare! They might be excused for thinking such thoughts.

Mutare was in such festive mood for the occasion that the City Fathers had agreed to our request – at our expense – to line the main street throughout the city with coloured lights and bunting. Great banners across the streets, both in the centre of the city and on all the approach roads from outside, together with thousands of red and white posters, gave the city a festive air that no one could fail to notice. However a Cabinet Minister's visit to the city just days before the start of the campaign proper put paid to the coloured lights and the bunting. He ordered the City Fathers to take them down as they were only to be used on 'national occasions'. Nevertheless, nothing could dampen the enthusiasm and excitement of the community. Despite the fact that the Mission was held in mid-winter, thousands and thousands of people braved the cold and poured into the city stadium for the opening and closing rallies.

It was only during the weeks before the crusade that Barbara Shepherd suddenly remembered that prophecy of 1972. This was indeed ten years later, and the city had never seen the like of it before. Some weeks later, Africa Enterprise hoped that a similar crusade might be held in Zimbabwe's second largest city, Bulawayo. They asked me to accompany them down there and share information with the pastors and clergy of that city about our own crusade. I was able to tell them of one incredible miracle that had happened. On one of the first visits of the Africa Enterprise 'set-up' team, led by David Richardson, he had shocked us rigid by telling us that we would have to raise all the local expenses, which they had anticipated at that time would be $13,000! Most of our Churches were unable to pay their pastors a full-time wage, let alone raise that kind of money. But, after much anguish, the Ministers' Fraternal as a whole decided that we had to just step out in faith and believe that God would provide the necessary resources. Within a week of making the decision to go ahead – and long before we had time to plan a campaign for funds from among our respective congregations – we received an anonymous donation of $11,000!

As I explained to the Bulawayo people, it was like a confirmatory sign from God that everything would be taken care of. In fact, because the Mission was far more extensive than we had at first planned, and because the costs of a six-month follow-up programme of literature for six thousand converts was way beyond our planned expectations, the final overall cost of the Mission to the Mutare Ministers' Fraternal was over $30,000! Not a cent owed when we finalised our accounts after the Mission!

A small group of Anglican ladies in Bulawayo then shared 'a picture' with us that they had been given during a prayer time a couple of years before, which seemed to be confirmation of the 1972 prophecy. The 'picture' they had seen was a map of Zimbabwe. At one point on the map that corresponded with Mutare on the eastern border, they saw an enormous shoal of fish pouring out and spreading all over Zimbabwe, overflowing our borders into the countries on all sides of us. Much of that promise seems to have been borne out by our experience.

Large numbers of people from neighbouring countries had come to Mutare for training, and the city itself is now a centre of mission work into the devastated areas of Mozambique. Trained Evangelists from Mutare have moved to many parts of Zimbabwe, and to countries bordering on Zimbabwe. Much work is being done in establishing new churches in rural areas of Manicaland by teams of evangelists going out from Mutare. Despite the government policy of setting up communist-type cells amongst the various age groups of children and teenagers to promote Marxist-Leninist doctrines, large numbers of young people are giving their lives to Christ, and there has been an unprecedented growth in Scripture

Union groups in Secondary schools in the area. The enthusiasm and dedication of these youngsters, and other young people who have left school, has to be seen to be believed. All night prayer and fasting is a regular feature of their determination to storm the gates of hell and win back the young for Christ! Even more inspiring than their ardent young communist counterpart, they will be found devoting every spare moment to working for the extension of Christ's Kingdom, using their well-thumbed Bibles as a powerful weapon, sharper than any two-edged sword (Heb. 4:12,13).

Under persecution and almost endless civil war, deprivation and hunger, the Christian Church is growing faster in Africa than almost anywhere else in the world. Much of that growth, just as in the 'House Church' movement in Western Europe and elsewhere, is sadly taking place outside the traditional churches – be it mainline or Pentecostal – possibly because these Churches have tended to become so bound by past tradition, or because of their unwillingness to consider change, to allow freer expressions of worship and manifestations of the gifts of the Spirit, and sometimes because they have ostracised from their ranks those who have had experiences which differ from their own.

One of the marks of the very early Christian Church was the freedom with which the new converts – with relatively little training in terms of many modern 'theological requirements' – brought new people to Christ through their infectious enthusiasm and excitement at what God was doing in their own lives. No doubt they made mistakes, and no doubt some of their theology was occasionally a little 'off-beam', but often such people do more to bring people into the Kingdom of God than whole battalions of poker-faced, theologically sound church goers (except when turning apoplectic at some innovation) who do little more than warm the seats of their pews on Sundays.

One of the tragedies of the 'Mutare for Jesus' campaign was that nearly three thousand of those who made commitments to Christ came form those who had some past connection with mainline Churches in Sakubva, a high density suburb of the city. Although many of us offered to bring in teams to help these Churches in 'establishing' these new or renewed members, they said they were able to cope themselves. A follow-up exercise some months later revealed that most of those people never went to those Churches, but went into limbo or joined up with fervent 'fringe-group' Christians. The reason? By and large it was discovered that the only action these Churches took was to send Church Councillors or elders to the people concerned. The visitors told them where to find their nearest church, gave them the times of services, and informed them of what they would be expected to give to the Church! The tragedy was that those

Churches had few, if any, members capable of undertaking the nurture of newborn babes in Christ.

CHAPTER TWENTY – TWO

THE POWER OF GOD IN LOVING THE BRETHREN

The coming together of teams of evangelists from different denominations served to underline other Scriptural principles of unity. No one can be happy about the divisions within the body of Christ. All too often, in all too many places, the only time denominations show any concern for the sinfulness of their divisions is during times like the Week of Prayer for Christian Unity (18-25 January) each year, but it only seems to go skin-deep and is forgotten about, for all practical purposes, immediately afterwards. Instead of ecumenism, to most denominations it is still a case of 'you-come-inism' – join us, if you like, because we are the true Church.

Worse still is the antagonism, which exists between the leaders of many Churches in many areas. We know that all disunity is deeply wounding to Jesus. In one of the most moving prayers of Jesus ever recorded, and prayed the night before He died, He spoke of the longing in His heart for all division to cease. It was a fact of life in the established (Jewish) 'church' of His day. There were groups that could not tolerate one another, or who 'looked down their noses' at one another, and it has split into many more groups since then. Jesus could also foresee it happening in the 'renewed' body that He had come to establish. And He cries out in that prayer:

"Holy Father! Keep them safe by the power of Your name, the Name you gave Me *so that they may be one* just as You and I are one…..I pray not only for them, but also for those who believe in Me because of their message. I pray that they may *all be one*, Father! May they be in us, *just as* You are in Me and I am in You. May they be one *so that the world may believe*…(John 17:11b, 20-21)."

There is an important principle about evangelism to be found here. Until we are *seen* to be working together in unity, *the world will not believe.* Nor will the world see the *glory of Jesus.* I believe that is why so many *inter*denominational ministries are seeing large numbers of converts being brought to Christ. I believe that is why the 'House-Church' phenomenon is growing, expanding and developing large numbers of new ministries while most of the mainline, and many Pentecostal, Churches are losing numbers, and continually retrenching men from the ministry

Those moving into the 'interdenominational', or 'non-denominational' or 'House Group' field have given up hope of denominations coming together in any kind of agreement – and many have pulled out of that kind of sectarianism (the, 'we are right and nothing is going to change' syndrome) and linked themselves with those who want to see God's Kingdom, and not denominational empires, built up,

In the same way many would argue that the 'charismatic' renewal, especially between the periods 1965-1980, had a profound effect on the lives of countless thousands of people in mainline churches almost simultaneously all around the world. Many had been nominal Christians before the Holy Spirit changed their lives. Many look for a greater freedom in the Church's worship, particularly in freeing the Church from much (as they see it) of its dead formalism, and longing to see everyone able to enter into worship by bringing prophecies, Scriptures, testimonies, hymns and spiritual songs to it. St Paul says:

"This is what I mean, my brothers. When you meet for worship, one person has a hymn, another a teaching, another a revelation from God, another a message in strange tongues, and still another the explanation of what is said. *Everything must be of help to the Church.* If someone is going to speak in strange tongues, two or three at the most should speak, one after the other, and someone else must explain what is said....two or three who are given God's message should speak, while others are to judge what they say. But if someone in the meeting receives a message from God, the one who is speaking should stop. *All of you* may proclaim God's message, one by one, *so that everyone will learn and may be encouraged.* The gift of proclaiming God's message should be under the speaker's control, because God does not want us to be in disorder but in harmony and peace (1 Cor. 14: 26 – 33a)."

The tragedy of the renewal was that it basically left the denominations, and their traditional practices and formal structures of worship, unchanged. Many lost heart. Many, believing that 'their' Church would never change, moved out and linked themselves with Church groups that were more open to the 'leading of the Holy Spirit', and to patterns of worship that allowed the full participation of the whole congregation – under the direction and leading of the Holy Spirit – as revealed, for instance, in the above direction laid down by St Paul.

It was quite remarkable that the great strides made by the Church as a whole in Mutare came about at those times when the denominations demonstrated their unity and love for one another – and sharing with, and learning from, their varied patterns of worship; by getting alongside one another and understanding why we believe this or that; and thereby often broadening our own understanding of Scripture and God's revelation to man; and even to the extent of not vying with each other over each new convert, just as long as the Kingdom of God was growing.

If we want to be with the Lord forever, then there is a need to love one another. 'If someone says he loves God, but hates his brother, he is a liar. For he cannot love God, whom he has not seen, if he does not love his brother, whom he has not seen. The command that Christ has given us is this; whoever loves God must love his brother also' (1 John 4:20, 21). Of course many try to get round that challenge in Scripture by saying that a 'heretic' is not a brother, thereby implying that 'our' Church has 'all' the truth; and therefore all other Churches are not really part of the true Body of Christ! What arrogance! Those who had adopted such a stance have made their denomination 'their God'.

To return to the Mutare for Jesus Crusade, one of the most positive things to come out of it was the desire of many of the denominations to work more closely together. Instead of being a group of Churches seen by the world as a group largely in competition with each other, there was a desire to be seen as a group that worked together in love – in order that the world may believe. In some ways that move was spearheaded by the lay people of the Churches. During the last three months of preparation leading up to the Crusade, we had opened a 'Mutare for Jesus' office in the centre of the city. Every day that office was staffed by volunteers from many different Churches. We had batteries of typewriters, telephones and display boards, and by the time the Crusade got under way, the pace was hectic. The office remained open for a couple of months after the mission to help cope with the mailing to six thousand people who had made decisions for Christ!

At the end of it, the lay volunteer staff had developed such a wonderful spirit of friendship, and such a desire to continue working together for the Kingdom of God, that the Ministers' Fraternal were asked to keep open a 'joint office'. However the office we had was not really suitable as a counselling centre, so it was agreed we should look for offices that would meet three important conditions: 1) It must be on Main Street in the commercial area. That almost seemed an impossibility because there were no shops vacant; 2) It must be at street level so that general public would see it when walking by; and 3) it had to be large enough to provide for all the various ministries we thought would develop out of such a co-operative venture. In faith we closed down the first office and began to pray for the right place.

Not long after Duane Udd, the new pastor of the One Way Christian Centre, rushed into my house one day and said he thought the ideal place was about to come on the market. He had been in to a very large photographic shop, with plenty of rooms and over 5,000 square feet of space, and they had told him that due to lack of business they were closing down.

We approached the Estate Agent who handled the property and could scarcely believe it when, soon afterwards, we were actually signing a long-term lease on the building. The agreed rental was $350 a month. In addition to two reasonably sized 'halls' which could be used for seminars and conferences, a third 'hall' was divided into sections, proving a large lock-up office for the Tape Library, an entrance foyer with chairs and tables for visitors, an 'office section' with desks, typewriters and duplicating machine, and also a tea and coffee section. Furthermore there were also other rooms which could be set aside for the prayer room – carpeted throughout – (the central 'power-house' for the complex, a Christian book lending library, storerooms and toilets!

A few months later we were in for another surprise – this time a totally unexpected bonus from the Government. The new Rent Act on commercial premises had just been brought into being. Legislation made it impossible for landlords to increase rents over what was paid at a certain period the year before. Because the previous tenants had been facing considerable financial difficulties, the owners of the building had tried to help them by reducing the rent in the hope that they would eventually get on their feet again. Therefore our new rent was governed by that figure, and we received a refund for all the excess rent we had paid! (The rent does increase each year, but even at the time of leaving Mutare in 1986 was still less than $300 a month!) What an answer to prayer those premises proved to be!

Over a period of time I had collected quite a large tape library, mainly teaching tapes from a large number of conferences and the like. I allowed many people to make use of it on a fairly haphazard basis. One day, feeling it could be put to much better use if properly organised, I approached one of my parishioners, Felicity Watkins. I could not have chosen a more dedicated and efficient person to undertake this task. She even visited a very large tape library in South Africa to get additional ideas for improving the library. When it was all catalogued, re-labelled (with master copies safely put away) and stored in well-designed racks in nice new lockable steel cupboards – together with a super catalogue for customers – I handed it over to Mutare for Jesus, to be used by anyone who needed it. Thanks to Felicity's excitement, interest and hard work, we began to get gifts of tapes from all over the world. One tape library in Queensland, Australia was so impressed by what they heard of our tape library through a friend of theirs who came to visit us that they sent us a complete set of teaching tapes (over 750 in all) by David Pawson, and thereby filled in some of the gaps I had in my own collection. Many International Visitors, on being shown around, were so impressed that when they got home they arranged for tapes to be sent to us. In no time at all we had over three thousand teaching tapes in the library for the people of Manicaland to borrow.

Another serious drawback in Zimbabwe is not only our lack of Christian literature, but also the inability to import it. This goes back to the days of Ian Smith's government and the 'sanctions' imposed on our country. Christian literature was given a very low priority, and so the import of Christian literature was severely cut back. Soon after Independence, with import restrictions getting progressively tighter, our own Christian Bookshop in Mutare was left with almost no allocation for the import of religious books. Virtually the only Christian literature that now comes into the Bookshop from outside the country is made possible by monetary gifts from outside the country – these are channelled to overseas publishers for the purchase of books, and then these books arrive as 'free gifts' from the original donor. Not surprisingly, there is little to buy.

However many of us had books on our shelves, which we had read once or twice and were unlikely to need again? I asked everyone in our Christian community to let us have anything they could spare so that we could establish a Christian Lending Library at 'Mutare for Jesus'. Once again we were wonderfully blessed by many gifts, and the gifted people we had in Mutare. Bette Olsen, another member of our congregation spent hundreds of hours with a team of helpers, cataloguing all the books, and handling the on-going business of operating a lending library.

The 'Mutare for Jesus' complex also became the centre for many teaching courses, seminars and the like. We used it as our base for the evangelism explosion clinic and for the on-going evangelistic outreach into the city. We also undertook clerical work for Churches that had no office equipment and produced bulletins and so on for their use. A small Reference Library was set up for pastors who had no reference books of their own.

The staffing of 'Mutare for Jesus' was done entirely with volunteer staff. *No appeals were ever made for funds* to operate the 'Mutare for Jesus' office, and yet we never needed for *anything!* Voluntary donations more than provided for the rent, general running expenses and everything else we set out to do!

The beginning of our working together as a group of Churches in Mutare probably goes back to the first 'Renewal' weekend we held as an Anglican parish at an hotel in the Nyanga Mountains in 1976. It was so talked about around the town that when we were planning a second one, some of the Pentecostals in the city asked if they might join us – as did a group of Roman Catholic charismatics.

(What a mix you might think!) But that too was a tremendous success, and helped us to learn more about one another.

About that time, one of our Anglicans bought a large property in the Industrial Sites on which to expand his business. Eric Carlsen, having sat on the fringe of the Church for many years ('I don't want to get involved' syndrome) gave his life to the Lord around this period. The change that came over him was truly miraculous. Having been the kind of person who was repelled by any infectious enthusiasm over religion, he suddenly became one of the most infectious and enthusiastic Christian I think I have ever met - and still remains so to this day. He and Jeanette, his wife, now have a large home that houses a Christian Community. His whole life is lived for the Lord. His business is dedicated to the Lord.

When we all attended a large renewal conference in Johannesburg, it was here that Eric became certain that God was calling him to set aside his new property investment as a centre where Christians of all denominations could meet together – as we had done at the hotel, and as we had done on an even larger scale in Johannesburg (Ten thousand present!), with Christians of every denomination and colour meeting together in reconciliation, love and harmony.

Over the next few years this new multi-denominational complex was wonderfully used in bringing the whole Body of Christ together. We held many such gatherings where people would take part in a time of renewal from Friday evening through to Monday afternoon whenever there was a bank holiday weekend. The only times we did not meet over such a weekend were on Sunday morning and evening when people were expected to attend their own services. Lunches, teas and suppers would be provided by groups of women from the different Churches right through the weekend. We were blessed with a wonderful key organiser for these events in Muriel Acott, who took care of registrations, setting up the programme and speakers, musical groups, crèches and children's programmes. Supported by her band of helpers, she ensured everything ran smoothly, with everyone obtaining the maximum benefit from their participation.

Because the complex was within the city boundaries, many people who might otherwise have been deterred by the expense (staying in a hotel), problems with transport out of the city, or being unable to leave husband or wife at home for the weekend, were able to attend. Some difficulty was experienced later in the war when the city's fuel storage tanks were at risk from rockets, and special permission had to be obtained to get through road blocks set up to seal off that part of the industrial sites during curfew times.

Eric, by now one of my churchwardens, had great difficulty in keeping his enthusiasm for the Lord in check (why should he?), and found the Anglican Church extremely restricting to someone who wanted to see so much more freedom in our worship, and much greater freedom in the ministry of the laity. Eric also believed that the One Way Christian Centre, as it was now called, should be utilised more fully.

When a new Pastor in the city asked Eric if he could borrow chairs from the Centre for the 'church' that was now meeting in his home, Eric immediately offered the use of the Centre as a place of worship. Naturally enough, it was snapped up! Also, not surprisingly, and because some deep hurts caused by people leaving a number of churches to join the new 'One Way' Christian Church, the large majority of churches felt they could no longer use the Centre as neutral territory for inter-church activities. Eric and a number of my leadership were amongst those who joined this new Church. To this day they have provided much of the key leadership of that new Church, and a great healing took place about a year later between this group and us. We have all worked together very closely ever since and probably to greater effect – as many of the lay people have developed wonderful ministries that probably would never have been possible under the restrictions imposed by the Anglican structures. And there can be no doubt of their being used mightily of the Lord in the building of His Kingdom. Deep and lasting friendships, and much sharing of team ministries, have deepened between myself and many pastors who have served in Mutare.

For some years now God has led us to cancel all our Sunday evening activities on the last Sunday of each month. In place of it, the whole Body of Christ gathered together for a joint service of 'Celebration'. A roster was drawn up in which one pastor was given the responsibility of leading the worship, and another the ministry of preaching at the service. Musicians from a number of churches would get together for practices and to play together. We got to know people in all the different churches, and a real love developed between us all. 'The Brethren' taking part in these monthly Celebrations certainly 'dwelt together in unity', and with a love that superseded the doctrinal differences we might still have. We learnt to accept and respect one another despite those differences. Perhaps more than anything else, our willingness to share our differences helped us to widen our understanding.

Each ministry operating out of 'Mutare for Jesus' had its own sub-committee made up of members of different churches, with each sub-committee reporting to me as the person responsible to the city centre pastors for the administration of the complex. At the centre of everything at 'Mutare for Jesus' were the prayer support groups for the various ministries. There was also, I believe, a really 'key' group brought together by the Lord, representing a number of churches, to specially uphold the churches, and all the priests and pastors in sustained intercessory prayer. They were called upon to pray for the various programmes being undertaken, for various difficulties being experienced in any one or more churches. They continued faithful in this for many years, meeting one afternoon a week virtually without a break for the whole period of time. For much of the time there were seven in the group – Claudia, Barbara, Jill, Betty, Ning, Vickie and Debbie – and the Lord laid on them the need to *fast and pray*. Each one took responsibility for one twenty-four hour period each week – and for more than two years a continuous unbroken fast was kept.

I believe that it was that kind if commitment to prayer and sacrifice, to be found in a number of parts of the city, that enabled us to see God working so mightily in our midst, and which explains why the brethren were able to dwell together in unity.

Only God, through His Spirit, could work the miracle of bringing together so many different groups of His people – usually separated by man-made walls of division – to experience such love and respect for one another. We praise His name for what He has done, and continues to do, in bringing reconciliation and healing.

CHAPTER TWENTY-THREE

'GO AND SELL ALL THAT YOU HAVE'

The contrast between the lack of enthusiasm with which I faced my return to the full-time ministry, and the excitement that filled every part of my being within a year of my returning, couldn't have been more marked. The job-satisfaction far exceeded anything I had ever known before. I found myself given gifts that were not natural to me. If there had been any indecision at all, it was only as to whether I could remain within the Anglican Church. There, too, I was firmly convinced that whatever the cost, God was calling me to remain and witness to the change that He had brought about in my life. Over the past eleven years I have been able to share with many people the story of how God brought about that change, and tell them how He could change their lives too. I was to share this not only with Anglicans who had never understood what God was really offering them, but also with people in many other mainline Churches in Zimbabwe and in neighbouring countries. Many have come to this experience of being born again, and of receiving the empowering of the Holy Spirit.

With the coming of this wonderful change in my life, I now had no thought of leaving Mutare. It was such a lovely city, surrounded by mountains in the most beautiful part of Zimbabwe. My predecessor had been there for nearly twenty years. As I talked with God on more than one occasion, I told Him how nice it would be if I could just stay there until God called me 'upstairs'. Surely He wouldn't mind, I would ask, even if I remained until my retirement? A matter of twenty-eight years?

In 1984, however, I came to believe God was telling me it was time to leave. In fact, I believed I was required to be willing to give up everything I had become so attached to in Mutare: the congregation we dearly loved, and the deep and loving relationships we had with people across many denominations. There was also our six-bedroom house, which we shared with such joy with a constant flow of visitors from near and far. There had been the challenge and excitement of seeing a new Diocese coming into being and beginning to spread its wings, and the privilege of being a part of that experience. Now I was being called to give up the security in which I had come to trust (although until that moment I had not realised how important a part it played in my life): the assurance of a regular stipend, and a pension to follow.

The rich man who met with Jesus in the Gospels was told to go and *sell everything he had* (because it was more important to him than almost anything else), and give it to the poor. Then, said Jesus, 'come and follow me'. Nevertheless, how can one be expected to give up everything when one has a family to consider? At the time our son Andrew was starting on his 'A' levels at School, Diana was in her second year of Secondary School, and Lynne – who was only three – plus my wife Jill were all dependent on me as well. As a result I decided that the suggestion I give up everything could not have come from God!

But the easy way with which I disposed of the thorny issue of putting my trust in that kind of security – just like the rich man in the Gospel – left a considerable unease in my spirit. It involved a similar principle to my not trusting God to provide the words for a sermon. I salved my conscience, for some time, by regularly asking my Churchwardens, Giles Wakeling and Robert Rugge whether they didn't think the time had come for me to move? It was a good way of 'chickening out'. I asked the same question of other leaders, members of the Church Council, and friends. Nothing pleased me more when each responded, 'Of course not, John…'

A few months later it was decided that Jill and I should go to the United States as 'ambassadors' for our Diocese and meet with the many people in our Companionship Diocese of Massachusetts in New England. As our Diocese was unable to afford such an expense, the parish most generously responded to the Bishop's suggestion and paid for the trip as a gift for us after ten years' service. As they informed us of the gift, they jokingly added a 'condition' to that gift and one can see how all my questioning had begun to make some impression on them: 'In making this gift to you, we expect you to sign on for another ten years!'

The gift made it possible for us to spend two months overseas. We were able to have our own holiday first in Israel, visiting the home of Jesus (the most memorable and heart-moving experience for both of us), before flying on to spend three weeks in New England, followed by three weeks in the United Kingdom on the way home. It was a truly wonderful experience. Bill and Liz Reynolds were kindness itself when they moved into our house and looked after the two girls while we were away. It was also a welcome break from all the anxiety and strain that had followed an earlier mass demonstration against the Bishop early in 1985, when Tekere and his supporters had, on this occasion, taken over the Diocesan offices.

However, on our return the issues had still not been resolved. I learnt from the leaders of the Diocese that they were determined to go ahead and press charges against the leaders who had been in rebellion, and who were strongly supported by their political friend Tekere, the former cabinet minister of Mr. Mugabe. I felt I had to make my own position on the question of charges clear, as I believed that Scripture clearly tells us that we are not to take a brother to court. I also warned (despite whatever assurances to the contrary were given to them by some government ministers and officials) that I could not see Edgar Tekere allowing these leaders, whom he had so strongly supported all along, to be prosecuted. If they were determined on this action, I said that I believed even worse demonstrations would follow.

The demonstrations took place as outlined at the beginning of this book, and on a far worse scale than anyone could have predicted.

The major reason for the publicity given to this desecration of the Cathedral was that this was not the first time that this type of tactic had been used. Similar, politically-motivated, pressure tactics had been used as a weapon against a number of denominations and church leaders in the immediate past. It was for just these reasons that both the Mutare Minister's Fraternal and the Roman Catholic Justice and Peace Commission also came out with strong statements supporting the cry to Government to put a stop to this kind of political thuggery and intimidation.

After the invasion of the Cathedral we spent a fortnight away from our home. A week after our return, Diana was rushed into hospital for an emergency appendix operation, but made a speedy recovery. Two days later a very senior member of the Party telephoned me about the publicity that had been given to the event overseas, and promised that I would be severely dealt with by the party for 'bringing the country into disrepute' (as he described it). The next morning a gang of thugs was waiting to ambush me near my office. I had had a dream the night before that warned me of impending danger, and I escaped with seconds to spare.

Strangely enough two different people were, that very morning in their quiet time, given the story of St Paul having to escape those who plotted to kill him, by being let down over the city walls of Damascus in a basket. The people given that reading, without having any knowledge of what was happening to me at the time, felt quite clearly that God was telling them that the story was for me. They shared it at a special meeting, which was called that night. They all agreed that I should disappear.

As the family left for Harare on indefinite leave a few days later, we discovered that God had begun to do a wonderful work in each of us, as each one realised that we no longer had any concern in our hearts, even if we were never to see any of our possessions again. It was almost as if God had taken away our dependence and trust on such things. We spent six weeks in Harare living in many different Christian homes to avoid being found and we were quite wonderfully loved and cared for by the wider Christian community

What came out of that stay away from home was that we became increasingly certain God was calling us out of the Anglican Church in Zimbabwe, and out of the country we perhaps loved too much. A whole range of prophecies was given to us, through many different people, all of them dovetailing together, – including twice being told 'return to the land of your fathers'. Both our Dads had come from England! All these provided plenty of confirmation for each decision that was made. 'All things work together for good….'?

Well, if there was no other way of getting me to let go of all the things I had been trusting in, then God could use the prevailing circumstances I found myself in to make it impossible for me *not* to resign. Now I would really have to start trusting in Him for everything.

Although peace was eventually restored between members of the Party and the leadership of the Church, and an agreement arrived at with those in the Church who had been in rebellion, part of that agreement led to the appointment of the Head of the Witchdoctors' Association as Chairman of the Board of Governors of one of our most prestigious Anglican Schools. It appears to me, and still does, that Scripture clearly points out that God's people can have nothing to do with 'supporting' things clearly shown to be contrary to God's Word.

"When you come into the land that the Lord your God is giving you, don't follow the disgusting practices of the nations that are there….don't let your people practise divination or look for omens or use spells or charms, and don't let them consult the spirits of the dead (*all* the things that witchdoctors do). The Lord your God hates people who do these disgusting things….Be completely faithful to the Lord (Deut. 18:9-12)."

"Fear the Lord your God and worship only Him, and make your promises in His name alone. Do not worship other gods, any of the gods of the people around you. If you do worship other gods, the Lord's anger will come against you like fire and will destroy you completely, because the Lord your God, who is present with you, tolerates no rivals (Deut. 6:13-15)."

The New Testament is equally clear on what the Church's stance should be on this matter:

"Many of the believers came, publicly admitting and revealing what they had done. Many of those who had practised magic brought their books together and burnt them in public. They added up the price of the books, and the total came to fifty thousand silver coins. In this powerful way the Word of the Lord kept spreading and growing stronger (Acts 19:18-20)."

As a matter of conscience I handed in my resignation to Bishop Elijah when it became clear that the decision to appoint the Head of the Witchdoctors' Association would not be fought. My resignation was accepted.

The resignation meant that I no longer had the security of a job or a salary. I would also be without a house and car, and would lose my Pension. Furthermore, given government regulations of the day, we would be able to leave the country with less than £400 to start a new life. It is possible to export *some* furniture and personal belongings, but at a cost of $700 a cubic metre! That we didn't have. Not that the government is wholly to blame. On leaving the country many people (going right back to Ian Smith's declaration of UDI in 1965) had done everything possible to get round regulations and exported far more than was allowed. The net result was that those who followed later faced tighter and tighter restrictions and allowed to take out less and less.

Another problem resulting from my resignation was being able to raise most of the cost of the airfares for the family to travel to England. We were aware of all these factors when I faced the consequences of resigning. It was a choice we freely made. We accepted it because we believed God was calling us to move to England – 'return to the land of your fathers'.

There was no way we could pay for those air fares *and* export our furniture. Apart from anything else, we did not believe we could in conscience spend considerably more than the furniture was worth in exporting it. We had virtually no savings, so we decided to sell all our furniture and many of our possessions, and used the money to pay for our fares, and to cover the cost of sending a limited amount of clothing, crockery, cutlery, linen, bedding and kitchenware by sea. That way we would at least have something with which to start a new home….eventually! The small life policies we had were cashed in and the money given to further the work of God in Mutare. What was refunded to us from a recently established Pension Fund for the Clergy in Zimbabwe provided the whole family with a wonderful 'farewell tour' round Zimbabwe before we left in July, 1986.

I was warned by an old friend and former Bishop, Paul Burrough, now retired in England that the prospect of getting a post in the Church of England could be difficult, as the Church Commissioners required the number of posts presently filled to be reduced. Bishop Paul was a great support during this time, writing us many letters of encouragement and helpful advice. He had been 'through the mill' himself before leaving Zimbabwe some years earlier, also at the hands of Tekere.

The decision to give up everything was probably the hardest decision in my life. To surrender everything I knew, and hand in my resignation. For what? An empty future? And what about providing for my family? Yet, over and over again, during that period of exile in Harare, God showed us in our daily readings (and in many of the prophecies given to us) that He would take care of our every need. All that was required of us (so easy to say, so difficult to obey) was that we entrust our future and ourselves to Him, and step out in faith.

There was one further complication. I believed that I could get a job in bookkeeping or administration, but we were convinced (and again this was borne out by prophecies given to us) that God was saying to me that I was *not* to take a job of any sort for some time (six months to a year seemed to be the time span) because He wanted me to deepen my relationship with Him. Like so many in ministry, my life had been so hectic working *for* God in the past ten or more years that my relationship *with* Him was not all that it could be. Perhaps it was David Watson's book *Fear No Evil* that had started this train of thought in me. Our work *for* God becomes so important in our eyes. Yet what God wants for us more than *anything* else is just to spend time *with Him*, alone. That, to Him, is as precious – even more so – as any two people deeply in love with each other. How fantastic! To realise that the God of the Universe calls you and me into an individual, *personal* love-relationship with Him.

Unbelievable! But how does one go to a new country with less than £400 in one's pocket, a family to provide for, and no home that one can call one's own, and not work for a considerable period while one spends time with the Lord?

God's clear answer to me was, 'Trust Me'! We took that leap of faith. By the time we left Zimbabwe, I had had almost nothing to do (work-wise) for over four months except to spend a lot of time with Him – and I have never heard Him speak to me so much before, or so clearly. I was also able to hand over all the responsibilities I had been carrying, and sell up everything.

For years I had handled all the administration of the diocesan Trust Funds – ever since the creation of the new Diocese of Manicaland in 1981 when I was appointed Dean of the Cathedral) – on behalf of my fellow Trustees. This covered funds held for the Diocese, for Parishes, for Missions together with all the property of the Diocese. It also involved the handling of many grants from overseas for specific projects – involving detailed applications, costings, and financial returns to donors and donor agencies. I also had the responsibility for the profitable and secure investment of those funds. As I handed over that responsibility, and the other Trustees signed for all the assets together with the audited accounts, a marvellous sense of peace flooded though my being.

My life as Dean of the Cathedral Parish, my primary task, had also been a very full one, and immensely satisfying and encouraging – as this account probably reveals. However, even as I handed over that task, there was the assurance that God had no more for me to do there, and that others had their part in bringing all God's people to their full stature in Christ. The Cathedral Church Council had always been very understanding about my deep commitment to working with all the Churches in Mutare, and to working *outside* the Body of Christ to bring the lost into the Kingdom. Whether I was travelling away to hold evangelism clinics, attend and teach at renewal conferences, or work on joint-Church projects in Mutare and in the wider Church, they generously allowed me complete freedom to act according to what I believed God's priorities for my time should be. Never once was there any suggestion that, because they paid my salary, all my time should be spent only on those 'who footed the bill'.

There was also a sense of shedding another load as I handed in my resignation as Chairman of the Ministers' Fraternal, and handed over – something that had become especially dear to my heart – all the responsibilities for the administration of the Mutare for Jesus complex.

It was all like having an incredible load lifted off one's shoulders as I released one job after another. Of course, one never really appreciates the load until that point, because it is something that has been gradually increasing over a period of time. It's like the analogy that was once told me about the frog. Put in a beaker of water over a flame, he doesn't realise how critical his situation is; for as the water temperature increases, his body adjusts to it. Only too late does he realise (if he realises it at all) that he has reached the critical point of no return! Similarly, it was only as I was freed of all these responsibilities that I realised what a weight I had been carrying, and I began to understand my family's complaint that I was a 'workaholic'. Those four months were one of the most wonderful periods in our life as a family. We had never seen so much of each other *as a family*, and we enjoyed it immensely.

It was not that I hadn't enjoyed doing all the jobs that I had taken on. I had done so tremendously. Naturally there were heartaches at saying farewell to those we loved so deeply, and many a tear. Even so, we felt a deep peace about our decision because we shared the belief with those close to us that this was of the Lord, and that even if we didn't meet up again in this life, we would soon be together again for ever.

As the day of our departure drew nearer we felt, understandably enough, some concern for our future means of support. We started to joke with friends that if nothing else materialised, we might be reduced to seeking shelter under the Severn Bridge! Not surprisingly our parents and other members of our extended family felt that it would have been wiser to have had a job lined up before venturing into the unknown in another country. Many of our Christian friends, because of their love and concern for us, also couldn't help but express some anxiety from time to time. We had to keep reminding ourselves that Jesus did indeed say, 'Take no thought for the morrow….Your Father knows you have need of these things'…..food, clothing, drink. The priority Jesus lays before us is crystal clear: 'Seek *first* the Kingdom of God', and *then* all these things (food, drink, clothing, jobs, homes, security and so on) will be added to you'!

It was only *after* we stepped out in faith and *cut all our ties* – and only then on the very eve of departure – that we received an unbelievable offer.

CHAPTER TWENTY – FOUR

'BEHOLD I MAKE ALL THINGS NEW'

The unbelievable offer came from a Christian Fellowship in Theydon Bois in Essex, England. They had heard of our difficulties and trials through mutual friends. We knew nothing of the Fellowship at that time, nor had we ever heard of Theydon Bois before. It's a little village just outside the northeast border of Greater London with a population about 4,500, and maintains its village character by refusing to have streetlights. These people had been led to pray for us, with the leadership being convinced God was calling on them to provide for us. Through John and Jenny – farmers in the Nyanga Highlands – they telephoned a message to us to this effect, and followed it up with a confirmatory letter. The Fellowship is under the leadership of three men: Alan Mutter (Deputy Director for Education in Enfield, Essex) and his wife Barbara; Mike Steward (Professor of Immunology at London University) and wife Lynne; and Vincent Wiffen (retired from Local Government) and his wife 'Jimmie' (Doris). What an unbelievable offer of Christian love, generosity and self-sacrifice to extend to an Anglican Dean and his family they had never met!

In the confirmatory letter, each leader and his wife added a personal message. Amongst other things they said: 'We'll just put ourselves in God's hands and do anything He asks'...Whatever is ours is yours if you need it'...We would like to assure you that we have some accommodation available and will be very happy to share it with you for as long as you need it'. (Another strange coincidence in this story is that Alan and Barbara had been virtually life-long friends of the leaders of the Elim School at the time of the massacre.).

This offer of help was a wonderful answer to prayer, and an assurance to us that God was already taking care of our 'provision' in England. Very soon after this news was received, we had our final Celebration Service (gathering of all denominations in our monthly corporate act of worship) in Mutare. Although most certainly not planned as such – I had drawn up the roster of preachers for those monthly services nearly a year earlier – I was down to preach for that particular service! Duane Udd, who led the worship, also turned a part of the service into a moving farewell for the Knight family. The 'One Way Christian Centre', where this service was held and which held so many treasured memories for us, was packed to the doors. The whole congregation prayed over us, and I was so emotionally moved by their love and concern for us, that I found it very difficult to preach. Immediately before doing so I told them, knowing the concern many had for our future provision, that we had received this wonderfully comprehensive offer.

I explained that we had agreed to go and stay with the Christian Fellowship for a short while after our arrival in England. This would be followed by a visit to Jill's brother and sister-in-law, Howard and Claire, in Duffield. Then the Fellowship would have time to decide – having met us – if they wanted to stand by their offer.

While I was telling the congregation about this unknown Fellowship, I had no idea that a young man was in the congregation, trying to summon up the courage to stand up, interrupt me, and tell the congregation that he not only knew the Fellowship, and the village of Theydon Bois, but also was actually part of that Fellowship!

One can imagine the kind of odds a bookie would offer on the chance of a member of that tiny Fellowship in a very small village in England six thousand miles away, being in a particular church in a very small city in Africa, at the very moment the preacher mentioned that Fellowship by name! Mark had, earlier that day been in Masvingo nearly two hundred miles away. (He knew nothing of me, or the offer that his Fellowship had made because he was already on holiday.) He had hitched a lift through to Mutare, and asked people he met there if there was a service he could attend that evening. He was brought to the place where we were meeting! Now that is what I call a God-incidence, rather than a coincidence. As he spoke with many of us after the service about the loving people we would find in the Fellowship in Theydon Bois, it seemed a final confirmation that this was God's way of telling us that *this was His provision!* There was no other way of explaining away all those God-incidences!

Early on Sunday morning, 13 July 1986 we landed at Heathrow Airport in England and were met by 'Jimmie' and Vincent Wiffen, and by the same Mark we had so recently met in Mutare. A few hours later that same morning (we did land very early) we were welcomed by the members of this vibrant Fellowship at their time of worship. For over six months, at the time of writing, they have showered us with love, been ever thoughtful of our every need, ensured that we needed for nothing, and embraced us as an accepted part of a really warm, caring and close-knit family.

Very soon after our arrival, those with education expertise in the Fellowship set about finding a solution to Diana's schooling problem. Her final 'O' level year had been shattered by an enforced four-month break from school, both during the two periods of exile from our home, and during the time of packing up to leave Zimbabwe. Through expert help and advice, the authorities concerned in England have been kindness itself – from the Cambridge School Certificate Board responsible for people like Diana writing overseas examinations, right through to the Davenant School Foundation in Loughton – next door to Theydon Bois. Staff at the school had gone out of their way to coach Diana, and help her in areas where her past schooling had been deficient. They even put her in the Sixth Form to make her feel more comfortable. Diana will now be sitting a new set of 'O' levels in June 1987. Lynne, too, has been equally well catered for, and is very happy with the place that was found for her in the Theydon Bois Primary School.

"The group of believers was one in mind and heart. No one said any of his belongings was his own, but they all shared with one another everything they had"...."there was no one in the group who was in need" (Acts 4:32-35). How wonderfully this Fellowship have lived that out in their daily lives, both with one another, and with us who have been made very much a part of the 'group of believers'. As we have spent time waiting on the Lord, renewing and deepening our personal relationship with Him, and allowing members of the Fellowship to minister healing to many hurts and scars that had inevitably been caused in recent times, we have tried to live one day at a time, *endeavouring* not to be anxious for anything.

The greatest sacrifice was inevitably made by 'Jimmie' and Vincent; for it was their home we invaded for nearly six months. They took us in and shared everything with us – not as lodgers or tenants, but as one would in a close-knit family. They were always there to pick up the pieces, to pray with us and for us, and to minister to our needs for healing. They were the ones who broke us in gently as we became accustomed to living in a new country (for most of the family), with its many cultural and practical differences.

When I got down to writing this book, they made over their caravan to me as an office, so that I could work for hours on end undisturbed. Even after obtaining a small flat for us to live in – almost exactly six months after our arrival – they remain very much a part of the family. Villagers are still seen to raise eyebrows when Lynne calls 'Jimmie' and Vincent 'Granny and Grandpa'

The Fellowship also discovered later, that even though I had spent so few years in England when I was a student, I was entitled to claim supplementary benefit. This indeed proved to be the case, and the DHSS (Department of Health and Social Security) provided much help as we set about re-establishing ourselves.

Times of worship in the Fellowship have often been something very special to us. The first impression that strikes every visitor is the warmth and love they have for everyone from the moment they begin to gather. No one remains a stranger for long. There are also so many young people – especially those in their teens and twenties, thirties and forties. Many have musical ability, and use it in playing a wide range of musical instruments. There is a freshness and spontaneity – that admittedly doesn't *always* come off – to their worship, with many in the congregation bringing along to the service a reading from Scripture, a psalm, a hymn, a spiritual song, a prophecy, a tongue, and an interpretation, and so on. The leading of the Holy Spirit in all of this becomes most noticeable when everything seems to blend together, without any kind of prior planning or consultation before the service, and presents the worshipper with something that convicts him of God's presence, and of something that God is wanting to say to each individual that is relevant to his life at that time.

There is a wealth of experience in this Fellowship, for quite a number have come out of leadership roles in mainstream churches, and have previously served those churches as preachers, elders and so on. They are also drawing in people with no previous church background. All the preaching I have listened to has been of a very high standard, deeply challenging, instructive, encouraging, and very soundly based on Scripture. More than anything else, and I have experienced this myself as an occasional preacher in the Fellowship, one recognises God's inspiration when the preached Word dovetails in so perfectly with all that the others have brought, and with its relevance to prophecies, tongues and interpretation, that have been given by others during the service under the leadership of the Holy Spirit..

A strong argument is sometimes put forward by people outside the fellowship that those who have moved out of other mainline churches would have done better to have remained there and worked for change in those congregations. I have been privileged to listen to the stories of many people in this and other similar fellowships. As with reformers of every age, one hears of agonising and very painful decisions that many have felt led by God to make. Many forget, or fail to appreciate, that such decisions are costly and painful. A decision of this kind often, and sometimes inevitably, leads to ostracism, ridicule and even persecution from former friends, neighbours and colleagues. In a small community it is a devastating blow to a family – to be cut off like a leper of biblical times. Many knew that that would be the price. Some took that step despite the cost, because in conscience they believed God required them to make a stand for truth as they saw it. But all too many were simply expelled from their churches, as were Luther and so many others in Church History.

It was the *Church Times*, in its report of a meeting between Anglican Evangelicals and the House Church Movement that said the renewal movement had to be seen as a vote of no confidence in the traditional Church. At that same meeting Dr John Stott is quoted as saying, 'we belong together in the Body of Christ' and that 'a lot of our divisions are due to caricatures we have of one another' (*Church Times*, 23/1/87). We ignore at our peril the challenge of such movements and what they are saying to us in the traditional Church. There is a need to get alongside and discover why so many good people in leadership have left, and why they are attracting many new members and we, on the whole, are not.

In the days of Jesus the Jewish Church, established and built by God, no longer moved with God despite continually going through all the rituals, ceremonies and forms of initiation. So Jesus Himself 'rebelled' and established something new, a Church that *would* move on with God under the direct and observable leadership of the Holy Spirit, and testified to by the miracles, signs and wonders that followed.

During November 1986 I applied for a number of posts in Para church organisations. The *"Reluctant Priest"* all over again? Yes! There was much that I found difficulty with in my Church. The fact that I was made the scapegoat for other people's problems and mistakes had caused much hurt; but God had been good and enabled me to forgive those who did that, and healing was given to each member of the family. What really has caused me concern, particularly on the part of many in leadership, is the lack of belief in miracles (both in Scripture and in the present); the lack of belief in much of Scripture as the Word of God; the denial of the unequivocal evidence in Scripture of the bodily Resurrection and Virgin Birth of Jesus and so on; the denial of the operation of many of the gifts of the Spirit in the twentieth century – and the ascribing of some of those gifts to the work of Satan; the failure to preach the Gospel in many churches, with services that are 'dead', because the work of the Person of the Holy Spirit has been deliberately restrained. So much of this points to the grave danger that 'reason' has become the new god of this age (the glorification of man's intellectual abilities). The Anglican Church has generally taught that truth is determined on three bases – Scripture, Tradition and Reason. Many of today's *avant garde* theologians give 'Reason' priority over the other two. All too many in the leadership of the Church today seemed to have overlooked our roots – for both the Book of Common Prayer and the Thirty Nine Articles of faith stress over and over again that *Scripture alone* is the fundamental base on which ALL truth is determined.

So, in seeking a job outside the Church was I simply trying to find something more acceptable to me? This became clear to me in the interviews that I attended. I felt decidedly uncomfortable each time I was asked the reason for leaving the full-time ministry. Although I could talk about Pauline 'tent ministry' (Paul was proud to earn his keep making tents while continuing his missionary work) I felt unease in my spirit, because at this point in time I could not see a part-time ministry being more effective than a full-time one I had in the past.

All denominations are imperfect, and their members are imperfect. As a Christian sticker has it, 'I'm not perfect; but be patient, God hasn't finished with me yet'! This was also made clear to me by two other things that I observed. Close friends were very unhappy in a lifeless Church where the Gospel was not preached and the priest antagonistic to renewal. Although they would have loved to look for a Church that would meet their needs and 'make them happy', they were brought up short with: 'How can we leave when so many in *this* congregation don't know Jesus as Saviour and Lord?'

The other thing concerned Sid Freeman, a member of the Fellowship. He had the seemingly impossible job of promoting Scripture in an atheistic environment, but instead of looking for a more congenial area to work in, each week he asked for prayer to remain faithful to the Gospel where he was, whatever the apparent odds against his team!

The Fellowship has been much involved in praying for our future ministry in England. When they said, 'Come and stay, no strings attached', they meant just that. They were delighted when I finally said I believed God was calling me back into the full-time ministry and that we were going to knock on the doors of the Church of England. So were the Anglicans we had come to know and love in the area, particularly at Coopersale where I had also preached and ministered. Ralph Harding (the Vicar) and his wife Elizabeth, who have so loved and supported us, were particularly thrilled.

Whether the door is opened for us to continue ministry in the Church of England, or whether God has some other full-time ministry in the wider Church, waits to be seen.

We seek only to be obedient to God's will and purpose for our lives. The truly astounding truth is that nothing happens by chance and, as the Psalmist says, 'the days allotted to me had all been recorded in your book, before any of them ever began' (Ps 139:16). 'I chose you before I gave you life, and before you were born I selected you to be a prophet to the nations' (Jer. 1:5). And that is true of everyone God calls into His service. His plan for each of us is perfect!

At about the time we were reaching these conclusions, a word was shared with us in one of our times of worship – through Sandra Walker – which I felt spoke specifically to my family and me in my situation:

"Driving along to work one morning, I was overcome by the sheer beauty of the trees in their autumn colours. I could not comprehend how God could create the many different shades of colour, and blend them all so well together. But then I felt a sense of sadness as the leaves began to flutter from the trees, and I was aware of the fact that soon the trees would be bare and unlovely."

"Then I remembered God's promise of new life, and it would all come alive again. God spoke through that picture and said, 'When you reach an autumn in your lives, and your leaves begin to fall, remember my promise. When all seems to be going wrong and life loses its colour, and piece by piece it crumbles and falls away, take hold of my promise: ' I will never leave you or forsake you', but put your hand in mine and I will reclothe you again. Spring will come to you again, and will give colour and beauty to your life….As the wind blows through the leaves and they flutter to the ground, I will blow my Spirit through you and all your unrighteousness will flutter away, and my Spirit will reclothe you in a new and wonderful way. Reach out now, and let my Spirit blow in, through and over you until you are completely immersed in my love."

Some of the seemingly cataclysmic events of recent times had indeed led us to 'an autumn' in our lives. Yet having experienced so much of this miracle-working God over recent years, and having seen the abundant outpouring of His Spirit on individuals, congregations and situations, bringing about startling and exciting changes – quite literally 'rain in a dry land' (Hosea 14:5) – we are absolutely convinced of His promise for the future: "Behold, I make all things new!"

EPILOGUE

Time after time I hear people say to me,
'Why don't we see miracles like there used to be?'
I still believe in miracles, God gives us when we pray,
For God is God like yesterday, and God is God today!

Chorus:

God can do it again and again and again
He's the same God today, as He always has been.
Yesterday, now, forever He's always the same,
There's no reason to doubt God can do it again.

The complete version of this song may be found in *Songifts* (Ed. Jeanne Harper, Hodder and Stoughton 1986) and is used with permission.

See next page for the first chapter…

Chapter 1

TO REIGN OR NOT TO REIGN?

"God moves in mysterious ways His wonders to perform"! That was certainly true of one of our daughter's Sports Days. Most young children are excited on such an occasion; seven-year-old Lynne and her School friends were no exception. However, when we arrived at the school, with the field beautifully marked and laid out for the event, it was to find enormous black clouds directly overhead. And if that was not enough, there was an even more ominous gathering of storm clouds over to the west, with a wind blowing so strongly in our direction that the willows in the field below us were bent almost double.

Lynne's school was a church school. No suggestion was made that the problem be committed to prayer. And I suppose that if the organisers had stopped everything and called on everyone to pray for clear skies, there would have been surprise and general embarrassment all round. Laughter, too, perhaps. The problem would not necessarily be with the children (many have a wonderful simple faith in God!); it would have been the adults. You can picture the scene for yourself. As rain drops begin to fall, the announcer calls on the crowd to join with him in prayer for clear skies...?

No! Rather, because so few expect God to work in that way (or, possibly, too frightened to lay their faith on the line in case such specific prayer isn't answered?) what we in fact heard was a very different announcement over the loud hailer. "You can see from the coming storm that we will not get through the programme. So we intend to rush through as many events as possible before the storm breaks!" The proposal was clearly accepted as perfectly reasonable. Certainly one that was in line with most people's perceived acceptance that nothing could be done to alter 'those facts'.

Three of us, sitting together amongst that large gathering of parents, often prayed together. So I said to Jill and our friend Janie, "Let's ask God for clear skies right now." I thought I had spoken fairly quietly, but a lady sitting next to me overheard my suggestion and chipped in: "I gave up praying for that sort of thing years ago; it never works!"

For our part, I told her, our experience in Africa had shown us a God who actually delights in answering prayer. We believed in the power of prayer; so we would pray in faith for the miracle needed to enable the children to enjoy the afternoon. Nothing ventured, nothing gained!

After two or three minutes the rain drops from the heavy clouds over us stopped. A short while later I looked up and saw that the willow trees were now bent over in the opposite direction! The clouds above us, and the storm following, moved off in that direction. A moment or two later the sky cleared. The remainder of the sports afternoon was bathed in warm sunshine. All the events on the programme were completed. Then, as the last presentation was made, the clouds returned; this time we had to run for cover! Most of us were drenched! But the children's joy was complete. "To God be the glory, great things He has done"!

Should it really surprise us that God cares for us on a personal level? No one was deprived of rain; only the timing was altered! Such incidents have become known. When good weather is essential for special events (like Diocesan events at Lamport Hall, or Church summer fetes) people have asked us to pray for good weather and been thrilled (indeed amazed) at having rain-free, or beautiful sunny, or even wonderfully hot, days for those events.

Should such things surprise us?

'The British Isles gets the weather the people deserve'! Could that be true?

None can be unaware of how pessimistic, even downright negative, the majority of the people of Britain are when discussing the weather! When a special event is planned, we often hear such comments as: "It's always cold and miserable then!" Or, "What will we do if it rains? Where will we then hold the event?"

Someone will be sure to cap that comment with one of those sweeping generalisations heard when the weather is discussed: "we no longer have the long hot summers we had when I was a child"...

The reverse is equally true. If better than average weather is experienced, people say "it won't last"; or "you mark my words, we will pay for this"! (and prophesy doom and gloom as a result).

I sometimes begin to think the British get the weather they expect and deserve!

It's true, isn't it? Few people act as if they believe anything can be done to alter the weather. Certainly few believe it seems to me, that prayer (and therefore God) can change it!

How short people's memories are! The British nation was called to prayer when their army had been driven back on Dunkirk by Hitler's lightning invasion of the

Low Countries. With no escape, and their backs to the sea, the whole nation prayed for those men. And then, do you remember what followed? Against all the odds, the Channel was "as smooth as a millpond" and the smallest of boats made it across to help in the dramatic rescue of the British Task Force. Without the miracle - and most accepted it was - the losses would have been appalling. Against all the odds, the great majority returned to fight another day.

Where is that faith in prayer, in a God who is able, in Britain today? The Scriptures challenge us about this state of affairs, and about the negative and unbelieving attitudes we so often adopt - often without being aware of what we are doing!

Look at something the Bible teaches. The psalmist reminds us of the close, individual and personal relationship God has with each one of us: "You made all the delicate inner parts of my body, and knit them together in my mother's womb. Thank you for making me so wonderfully complex! It **is** amazing to think about. Your workmanship is marvellous - and how well I know it. You were there while I was being formed in utter seclusion! You saw me before I was born and scheduled each day of my life before I began to breathe" (something the pro-abortionist lobby needs to consider?). "How precious it is, Lord, to realise that you are thinking about me constantly! I can't even count how many times a day your thoughts turn towards me. And when I waken in the morning, you are still thinking of me..."!

If God is so intimately involved with every moment of our lives then surely He is willing, where it is right, to bring about change - in even the smallest detail - in the lives of those He loves? Yet despite the truth of all this, the tendency is to laugh it all off. We believe, simply by failing to do anything, that there is nothing we can do to change the circumstances surrounding our lives - be it the weather, or a headache, or whatever. Be honest! Are you, if only occasionally, negative or pessimistic about such things? It is certainly often true of me. Particularly at times when my faith level plummets for one reason or another! If *your* answer is "yes", you too may have a spiritual problem. Think about it...

It has to do, for want of a better description, with what one might label as a "mind-set". Some people seem to be critical of everyone and everything? Criticism becomes such a habit that eventually the person is oblivious to what he is doing and becomes a 'pain in the neck'. It is avoidable because, in part at least, it results from the person's on-going negative, unforgiving, (yes, sometimes even hateful) attitude towards an individual or individuals; or is brought about by events or circumstances connected with that person's life.

Now the same kind of "mind-set" can apply to our attitude to the weather. Just as we have to do something positive to deal with a critical or carping spirit, so we need to be positive over attitudes about the weather; to put a guard on our lips; to say nothing unless we have something positive to say. But there is still more to it than that.

Once we become negative and critical about the weather (or anything else for that matter), that critical or negative attitude doesn't stop there. It insidiously begins to permeate, as a "mind-set", every other area of our lives. It might be our daily complaints about government, the hole in the ozone layer, the Church, the vicar, a member of the family or erstwhile friend, our anger over straightened circumstances, or about any number of issues. If you find that difficult to believe, spend a little time observing the faces, the words used - and the spirit in which they are said - of those involved, for instance, in present-day politics, or those involved in television interviews!

And it goes much deeper than that. Jonathan Miller wrote: "nowhere else is the cult of misery so entrenched and nowhere else is so much pleasure taken in a zeitgeist of gloom. The British are not merely miserable, they are brilliant at it...it cannot be coincidental that two of the biggest television hits, 'One foot in the grave' and 'Inspector Morse', both revolve around characters who have elevated woe to an art form." He concludes, "If we can be conditioned to misery, why can we not condition ourselves to take a more balanced view: to exalt in achievement, rejoice in success and value those things about Britain which remain good...?" In his article Miller quotes Laurie Taylor - professor of sociology at York - who says, "It's all part of what Norman Tebbit called the culture of negativism. We've turned grumbling into an art form".

If that negative or critical spirit in an individual is not checked, the subject eventually becomes so embittered that he loses friends, and much else besides. So we know it is important to lovingly show the person what he is doing to himself. Then it's up to the subject to start changing that "mind-set" - not only by biting his tongue every time he is about to say something critical, but by thinking of something good, positive or complimentary to say in its place!

Surely the most important thing of all is to see that a negative "mind-set" effectively denies God's control or ability to bring about change - whether it be in respect of a person, situation or circumstance. Let me repeat that. Intended or not, we effectively deny God's ability to bring about change! Now you and I can only change that "mind-set" when we acknowledge that there is nothing we can do about it; but God can! When we positively turn that person or situation over to God, we ask God to bring about whatever is needed.

Before reaching that stage, however, we have to ask ourselves the question: "Do we actually believe God can bring about such change, or perform such signs?" And because that faith level can be so mercurial, we have to review the question continually. It reminds us to look to God, not to ourselves, to bring about whatever is needed.

It is very important to note that this has nothing to do with the power of positive thinking, nor has it anything to do with autosuggestion. It has everything to do with the acceptance of, and belief in, God's promises to us as contained in Scripture, and that with Him "nothing is impossible".

"Oh yes! God can do signs and wonders, or work miracles," we may be willing to admit. Yet, isn't it true, that the areas in which we have the greatest difficulty concerning them is when it has to do with just the ordinary, everyday things - like the weather, or a cold, or a headache, or regular monthly menstrual pain or PMT? Some find it easier to think of God getting involved in such miracles as 'walking on water' or 'raising the dead'.

"Stop your doubting and believe", Jesus said to Thomas. On another occasion He said to his disciples: "Ask" (literally "go on and on and on asking", the original Greek implies) "and you will receive". James, one of the disciples, wrote: "you do not have, because you do not ask"!

It's easy to illustrate why doubt and unbelief can have such a crippling effect. It's important to recognise the mercurial nature of our believing and doubting. Our human nature being what it is, we find ourselves - if we recognise the syndrome - waging an almost constant battle with those negative attitudes that so easily rise to the surface. No sooner do we think we have got our act together - and we really begin to believe in, and trust, God to undertake - than a new set of circumstances presents itself. In a flash our doubts, and consequent failure to trust God for the solution, take control of us once more.

Probably one of the most dramatic illustrations of this - with equally devastating consequences - is the story of the people of Israel standing with Moses on the threshold of the Promised Land. Of all people, they really had no excuse for what was to follow.

A further title from John, "Who Holds Your Reigns" which will be released in the Autumn of 2011, details his experiences following the pilgrim route to Santiago de Compostela.

Here is an extract from Chapter 1:

NEW HORIZONS

Stranger than fiction, perhaps, but having served in the Christian Ministry for close on forty-five years it was a self confessed atheist – someone who does not believe in God – who opened up a new and exciting area of ministry and pilgrimage for me. One that would bring many new challenges, not least the fact that I was ill-equipped to consider it, for I was experiencing increasing difficulty in walking for more than a few hundred yards without considerable pain.

For some years I had enjoyed reading some of Ken Follett's novels. Then about six months before my retirement from full-time ministry, I came across his book 'The Pillars of the Earth'. It was the story of the building of a large imaginary Gothic Cathedral somewhere in South West England in about the 12th Century.

Ken Follett had shown an extraordinary interest in the architectural history and development of Gothic Cathedrals. Such was his interest that, as a result of all his research in this field, he started to write "The Pillars of the Earth". His publishers showed little interest in this new work, believing that the subject matter was too far removed from what his reading public expected of him. It was only some years later that a German Publisher agreed to publish this work and it was an instant success – so much so that sales of this book have now outstripped that of most, if not all, of his other novels.

I, too, probably because I was brought up in the heart of Africa for most of my life, have had a great fascination for these wonderful Gothic Cathedrals built around England and Western Europe nearly a thousand years ago. What extraordinary feats of engineering they are! If you are an admirer of these amazing architectural feats of engineering; if you are fascinated by what life must have been like in those far off days; if you are curious as to how they built these vast edifices without the technology, cranes and scaffolding we use today, then this book is for you because it is so informative.

But I also learnt something else – and that was about Christian pilgrim routes that were well used and to be found at that time throughout Britain and Europe. In the second half of the novel "The Pillars of the Earth", Jack - the step son of Master Builder Tom of the imaginary Cathedral - followed the Pilgrim Route from Paris right down to the South of France, over the Pyrenees, and right across Northern Spain from East to West to Santiago – 'Sant Iago' meaning 'St. James' in Spanish - the place where St. James the Apostle was buried.

Unknown to Jack when he left Kingsbridge, he had fathered a child 'out of wedlock'. Even more amazing, sometime later his 'girl friend' and baby set out to find him. First she travelled to Paris, then all the way to Santiago – only to discover that he had already left for Toledo. Again she follows, only to find that he had left Toledo and was now headed back to Paris. So nothing daunted, she heads off back to Paris. Some distance – even on horseback! And with a baby! Well, it ***was*** only a novel!

But the idea of ***pilgrimage*** fired something up inside me. Having led a very full life in ministry, the idea of having time to be away from everything that ties one down and keeps one so frenetically busy seemed too good to be true. Just imagining oneself far removed from one's place of work, with real prime time to reflect, and pray. And the icing on the cake, if you like, was the opportunity to meet with people from many parts of the world who have similar aims of discerning God's will and purpose for one's life. And to be able to do this over a period of perhaps several weeks or more - on a journey - seemed to be just what was needed for real renewal and refreshing. In the real world it is hard to find such uninterrupted time to draw close to God.

As I continued to ask around about this pilgrim route, John and Susan Guy – parishioners of mine at Litchborough – told me that they had walked a part of one of the pilgrim routes, and were able to give me a route map of that section.

But clearly any thought of undertaking some form of pilgrimage would have to remain the pipe dream it had to be. Only the previous January, when we were visiting our daughters in Zimbabwe, we had gone out to one of their farms for a picnic. When we could no longer drive, we had to get out and walk. First we climbed a small rocky outcrop. My daughter (all 4ft. 11 inches) and a grandchild had to help me – and even then, by the time I struggled to the top – I was puffing and blowing to such a degree that I was finding it difficult to catch my breath at all. I was spared having to carry anything. By the time we reached this wonderful picnic spot, I really wondered if I would ever make it back to the cars again. I was so unfit I would clearly never cope with the mountains in Spain, let alone long distance walking and climbing – and carrying everything on my back as well!